NEITHER
Liberty NOR *Safety*

A Hard Look at
U. S. Military Policy
and Strategy

GENERAL
NATHAN F. TWINING
USAF (Ret.)
Chairman, Joint Chiefs of Staff
1957 – 60

HOLT, RINEHART AND WINSTON
New York   Chicago
San Francisco

Published simultaneously in Canada by Holt, Rinehart
and Winston of Canada, Limited.

Library of Congress Catalog Card Number: 66-21628
First Edition

Dear Howell:
I hope you like Nate's
book, as I have —

Ira

Designer: Ernst Reichl
88600-0216
Printed in the United States of America

On Liberty

They that can give up essential liberty
to obtain a little temporary safety deserve
neither liberty nor safety.

BENJAMIN FRANKLIN

CONTENTS

CONTENTS

CONTENTS

PREFACE

This book, I hope, will assist the American people in understanding the problems of national security at home as well as the effect of the policies resolved therefrom on the peaceful lives of men everywhere. I intend to lay out here, for appraisal, current trends in political-military relationships which undoubtedly will have a profound impact on the future of America—indeed, the world.

To give dimension and meaning to the events and attitudes of today, it is necessary to step back some twenty-five years in time in order to examine the basic factors leading to their development.

In 1939, almost three years before Pearl Harbor, Adolph Hitler took specific steps toward conquering the world. The Russian Bear became nervous, John Bull tightened his belt in preparation for a protracted war of attrition, La Belle France hastily stocked her Maginot Line, and a lethargic America was beginning to realize that all was not right with the world. Charles A. Lindbergh, the Lone Eagle, feted and honored by virtually every nation in the world, returned from Europe in the spring of 1939, after having issued numerous warnings of the overwhelming power building in Nazi Germany. He was indeed a "lone" Eagle because his comments had incurred the displeasure of President Roosevelt, many influential people in Great Britain and France, and the government of Russia. He was accused of "intermeddling in Europe."

What Lindbergh had said was that Nazi Germany's air power was greater than any combination of air power that could be assembled against her by European countries, including Russia. Further, he declared that the Russian air force was inefficient.

History, of course, records the bitter truth of Lindbergh's estimates of Germany's 1939 strength. In September, 1938, Prime Minister Chamberlain had traveled to Munich to "shake his umbrella in Hitler's face" and to issue an ultimatum that Hitler halt his aggressive moves in Europe. In the face of the appalling German war machine made clear to him at Munich, Chamberlain miserably switched to a policy of appeasement.

In May of 1939, America flexed her muscles slightly, increasing the number of Army Air Corps primary flying training schools from one to eleven and permitting a similar expansion in the Naval flying establishment.

Time and events afforded further tragic proof of the accuracy of Lindbergh's estimates. Russia's disastrous, although finally successful, campaign in Finland proved that its air force constituted no menace to Germany and that it would be nothing more than a broken reed for Britain to lean on in any alliance with her. The blitzkrieg in Poland substantiated all that Lindbergh had said concerning Germany's might. The operation against Norway dismally burst the myth that British seapower could prevent German occupation of the Scandinavian countries and, after the uncertainties of the winter of 1939–1940, real war finally broke out in Europe with the German conquest of Holland and Belgium and the subsequent disaster in France.

In 1964, after a decade and a half of Cold War, Americans facing a presidential election saw clearly defined at last the fundamental issues of contemporary military policy. During the time bridging these years, we had undergone four distinct stages in our political-military development. These four periods are:

1939–1945 The period of the magnificent and unified effort of World War II.

1945–1949 The incredible years during which we lost the reins of peace, permitted our military posture to decline, and returned to a happy lethargy.

1950–1960 We recognized the Communist threat, searched for a new theory of strategy, and actually developed the power base necessary to place that strategy into operation.

1960–1964 (and possibly extending some time into the future)
A period during which a startling belief developed at high levels of government that the Russian Bear had become a fun-loving, happily domesticated beast; that peaceful coexistence was desired by the U.S.S.R.; and consequently, that we must search for means of disarming.

The significant political-military events and actions during 1965 are briefly covered in the concluding pages of the book, but no attempt is made to provide a searching analysis of the military policies of the Administration of the thirty-sixth President of the United States. An informed judgment cannot yet be formulated, simply because not enough time has passed.

In discussing these various time periods, and in the attempt to bring our military philosophy into sharper focus, I shall not draw upon the rigid sequential discipline of the historian. Instead, I will indicate the basic pattern of the political-military factors and considerations of the past quarter of a century, adding where necessary other aspects of the history of our times in order to make the story comprehensible.

In view of the fact that during the quarter of a century under discussion we had a Democratic administration for seventeen years and a Republican one for eight, there seems little point in associating the policies of national security with any one political party. The evidence would indicate, nevertheless, that there were four dominant factors which did have an inevitable effect on the shaping of national security policy during the various time periods:

1. Actions taken by the Communist world to which we, as a nation, reacted.
2. National mood at the time.
3. Leadership afforded and the power direction provided by the Chief Executive and his immediate staff.
4. Political problems created by the progress of military technology and military intelligence on both sides of the Iron Curtain.

The importance and relationship of these four factors will emerge as we trace the background to the strategic decisions which have been taken. Their effect will become more apparent as we explore the conditions under which we must search for and secure a viable theory of international strategy to safeguard the freedom of mankind in the precious years ahead.

—NATHAN F. TWINING

PART ONE

BACKGROUND FOR

Strategic Decision

Chapter I

THE AMERICA
OF WORLD WAR II

World War II carried the United States to a pinnacle of self-confidence and world respect. We had started late, but, once engaged, put on a performance that was so good we startled even ourselves. The ease and alacrity with which our industry was able to marshal its mass production power in response to the call to arms made us the arsenal of democracy. It was a hectic thing at first—often frustrating and, in retrospect, sometimes ludicrous. But soon scores of thousands of guns, tanks, ships, and aircraft rolled off production lines in unending quantities. In addition, stupendous stocks of oil, gasoline, munitions, spare parts, foodstuffs, clothing, and combat gear of all types and descriptions were made quickly available.

What's more, all of this was done without materially reducing the American standard of living or altering—in a major sense—our way of life. The trials of war were remote; their exigencies unreal. Our war economy was, for the most part, superimposed over our peacetime economy. The capacity for phenomenal growth lies in the roots of our economic system, and we responded to the challenge and to the opportunity as much like businessmen as patriots. Of course, inconveniences were encountered, such as gasoline rationing and difficulty in buying a new car every year, but withal, it was a period of booming prosperity and full employment. The shooting war was a long distance away for most people.

However, on the battlefields of the world, on land, in the air, and at sea, it was a rough, dirty, and bitter fight, and the sons of thousands of families failed to return. Those families knew in tragedy the full measure and meaning of war far better than their more fortunate and more numerous neighbors. In retrospect, none of us can really deny that, with all of the effort on the civilian front and all of the sacrifice and heroism on the fighting front, we, as a nation, treated the affair, particularly in its closing days, more like a football game than a deadly contest for survival.

As the war drew to a close and our team was six touchdowns ahead with five minutes to play, we got up and left the stadium without even gathering up our things or putting on our coats. We had tired of war. Possibly we misjudged the oncoming battle for peace and assumed its happy outcome inevitable. More probably, we simply could not understand the new kind of world which was breeding malignantly in the disaster and wake of war. Historians will judge the reasons. Whatever the explanation, when the last shot was fired, we saw a "new" team coming out and failed to recognize the players in the red suits.

We reacted as though we had fought and won the very last great war which would ever be fought for humanity, decency, and freedom. We acted as though we had never heard of the Soviet Communist conspiracy, dating back to November, 1917, which has always been aimed unerringly at the heart of democracy and the utter annihilation of our way of life.

Politically and militarily, Americans on the home front, with a few notable exceptions, seemed to think that by winning the war they had magically created a utopian world in which the enemies of free men no longer existed.

4

Closing Days of the War in Europe

On the European fighting front our forces stopped at the Elbe River and allowed the Russians to take Berlin. Our failure to take Berlin was due to earlier political arrangements which had been made for the postwar disposition and control of Nazi-occupied territory. Simultaneously, we entered into a number of ill-defined political understandings which, in short order, were to lead to the enslavement of Eastern Germany, Czechoslovakia, Poland, Rumania, Bulgaria, Hungary and create the thorny problem of Berlin.

Speculation about the division of postwar Germany and the isolation of Berlin behind the Iron Curtain has been hot, often tedious, and always arduous. Some experts have blamed the slowdown of U.S. and British forces during the latter days of the war on the excessive caution of British Field Marshall Montgomery, who, it has been alleged, did not fully appreciate the drastically weakened condition of the German ground forces. This condition had been brought about by Allied air strikes stabbing deeply at the industrial heart and transportation system of Germany over a period of many months. The dreadful success of these blows was not entirely susceptible to accurate analysis by the standard intelligence techniques of the ground forces of the time. Others have stated with the same heated conviction that General Eisenhower's direct negotiations with Soviet authorities resulted in an unfortunate decision to hold up on the Elbe River— and to allow the Soviet forces to take Berlin. Sir Winston Churchill, to name but one, is known to have been upset by General Eisenhower's dealing with the Soviets at the political level. With a prophetic understanding of postwar problems with the U.S.S.R., Churchill strongly believed that Berlin should have been taken by American forces.

Many United States operational and strategic planners, foremost among whom were Army General George S. Patton and Lieutenant General Albert Wedemeyer, also believed at

5

the time that U.S. forces, not the Soviets, should take Berlin. Still others have held that the costly attack on Nazi-occupied Europe from the south, across the Mediterranean, was unnecessary and weakened the Allied drive through central Europe.

The problem is a complex one and I have neither the intention nor the requirement, in this book, to take issue with what finally happened. This is a matter for historians far removed in time from the battlefield. But I do believe that, regardless of the judgment of historians as to any individual responsibility which may have been involved, it is clear that massive combined war operations involving two or more nations are difficult to work out in a military sense and much more difficult to work out in a political sense. Possibly the world of today could have been vastly different and far less dangerous if our highest political officials had fully recognized and supported the postwar objectives as seen by Sir Winston Churchill. Second, if military commanders in the field, such as General Eisenhower, were actually participating in political decisions with Soviet officials, the essential fact emerges that there must have been no firm guidance from the responsible civilian leaders in Washington. Apparently, as a nation we did not think the problem through; America seems to have had no real wartime objective other than unconditional surrender.

Unconditional surrender may have been a valid wartime military objective, but this becomes inadequate when there are no appropriate postwar objectives as to the nature of international political arrangements and power positions which can emerge. So, it seems to me that in planning for this nation's future security, little is gained in attempting to fix the blame for past mistakes on the dedicated individuals who were caught up in the vortex of war. However, our nation would gain much if its citizens would trouble themselves to recognize that they are ultimately responsible. Political leaders in times of grave national crisis are inevitably influenced by the popular national attitude. If Americans could remember that they are fighting for life, liberty, and the freedom of men everywhere, and would not give up the fight until the long-term objectives of humanity are secured, then this nation might sometime win a war without losing the peace.

The tragedy of the closing days of World War II in Europe lies in the fact that the Free World Allies had already paid the price in blood and treasure to secure legitimate and humane objectives which were not achieved. All we really did was to destroy one system of dictatorship and idly permit the strengthening of a dictatorial system much more dangerous to man's freedom.

Closing Days in Asia

Meanwhile, on the other side of the globe, the United States invited the Soviets into the war against Japan—a war to which, I might add, the U.S.S.R contributed absolutely nothing. This invitation, together with its immediate acceptance by the Soviets, came at a time when our enemy in the Pacific was actually seeking the means to negotiate an end to hostilities.

Other statesmen at home, apparently not to be outdone and looking boldly and blindly ahead, promptly initiated a program of appeasement of the Chinese Communists. Some few* in the Far East theater of war and all too few at home saw the catastrophe which was building and tried to stop it. Their belief was that America could not possibly abandon a friendly China until we had reached a firm understanding with the Soviet Union guaranteeing a free China. The efforts of these few Americans, though utterly futile, are worth remembering and noting here. This unfortunate program of appeasement set the stage for the eventual loss of China to Communist domination and created the circumstances for the Korean War,

* Lieutenant General Albert Wedemeyer and Major General Albert Hagenberger, to name but two.

the French loss of Indochina, and today's untenable situations in Vietnam, Cambodia, and Laos.

Initially, at war's end, the plan was to safeguard China's freedom. The first phase of this effort in the Far East was the movement of four of China's best armies, comprising nearly 500,000 men, into the Peiping-Mukden area. This was accomplished at great cost between August and December, 1945. Two of these Chinese armies were airlifted from Burma by U.S. Air Forces, and two were moved by land, sea, and air from the Chihkiang front in eastern China. These armies, with U.S. logistic support, were to accomplish four tasks:

1. They were to accept the Japanese surrender in the northern China-Manchurian area.
2. They were to seize Japanese war material which was estimated as sufficient to support an army of a million men for ten years.
3. They were to immobilize the Chinese Communist forces in the area. (These forces also sought to obtain the Japanese war booty.)
4. They were to stabilize the military situation as a basis for working out political understanding with the U.S.S.R. and the Chinese Communists.

The movement of these four armies was successfully accomplished but under heartbreaking conditions. Those conditions were the result of the so-called "point system" which came into being in the autumn of 1945. The point system, sentimentally conceived, militarily quick, and deadly as the plague, rapidly decimated all elements of the greatest fighting force—land, sea, and air—which had ever been assembled.

I would like to believe that the point system represented the first great propaganda victory of the U.S.S.R. in its ceaseless campaign to disarm the Western World. Unfortunately, I'm afraid, the responsibility lay nearly completely with the American people.

8

The point system for demobilization was devised as the basis for determining who in the fighting forces would get to go home first. Credits were granted for months in service, combat duty, and so on. It was not applied to the Regular Army and Navy personnel—but there were few "regulars"— and it meant that the most experienced of the citizen armies would leave first.

At any rate, the military services, charged with bringing some order out of the incredible chaos of war, were left only a few regulars and unseasoned new arrivals to perform the critical and sometimes delicate tasks which are war's inevitable aftermath.

Nonetheless, the transport of the four Chinese armies to northern China was carried out by this handful of Americans. It was done as the point system rapidly drained our military forces of vital "know-how." It was accomplished even as our nation "got up and left the stadium." But the four armies were put in place *in time* to do the four things that they were intended to do. Ironically, time would soon show that the entire operation was tragically in vain.

The ink was scarcely dry on the Japanese surrender, signed aboard the battleship *Missouri* in Tokyo Bay on September 2, 1945, when United States government representatives arrived in Shanghai determined to force the establishment of a Chinese Nationalist-Chinese Communist Coalition Government.

This marriage was, of course, bitterly opposed by Generalissimo Chiang Kai-shek, who had long known the nature of communism. He knew that a coalition government would mean quick and certain absorption by Communists. But his pleas went unheeded by the American State Department representatives, already tone-deafened by the music of appeasement and coexistence. Most of all, our government had a pressure lever to help bring our friends and allies, the Chinese Nationalists, around to its way of thinking. It reminded Chiang that we had leap-frogged China's four best armies into the north country— far beyond his government's capacity for logistic support. If

9

America withdrew her support, these armies would soon become ineffective, because they were American trained, American equipped, and dependent upon American logistic support.

Without further ado, this political expedient was then ordered by our government, and support was withdrawn from the operation in northern China. This was a political decision —not a military decision. As a consequence, much of the Japanese war booty fell into the hands of the Chinese Communists. The main force of the Chinese Communist army was permitted to escape through the Kalgan Pass. Meanwhile, Nationalist China's four finest armies of 500,000 or more men fought to the best of their ability for over three years. They were short of supplies, abandoned by the United States, cut to pieces by Soviet artillery, in unreinforceable positions and eventually died, collapsed, surrendered, or defected to the Communists by the tens of thousands. Thus American policy —actually the lack of it—in the closing days of World War II and its aftermath set the stage for the loss of a friendly China to the heavy yoke of communism.

The real tragedy of this callow diplomacy is that it occurred during a time when we occupied a truly impregnable position. As the war ended, we had powerful armies and thousands of aircraft on both flanks of the U.S.S.R. We had undisputed control of the seven seas and the airways of the world, we completely dominated air and surface communications the world over, and we had friendly, co-operative allies everywhere. Our World War II enemies were totally defeated, and the U.S.S.R., battered and bruised, needed time to regroup, consolidate, rebuild, and dig out from under the wreckage of war.

Ironically, much of the remaining Soviet military strength had been provided by U.S. military aid and Lend-Lease*

* As far back as 1943, some far-sighted military planners had suggested that Lend-Lease to the Soviet Union be stopped—stopped because we were already certain of victory and knew the U.S.S.R. could never be trusted. Obviously, these views did not prevail.

10

Nevertheless, in addition to all of our military and political advantages from a conventional land, sea, and air viewpoint, we had two other tremendous assets: our population base and industry were undamaged and we alone had the atomic bomb.

It would be difficult in the entire history of humanity to find a more favorable climate for the practice of thoughtful diplomacy. Not only could we negotiate from a position of unchallengeable strength, but we had fought and won a just war; a war fought in the interest of humanity at large. Our military, political, economic, psychological, and technical advantages were indeed overwhelming.

Our failure to nurture the seeds of democracy, which we had strewn across the world, was symptomatic of our national attitude and, therefore, our national policy in the months following the armistices in Europe and in the Far East.

Unilateral Disarmament

Accustomed to setting records of one kind or another, the United States promptly established a new world's record for unilateral demobilization and disarmament. Never before in the history of the world had a great fighting force been destroyed so quickly. It melted away as though it had never existed. So frantic was the demobilization of U.S. forces that uniformed people disappeared from the four corners of the world before the matériel of war could be disposed of properly. Billions of dollars' worth of supplies and equipment were burned, pushed overboard, plowed into the soil, abandoned, buried, stolen, and otherwise neglected and wasted. Thousands of opportunists the world over became rich overnight with the hardware left scattered across battle arenas everywhere. There simply were not enough military personnel left to safeguard, process, package, crate, and ship the things of value which could have been saved and put to good future use.

While the stripping of our military forces was going on, the U.S.S.R., of course, did not disarm.

11

The extent and speed with which we shed our arms and demobilized is shown below:

	1945	1946	1947	1948	1949	1950
Men under Arms	12,123,455	3,030,088	1,582,999	1,445,910	1,615,360	1,460,261

	1945	1946	1947	1948	1949	1950
Military Budget, in Millions	$79,877,000	$42,021,000	$13,811,000	$11,094,000	$11,987,000	$11,877,000

(All figures shown are as of June 30)

Thus, we disarmed ourselves—disarmed ourselves before we had achieved the very fundamental political objectives for which we had fought. True, we had defeated the Axis powers. But in this battle we had fought for the liberation of Poland, Czechoslovakia, Rumania, Hungary, and Bulgaria—as well as for France and the protection of England. In the Far East we had also fought for the liberation of China—as well as the Philippines and the protection of Australia. Our postwar diplomatic inadequacies defeated these political objectives. The end of the war saw merely the transfer of many nations from one system of tyranny to another.

Disinterest in national security and a national preoccupation with the problems of returning to "normal living" continued at a breathless pace during the five years between 1945 and 1950.

The United States military establishment had been required to work closely with the Soviets during the war years. But it was an uneasy example of "togetherness," to say the least. Following the war, the military services, certain of the ultimate Soviet intent, sought but achieved little Congressional or public understanding of the critical state of the nation's defense posture. In fact, accused of "empire building," "goblin hunting," and so on, the military services battled largely to justify their very existence. Our legislators and Administration officials placed very stringent limitations on military budgets and manpower. The net result of this financial starvation was an intense competition among the armed services to obtain what little resources were made available. It was a bitter and hopeless task because there was simply not enough available to meet even the minimum requirements of an emergency.

Chapter II

BIRTH OF
A NUCLEAR STRATEGY

During the period 1945–1950, existing world circumstances and governmental power factors gradually forged a nuclear strategy for the United States—even though such strategy had not yet been formally enunciated. National Security Council actions taken during this critical period have been well documented by the military services as well as by independent writers. Therefore, most of this history is now available to any interested student or research group. While I will not repeat this history in detail, I want to make brief comments on a few topics because of their importance to the actions of that time and because of their lasting impact on the world today. The circumstances, events, and decisions of that time which appear to me to be of paramount importance are: the tight postwar budget, conflicting military interservice concepts and requirements, organization problems in the aftermath of war, conflicting technical viewpoints of the time, and positive actions taken by the Communists.

Accordingly, this chapter analyzes the broad impact of these factors on the formulation of a basic National Security policy which still exists, to some degree, today.

The Post-World War II Budget

The military budgets during the postwar years from 1945 through June 30, 1950, are somewhat difficult to define due to the fact that the Air Force did not gain autonomy from the Army until September 18, 1947. During that year and, of course, in prior years, Air Force procurement was administered by the Army. A further complicating factor is a separation of new funds and expenditures reflected for those years. The tremendous withdrawal of funds allocated for the military services resulting from the promise of peace actually occurred in 1944–1945. In fiscal 1944, *new* funds allocated to the military services amounted to a whopping 83.1 billion dollars. In fiscal 1945, these funds dropped to 36.3 billion dollars. Nevertheless, *expenditures* of the military services between 1945 to 1950 do provide an interesting assessment of the military force structures in-being during those uncertain years.

Military Expenditures
(in millions of dollars)

	1945	1946	1947	1948	1949	1950
Off. Sec. Defense					7	190
Army	$49,750	22,900	7,228	5,663	6,482	3,985
Navy (& Marines)	30,128	14,844	5,784	4,297	4,446	4,102
USAF	—	4,276	799	1,134	1,059	3,600
Totals	$79,877	42,021	13,811	11,094	11,987	11,877

The austere national defense budget of those years was not only the work of an economy-minded Congress. It appeared to me to be Administration policy. Secretary of Defense Louis Johnson would not fight for larger defense appropriations. In fact, he seemed to believe that a total of about nine billion dollars a year was adequate. The first Chairman of the Joint Chiefs of Staff, General Omar Bradley, collided with Secretary

15

Johnson on this subject often. Bradley has been asked since why he did not resign in protest, but he felt that he had a better chance to obtain increased appropriations than a new man would have. Actually, an increase was in prospect when the Communist attack in Korea occurred, and the appointment of General Marshall to succeed Secretary Johnson as Secretary of Defense automatically solved the problem. However, a considerable period of time is required to translate new appropriations into combat force-in-being, and at the time, there was not enough strength in our military structure to meet our burgeoning military requirements. The folly of the indolent years following World War II had caught up with us.

Concept of War

Added to, or perhaps a part of, the problems imposed by limited military budgeting of the entire postwar era from 1945–1950 was the general confusion and moral debate that existed with respect to military policy. The fact is that the United States had no specifically articulated military policy; there was only a general public conviction that the nation was in no danger. As a nation, we possessed the vague and entirely empiric view that the atomic bomb in our arsenal solved everything. Unfortunately, some very learned men—scientists and statesmen—inaccurately assured our people that this was so. Some of the issues of that time are significant, because they represent the initial groping of our society in a new world, a nuclear world, for a formula for security and survival.

Traditionally, up through World War II, the United States had relied on its position of geographic isolation as a major security advantage. America was protected by great distances and vast oceans on both critical flanks. During periods of peace, the U.S. Navy, therefore, became the first line of defense and was generally maintained in better fighting posture than the Army or the Army Air Forces.

16

This traditional concept of United States military preparedness came to be known as the "post D-Day mobilization concept," D-Day being the day of decision to become involved, and to be followed with the major effort in mobilization of men and material to meet the demands of a national emergency.

It was inevitable during this period of time that both the Army and Navy leaned toward the post D-Day mobilization theory of war, while the Air Force strongly advocated a "force-in-being" concept. Under a three-way split of available resources, neither the Army nor the Navy could maintain force-in-being adequate to a general war situation. The Air Force, on the other hand, with long-range strategic aircraft and the atomic bomb, envisioned a peacetime force which mounted "capability-in-being" to inflict massive damage on an aggressor. The Air Force argument further asserted that the post D-Day mobilization concept of war had become obsolete; that there would be no time to mobilize, in the traditional sense; that in any future general war, national resources going into a "mobilization base" would be largely wasted.

Historically, because of the protection afforded by the oceans, no enemy could build a military force and the necessary sea power to mount a successful invasion of the United States without it being known in sufficient time to mobilize American forces for defense. Therefore, we relied upon a very small regular Army and Air Force (at that time a part of the Army) and depended upon mobilizing manpower only in event of a national emergency. This concept can be defended as sound and economical prior to the maturity of air power and the advent of the atomic bomb. At the same time, no doubt America's lack of actual military forces-in-being, and failure to make a political precommitment of intentions, tempted enemy powers to initiate both World Wars I and II. With considerable rationality and historical backing, I am certain that Kaiser Wilhelm and later Adolph Hitler gambled

17

that either the United States would not enter these wars, or that if we did, our entry would be too late to frustrate German objectives.

The interservice argument with respect to this concept of war was not an academic exercise. It had real meaning in relation to how budget-limited defense dollars would be spent. The post D-Day mobilization program required a considerable outlay of dollars for the maintenance of reserve industrial tooling and industrial plants, the stock-piling of long lead time vehicles and material, equipping reserve and national guard organizations, providing for the early equipment of new units which might be brought into being, and a generally heavy investment in latent mobilization strength, as opposed to investment in existing force-in-being.

Which of these two judgments, if either, is completely or partially correct is a matter for historians, and need not be defended here. The point is that the traditional concept of United States military preparedness carried into the post-World War II years with considerable strength and this produced wide differences of opinion among responsible military and government leaders.

Two brilliant officers, with whom I often worked, wrote about these problems during the genesis of our post-World War II political-military policies. They were General Muir S. Fairchild and Major General Orville A. Anderson. General Fairchild died of a heart attack, probably the result of overwork, in 1950, while Vice Chief of Staff of the Air Force; General Anderson "prematurely retired" in 1950 under the Truman Administration.

In 1943, General Fairchild, serving as a member of the Joint Strategic Survey Committee in Washington (he was then Major General), incurred the wrath of high-level politicians by suggesting that Lend-Lease to the U.S.S.R. be suspended. It was already clear to strategic planners that the ultimate course of the war had been determined, and that America and its allies would win. General Fairchild always

18

viewed the U.S.S.R. as a wartime cobelligerent—but not a true ally; he did not trust the postwar objectives of the Soviet Union and he did not wish to see Russia emerge from the war in a power position which could threaten the freedom of Western Europe. Consequently, he made the unpopular suggestion that Lend-Lease to Russia be immediately halted. He was fired from his job because of these views.

General Anderson's difficulty, in the postwar years, lay in his outspoken evaluation of the basic moral issue involved in our confrontation of the Communist conspiracy. The basic question, as he phrased it, was: "Which is the greater immorality—preventive war as a means to keep the U.S.S.R. from becoming a nuclear power; or, to allow a totalitarian dictatorial system to develop a means whereby the free world could be intimidated, blackmailed, and possibly destroyed?"

General Anderson was convinced that the greater immorality lay in our decision to permit the development of a militant system of power capable of destroying the Free World. He regarded the "immorality" of a preventive strike against the U.S.S.R. as the lesser of two moral evils. His views were, of course, unpopular, because they contradicted the Administration's desire to maintain a *status quo*, and they were never given a fair hearing by the State Department, or for that matter, by the military establishment.

General Anderson did not advocate a sudden nuclear attack on the Soviet Union. What he did advocate was a power maneuver in which an ultimatum would be delivered to the Soviets to free the enslaved satellite countries of Europe and to stop subversion and aggression on the land mass of Asia. In terms of his logic, if such an ultimatum had been delivered to the Soviets, who were then in no position to offer effective resistance, Russia would have been forced to free both Eastern Europe and Southeast Asia. If such an ultimatum had been delivered and not accepted by the U.S.S.R., the United States could undoubtedly have eliminated Russia's power base for generations to come.

19

The debate and the dilemma of the time are well illustrated by the passages which follow.

Throughout recorded history, evolution in the nature of war has been associated with evolution in the technical and mechanical characteristics of weapons. Over a period of some thousands of years, we have progressed from the stone and club age, through the spear, bow and arrow, crossbow, and gunpowder periods, finally to arrive at the atomic era. Each major advance in weapons has been marked by either an increase in the range of weapons or by an increase in its lethal capacity. We have gone from the war capability of the club—the capacity to bruise a single individual at a range of a few feet—to the war capability of modern air weapons—the capacity to eliminate whole cities at ranges of thousands of miles.

This frightening increase in the potential of weapons has been matched with an evolution in our social and economic structure which adds further hazard to modern existence. The simple agrarian life, with humanity living close to the soil, dispersed and largely independent, has been replaced with a complex social and economic fabric which is super-vulnerable in many critical areas. As the power of weapons has increased, concentrations of population, industry and transportation have developed which invite destruction by an enemy. Thus, the evolution of our social order into a mechanized structure has placed us in double jeopardy. First, it has produced long range weapons capable of great destruction, and, second, it has created the targets for these weapons.

We know that our only possible military enemy in the foreseeable future is a land mass power—operating on interior land and river lines of communication. We know that this power, geographically and economically, is not particularly vulnerable to sea blockade and strangulation . . .

We also know that the U.S.S.R. has a powerful land force,

in being today, on the Eurasian continent. This land force is backed up by secure and relatively short land lines of communication. We know that, today, if we wanted a numerical land power equality with this Russian force, we would be required to maintain an army on the continent of Europe as large as the one we built for World War II. We know, further, that even this force would be outnumbered . . . with the full mobilization of Russian land power potential. We know that the continued maintenance of an army of this size would impose such a staggering load on our economy that our standard of living and our democratic way of life would be seriously affected. We know also that the projection of land power, in mass, across the seas requires control of those seas, and we know that—while Russia is herself relatively invulnerable to a sea power attack—she has a submarine potential which could seriously interfere with, and possibly defeat, any opposing force requiring vast movement of logistics across the ocean. All these things, then, involved in an offensive land power strategy, make it look extremely costly, hazardous, and uncertain of success.

By logic, therefore, we are forced to the conclusion that a basic strategy of neutralization is our chief hope of balancing the equation—of balancing the equation to such a degree that we can hope to defend ourselves successfully.

Such a strategy—a strategy of neutralization—does not mean that land power and sea power are excluded from the operation. They would participate in roles appropriate to the support of that strategy. All of our military forces would be integrated toward the common strategic objective of neutralization. This strategy would permit maximum utilization of our technological superiorities and maximum exploitation of enemy weaknesses. It would avoid the areas of greatest enemy strength. It would be designed to the geography of the situation, to the enemy's weaknesses, to our own strengths, and to the achievement of our post-war objectives, if a war were to be forced upon us by enemy aggression.*

Along these same lines General Fairchild wrote the following, in June, 1948:

Out of the smoke and shambles of Europe and Asia, from Pearl Harbor to Hiroshima, loom two major implications:

If in the future era of atomic and global warfare the United States should again become involved in war, the enemy will not strike the first blow at an isolated outpost. He will, without warning and with devastating suddenness, direct many blows against our homeland itself, our vital centers, our industries and our people.

After the outbreak of hostilities in such a future war, there will not be time for us to learn from either enemy or ally or to train millions of men, or to start from scratch and convert our enormous industrial potential into actual military power.

These two starkly realistic lessons must be made the basis of all our thinking and planning for the future. Should we disregard or misinterpret them, should we permit our thinking to become outdated and our planning to produce an obsolete air force incapable of forestalling, or warding off, of mitigating that powerful and sudden initial blow, any future war may be all over with a neatness and dispatch which will allow time for only three tragic realizations: we were wrong; we failed; we betrayed our country and our way of life to complete destruction.

Since these words were written, much has happened to document their prophetic nature. The loss of the Chinese mainland to communism became complete. The U.S.S.R. ex-

* From a 1947 paper by Major General Orville A. Anderson, Commandant, Air War College, forwarded to me at the time it was prepared.

22

ploded its first nuclear device (which both men accurately predicted in other works of the time); the Korean war came along and America settled for an inglorious stalemate; "limited war" became a fad and a convenient excuse for deferring hard decisions and sweeping fundamental principles under the rug. I am not an advocate of "preventive war," but believe it is obvious that we must take a hard look at our political-military strategy.

Nuclear Weapons

Despite interservice differences of judgment, the military services were in agreement on two basic points throughout the postwar period: none trusted the Communist theme of peaceful coexistence; all recognized the tremendous fire power afforded by nuclear weaponry.

Consequently, the Air Force sought to strengthen its position in nuclear delivery capability and both the Army and Navy initiated vigorous programs to adapt nuclear fire power to their traditional land and sea weapons systems. These efforts created additional interservice problems because, at that time, we found ourselves in a position of "nuclear scarcity." Not much is heard about nuclear scarcity at the present time, but what it meant in those days was that the United States had a very limited amount of nuclear materials which could be fabricated into weapons of war.

The first generation of weapons developed for Army and Navy delivery were smaller and far less efficient in the use of scarce nuclear material than were the larger bombs which the Air Force could use with its existing bombardment forces. Because of this the Air Force desperately fought to channel nuclear products into weapons for the strategic striking bombardment forces, while the Navy and Army insisted on a substantial allocation of nuclear material to weapons which they could employ.

These first five years of the Nuclear Age created many diffi-

23

cult problems for the military establishment aside from allocation of limited available nuclear materials for the manufacture of existing or possible weapons systems. Two of these problems deserve special mention: first, intelligence estimates as to the rate of probable progress of the U.S.S.R. in the nuclear field; and second, the requirement for a United States nuclear detection system to find out how well the Soviets were, in fact, doing.

With respect to intelligence estimates, a large segment of the United States scientific community believed that Soviet progress would be very slow—that we had plenty of time. The leadership of the Army and Navy generally tended to agree with this estimate. All government leaders, military and civil, had a high regard for the contribution of science and technology to military preparedness; and if the Soviet build-up in nuclear technology was to be slow, there was no urgent necessity to build up our air defense system or expand our strategic nuclear forces. Therefore, more resources could be allocated to ease the pressing requirements of the land and sea forces. The Air Force took the opposing view. It insisted that Soviet nuclear technology would move rapidly and, accordingly, more of the nation's available resources should be channeled into strategic strike and continental defense forces.

The second problem, the need for a technical system to detect Soviet nuclear experiments was directly related to the intelligence estimates. If Soviet progress were to be slow, there was no immediate requirement to spend dollars needed elsewhere on a system to detect a nonexistent threat.

Documented history of this period, much of it still unnecessarily classified, indicates quite clearly that the Air Force put up a one-service fight on this issue, but finally carried its point. If our decision on this question had been otherwise, the government would not have known when the Soviets, in 1949, did, in fact, explode their first nuclear device. I will always have the greatest respect for the military officials from the intelligence community and for those among the nuclear spec-

24

ialists whose vision in this matter and whose dedication to duty brought the U.S. nuclear detection system into being.

Over the years which followed, nuclear material became more plentiful and nuclear weapons technology advanced with great speed. Army and Navy nuclear weapons delivery became more efficient and more effective during these same years, and gradually interservice divergence of views on nuclear energy matters was greatly reduced. In looking at the resolution of these issues from the vantage point of 1966, I am inclined to think that our military system of checks and balances worked very well under the circumstances which existed in those years. Every responsible military man had his day in court. The highest executive-level decisions were based on decisions made by competent lesser staffs. Certainly, the Army and Navy were right in fighting for the development of nuclear fire power adaptable to their basic missions and weapons systems. Certainly, the Air Force was right in fighting to build up a powerful strategic nuclear force and in fighting for a nuclear detection system which would keep the nation informed on Soviet progress. None, at that time, gainsaid the right of military leaders to speak out on service issues.

If, in those days, the military had had an autocratic single military chief of staff over all the armed forces, he might have favored one viewpoint or the other—and could have proven wrong in whichever decision he made. Likewise, if the military services had had an autocratic Secretary of Defense, he might well have made a judgment disastrous in its implications for the future. I do not believe in compromise simply for the sake of agreement, nor do I believe in pampering individual service judgments. However, forty-four years of military experience has indicated to me that no one man can see around all corners. The professional judgments of dedicated career men who fight on land, at sea, and in the air should not be taken lightly.

In looking back at the problems of those first hectic years of the Nuclear Age, it is a source of personal satisfaction to

25

I I 3 0 I

me that during my last year of active duty (1960) the Joint Chiefs of Staff were unanimously agreed on the allocation of 99 percent of the kilograms of nuclear material which was available for weapons purposes. We were all agreed on the nature of Communist nuclear capability and the status of their nuclear technology.

Organization for National Security

In addition to the planning, management, technical, budgetary, and intelligence problems of the postwar years, the White House and the armed forces faced monumental tasks of government reorganization. The structure of government had been improvised during World War II by the appending of many temporary boards and committees to assist in the prosecution of the war effort on the home front. These temporary groups and committees had to be dissolved, integrated, or replaced with more permanent organizations and procedures to deal with the new burdens imposed by our burgeoning international responsibilities.

Organization is a tedious subject. This being so, I am noting here only three topics which must be fully understood if the implications of the events which followed are to be appreciated. The first is the enactment of the National Security Act of 1947. This Act provided for the establishment of the National Security Council, the Joint Chiefs of Staff, the Office of the Secretary of Defense, the Central Intelligence Agency, and the establishment of a separate Air Force, and finally the roles and missions of the military services. The second of these important organizational actions, from a defense standpoint, was the Key West Agreement between the services which spelled out what each service would do to prepare for and maintain the security of the United States. The third and more or less concurrent action was the establishment of the United Nations.

The firm intent of the National Security Act of 1947, as

expressed by the Congress, is well worth repeating as the people of the United States look toward the future.

In enacting this legislation, it is the intent of Congress to provide a comprehensive program for the future security of the United States; to provide for the establishment of integrated policies and procedures for the departments, agencies, and functions of the Government relating to the national security; to provide three military departments for the operation and administration of the Army, the Navy (including naval aviation and the United States Marine Corps), and the Air Force, with their assigned combat and service components; to provide for their authoritative co-ordination and unified direction under civilian control but not to merge them; to provide for the effective strategic direction of the armed forces and for their operation under unified control and for their integration into an efficient team of land, naval, and air forces.

In accordance with this statement of Congressional intent, the 1947 Act established the National Security Council (with the President presiding) as the agency to advise the President on national security matters. It established the Central Intelligence Agency as the principal office to advise the National Security Council on intelligence matters affecting the national security, and further, to advise the National Security Council on matters of co-ordination of the various intelligence activities of the government. It created the National Military Establishment (Army, Air Force, and Navy—to include the Marine Corps) and the position of the Secretary of Defense, who was to establish general policies and programs for the National Military Establishment and to exercise general direction, authority, and control over such departments and agencies. It created a separate Air Force, coequal with the Army and the Navy, within the National Military Establishment. It established the Joint Chiefs of Staff and their Joint Staff within the

27

National Military Establishment—but it did *not* provide for a Chairman of the Joint Chiefs of Staff. Under this Act the original Joint Chiefs of Staff consisted of the Chief of Staff of the U.S. Army, the Chief of Naval Operations, the Chief of Staff of the U.S. Air Force, and the Chief of Staff to the Commander in Chief, should there be one. This latter position, incidentally, has not been filled since the retirement of Admiral Leahy in 1949. Under this original Act the Joint Staff was to be composed of no more than one hundred officers selected in approximately equal numbers from the Departments of the Army, Navy, and Air Force.

The National Security Act of 1947 also provided that the members of the National Security Council would include the President and the Secretary of State, the newly created Secretary of Defense, and the Secretaries of the Army, Navy, and Air Force. The council also included the heads of important wartime boards which were yet in existence, principally the National Security Resources Board, the Munitions Board, and the Research and Development Board.

The original composition of the National Security Council is important to remember because the framework which has evolved today shows a far greater centralization and concentration of power in the office of the Secretary of Defense than was initially intended by the Congress. The National Security Resources Board, the Munitions Board, and the Research and Development Board have disappeared and their former functions are now directly under the control of the Secretary of Defense. Likewise, the Secretaries of the Army, Navy, and Air Force are no longer members of the National Security Council. This subject will be discussed later in more detail.

The gradual evolution toward the centralization of control of defense matters had its first milestone in an act of the 81st Congress in 1949. This 1949 amendment to the Act of 1947 established the Department of Defense (in lieu of the National Military Establishment) as an "Executive Department of the Government"; it reduced the status of the Departments

28

of the Army, Navy, and Air Force from Executive Departments to Military Departments of the Department of Defense; it provided that the Secretary of Defense should have a Deputy Secretary of Defense and three Assistant Secretaries of Defense; and it somewhat strengthened the hold of the Secretary of Defense over the Military Departments and the Military Forces. However, the Secretary of Defense was still denied by law the authority to transfer, reassign, abolish, or consolidate any of the combatant functions assigned by law to the military services.

The 1949 amendment also created the position of "Chairman of the Joint Chiefs of Staff" as a separate office, but provided that the Chairman should have "no vote." The "no vote" provision of the law made no sense to the military because the Joint Chiefs of Staff do not operate on the basis of majority vote. There is a free expression of opinion in JCS deliberations, and a line-up may occur in which there is a lone dissenter on a specific issue. However, in such cases the majority "vote" is not binding. A lone dissenter then had, and still has, the authority to take his views to the Secretary of Defense, to the National Security Council, and ultimately to the President, if he so chooses.

The intent of the provision (that the Chairman of the JCS had "no vote") was coupled with another statement that there should not be a single Chief of Staff superimposed over the armed forces. Probably this reflected the traditional U.S. fear that a "man on horseback" would take the country over if the nation were not extremely careful. Nothing, of course, in U.S. military history has ever justified any such fear. The military leaders of the United States believe in civilian control, have fought for this principle, and would be the first to object to any changes which might lead to a military dictatorship. However, these ancient fears still persist in some quarters—and are sometimes used by individuals as a deliberate means of downgrading the professional military establishment.

Finally, the 1949 amendment to the National Security Act of

29

1947 increased the size of the Joint Staff from 100 officers to 210 officers, while at the same time providing that there should be no "Armed Forces General Staff." This may seem like a contradiction—but it was not. Many lawmakers in the United States feared a "Prussian-type general staff" in the same way that they feared the emergence of a military "man on horseback" who would take the country over.

Probably no military subject has ever been more misrepresented by writers and amateurs on military subjects than the nature and functioning of the German General Staff. The German General Staff of World Wars I and II bore no resemblance to our "Joint Staff" system. The German General Staff was predominantly an army staff, and it was composed of career staff officers who were selected very early in their lives for more or less continuous staff duty. On the other hand, the U.S. Joint Staff is a staff balanced among officers experienced in land warfare, sea warfare, and air warfare. These men are on the Joint Staff from two to four years in Washington, then return to operational duties in their own services or with other joint field commands.

In 1948 the Nation's first Secretary of Defense, James F. Forrestal, ordered the Joint Chiefs of Staff to take a sabbatical at Key West, Florida, for an intellectual reassessment of roles and missions of the armed forces. He hoped for a solution to the increasingly ugly internal struggle for resources. Unfortunately, no such solution came from the meeting. When reduced to the actual meaning of the many words of the document, the mission of the Army was only restated to be the defeat of enemy ground forces; the Navy's was to be control of the seas; and the Air Force was charged with securing and controlling the air. These missions and their service assignments were, of course, precisely the same prior to Key West. The promise of equal budgeting for the three services to maintain the *status quo* of the balanced forces concept was also strongly implied.

This redefinition of the roles and missions apparently failed to consider, or to strike at, the real core of interservice rivalry. It would seem, from agreements reached, that some fears had been expressed that one service might cannibalize another. But I don't believe that any responsible military chief of service ever actually entertained such an intention except, perhaps, as a "paper exercise." The complexities of modern war would absolutely prohibit a one-service or two-service system. The decisions inherent in splitting away the Air Force from the Department of the Army during World War II attest to this.

No, the real cause of interservice rivalry was—and is today —due to the fact that the power and speed and range of modern weapons have virtually annihilated space and time which traditionally provided neat distinctions between ground warfare and sea warfare. As a result, each service, forced by expanding technologies and constricting budgets, inevitably found its weapons systems delivery plans overlapping another service's mission. The Key West agreement, therefore, did not allay the restive interservice rivalry for limited resources and "first line of defense" recognition.

Interservice Problems

The rivalry of these early postwar years is probably best exemplified by the feud which mushroomed between the Air Force and the Navy regarding the B-36 long-range bomber and the strategic doctrine which it served. The feud, with its attacks and counterattacks becoming more and more heated, and finally resulted in a full-scale Congressional investigation of the B-36 program.

An appropriation urgently desired by the Navy for a 65,000-ton aircraft carrier, United States, and, in addition, progressive modernization and support for its aircraft carrier force was denied by an economy-bent Congress at the suggestion of

Secretary of Defense, Louis Johnson. At the same time, funds were made available to the Air Force to continue the B-36 program at a slow pace.*

Some officials of the Navy and of Congress decided to attack the B-36 as a "billion dollar blunder," hoping to stop the program and thereby release the monies involved for what they sincerely believed to be more important defense requirements. So virulent were the attacks against the Air Force and the contractor to whom the award was made, that the House Armed Services Committee was called upon in 1949 to conduct full-scale hearings on the plane and the backstage charges.

The results of that Congressional investigation are a matter of history.† Both the White House and the Congress favored the Air Force view. During the next decade, 385 B-36 long-range bombers were delivered to the U.S. Air Force and during that decade menacing words from the Kremlin and the march of communism across Southeastern Asia and toward Europe raised the strategic bombing theory to overwhelming military importance.

---

* It might be well, incidentally, to note here that genesis of the B-36 dated back to April, 1941, before the United States entered World War II. The first bomber rolled off the production line in late 1945 and, following more than two years of tests and "de-bugging," was delivered to the Air Force in August, 1947.

† *Report of the House Committee on Armed Services 81st Congress, "Investigation of the B-36 Bomber Program."*

"It is the unanimous judgment of the committee that the B-36 bomber was selected and procured regularly, based on an honest conviction that it is the best available aircraft for its purpose in the defense of the United States today, and that there is not a scintilla of evidence to support the charges, reports, rumors, and innuendoes which have been the subject of inquiry under item 1 of the agenda. In order that there might be no delay in clearing all those who have been unwarrantedly or erroneously charged, this judgment was made public by the following resolution adopted unanimously by the committee at the close of the hearing on August 25, 1949:

The White House and Congressional decisions regarding war deterrence via the long-range delivery system of the B-36 also heralded the first significant post-World War II move toward adoption of a foreign policy based on nuclear weapons delivery. At the same time, the Air Force was politically favored because at that time only it had the capability to deliver the atomic bomb. From the point of view of a stringent defense economy, the long strategic reach of the B-36 was also the cheapest way to insure some measure of strength via the atomic monopoly—far cheaper than attempting to keep millions of men under arms.

Had defense appropriations been greater, this argument might not have progressed to its logical conclusion. However, military policy at that time was directed toward only two possibilities which could seriously threaten the United States: first, direct attack upon the United States, and second, direct attack upon Western Europe. U.S. policy at that time offered no solutions to gradual reversal of the balance of power through subversion and political infiltration of weakened governments or emergent nations. In fact, national policy at that time generally denied that these possibilities were of any real military concern.

There has not been in the judgment of the entire committee one iota, not one scintilla of evidence offered thus far in these hearings that support charges that collusion, fraud, corruption, influence, or favoritism played any part whatsoever in the procurement of the B-36 bomber.

There has been very substantial and compelling evidence that the Air Force selected and procured this bomber solely on the ground that this is the best aircraft for its purpose available to the Nation today.

At this time we feel that the Nation should know that the Secretary of the Air Force, Mr. Symington, the leaders of the Air Force, and Mr. Johnson, the Secretary of Defense, have come through this inquiry without the slightest blemish and that these men continue to merit the complete confidence of the American people in their past actions and in the future."

33

Deterrence through strategic delivery of nuclear weapons thus moved into the forefront of our military policy. So much was it in accord with popular national thought that not only did the incumbent Administration concur, but so did the opposing political party through former President Herbert Hoover. The policy also found great favor with Secretary of Defense Louis Johnson, who was convinced that the Soviets hoped to induce the United States to spend itself into bankruptcy.

Our military stance during the late forties is probably best summed up in the words of the Chairman of the Joint Chiefs of Staff as delivered to the First Session of the 81st Congress in 1949. Paraphrased freely for brevity here, General Omar T. Bradley declared:

We assume that the only dangerous force in the world today is Communism, and the only nations whose postwar actions have indicated an opposition to the tranquility we seek are the Soviet Union and her Satellites.

The North Atlantic powers, opposing this, now combine in natural resources more of the vital factors for defense than the Soviet combination, except in the case of manpower. Geographically, Russia and her satellites stand next door to western Europe, undoubtedly a desirable commercial, industrial, and cultural prize. The Americans have joined with allies to save this prize from interests opposed to our own.

Our basic concept for defense includes protection of the United States and this continent in case we are attacked. It provides for early retaliation from bases which we hope to have ready at all times. This concept includes a decision that we shall have to be ready to seize other bases so that we may attack the enemy country at shorter ranges. Strategic bombing, therefore, has high priority in our military planning, because we cannot hope to keep forces in-being of sufficient size to meet Russia in the early stages of war.

This is particularly true since we are never going to start the war.

General Bradley's assertions concerned themselves with the political objective of preservation of the status quo, with the economic problems of the day, and implicitly with our nuclear superiority. The military doctrine of that time was thus dictated by the political and economic factors and was given support and meaning by virtue of our superiority in military technology.

Like the Air Force and the Navy, the United States Army had its problems during this five-year period. As a result, the Army, too, vigorously contested for what defense resources were available—and with considerable justification. The Army had most of the responsibility for occupation duties and for directing the various occupied governmental activities back into normal civilian control. That service distinguished itself in the performance of this thankless task in the face of constantly dwindling manpower and dollars.

The progressive reduction of Army strength in Korea during the late forties, and the conversion of its remaining units in that area to not much more than training cadres, was one of the major factors which led to the Soviet decision to initiate the Korean War. Simultaneously with the reductions in Army forces, the tactical air forces required to support Army forces were likewise being disbanded or denied logistical support to the point that they lost combat effectiveness.

The practical elimination from Korea of Army and tactical air force capabilities to fight effectively was tantamount to a U.S. political announcement that South Korea was of no vital strategic significance to America.

In fact, in a speech before the National Press Club in Washington on January 12, 1950, U.S. Secretary of State Dean Acheson offered an answer to this question. He declared that the defensive perimeter of the United States ran from the Aleutians to Japan then to the Ryukyus and then to the Philip-

35

pines. The United States military forces held defensive positions along this line, and this perimeter of defense would be unilaterally defended by the United States. Should an attack occur in some other area in the Pacific, Acheson stated that initial reliance on resistance to such an attack would be expected from the people subjected to the attack and "then upon the commitments of the entire civilized world under the Charter of the United Nations, which so far has not proved a weak reed to lean on by any people who were determined to protect their independence against outside aggression."*

Secretary Acheson's speech was criticized by those who said that it informed the Communists that the United States did not intend to defend Korea or Formosa. But in the *soft-spoken* language of diplomacy Acheson had actually stated that the United States would unilaterally defend areas which were strategically important to it and would participate with the United Nations to check aggression against other free peoples in the Pacific.

This combination of affairs apparently convinced the U.S.S.R. that a movement from North to South Korea was invited and would not be resisted by the United States. Therefore, I think that it can be fairly stated that our frantic unilateral demobilization following World War II and our tight postwar budget, coupled with an indecisive foreign policy— particularly as it affected Asia—brought on the Korean War.

Technical Viewpoints in Conflict

In addition to our problems with the budget, various concepts of war, nuclear energy, reorganization, and specific interservice problems such as the B-36 investigation, we had our problems with a part of the scientific community.

That part of the scientific community which was most active in political affairs was attempting to influence national policy on the basis of their belief that the U.S.S.R. was so

* Present at this luncheon were several members of the Soviet Press.

technically backward and retarded that it would take at least a generation for them to create an atomic device.

The foremost defense scientist at the time, Dr. Vannevar Bush, was one of the leaders of the scientific group which tended to underestimate Soviet capabilities. Dr. Bush had headed the Office of Scientific Research and Development during the war, and his views on defense matters carried considerable weight. These views were laid out in their entirety in a book entitled *Modern Arms and Free Men*, published in the fall of 1949. It came off the press during the month that President Truman announced that the U.S.S.R. had detonated its first atomic device.

Ironically, the book presented a very lengthy explanation as to why, in all future wars, the "defense" would probably always be ascendant over the "offense"; why the ballistic missile would never be a significant instrument of war; and why the organizational environment within the U.S.S.R. would make progress in the nuclear field uncertain and slow.

These mistaken judgments on the part of one of America's greatest scientists must be candidly stated because of a similar mistake which we seem to be making today with respect to military space technology. Those in Government who are actively holding back U.S. military space programs are cautiously asking for a definition of the precise military mission to be performed in space. At the same time they are over cautiously wedding space vehicles to armaments which they understand—such as nuclear warheads. In their thinking they are allowing one technology to move ahead, that of space propulsion and space vehicles, but they are not taking into account the progress in weaponry which will also occur.

Shortly after the book, *Modern Arms and Free Men*, was released to the public, one of my colleagues* wrote me this candid analysis:

* Ramsay D. Potts, Jr., a World War II combat pilot and staff officer with a distinguished military record, later Military Executive to the first Secretary of the Air Force, Stuart Symington; at the time

Several reviewers have stated that they thought the book should have been revised prior to publication in the light of President Truman's announcement that the Russians had set off an atomic explosion. As a matter of fact, some of the advanced copies did carry statements in general terms which indicated that Dr. Bush thought the Russians would have the bomb about 1960. These statements were deleted from the version issued to the public, but apparently no other revisions in context were made. This 1960 date seems to agree with some earlier forecasts which Dr. Bush had made as to the estimated time when the Russians would have the A-bomb.

In emphasizing the ascending power of the defense, the author uses a weapon vs. weapon approach, rather than considering the question by making a weapons system analysis. There seems to be no appreciation in the book of the difference between this proving ground approach of the author, and the weapons system approach which military planners must use. This approach is to be expected from a man who is primarily a gadgeteer and inventor, but it nevertheless impairs the value of the book as a guide to the professional military student.

In considering weapons the author classifies them as either offensive or defensive. This is a fallacious technique since it is not the weapons but the use to which a weapon is put which determines whether it is "offensive" or "defensive."

There are other reasons why it is basically fallacious to attempt to analyze modern warfare from a unit weapon point of view. Other factors, such as the state of training of the using personnel, the tactical employment of the weapons, and the quantity and replaceability of weapons

---

of his analysis of *Modern Arms and Free Men*, an Air Force Reserve Colonel on active duty; presently an Attorney in Washington, D.C., and a Major General in the Air Force Reserve, Inactive Status.

are equally as important as the potential capability of the individual units of hardware.

The Atomic Bomb. The author seems to have made two grave errors in his discussion on this subject. First, he states that the prospect of two nations facing each other, each possessing a substantial quantity of A-bombs, is still farther into the future than we think. This is in line with Dr. Bush's forecast that it would be 1960 before the Russians had the atomic bomb. A second error is the statement that atomic bombs are "scarce and highly expensive in terms of destruction accomplished per dollar disbursed." In refutation of this, a statement from J.R. Oppenheimer in Chapter V of *One World or None* is pertinent. Oppenheimer says that in World War II the cost of delivering high explosives to the enemy target was about $10.00 per pound. Thus it would cost about $400,000,000 to deliver 20,000 tons of high explosives. Unofficial estimates of the cost of present A-bombs having 20,000 tons of TNT explosive energy equivalent, give a cost figure of $1,000,000.

Atomic Propulsion. He sees this as being of no great tactical advantage to the United States either in ships or aircraft since, to his mind, the unlimited extension of range is not a critical factor in the present world situation, our foreign policy being what it is.*

Many scientists, generally those less active politically, did not agree with the group who seemed determined to push the United States toward unilateral nuclear disarmament. Among these, Dr. Edward Teller stands out. Dr. Teller lived, and still lives, in a real world—not in a dream world. Without his services our government possibly might have been bullied by the "soft line" group into a decision not to build the H-bomb. Dr. Teller has not tried to run away from the nuclear

* Author's Note: If this judgment had been correct, the Polaris Submarine would not be here today.

problem, or to sweep it under the rug. He has helped to master these new forces for the long-term good of humanity.

Also on the "plus" side, one of the foremost contributions to national security planning of this period resulted from the establishment by President Truman of a commission to make an "objective inquiry into national aviation policies and problems" and to assist the President in "formulating an integrated national aviation policy." President Truman established this commission in 1947. It was headed by Mr. Thomas K. Finletter. The far-sighted and distinguished work done by the Finletter committee was reported in a document entitled "Survival in the Air Age." This document was the formal report of the commission to the President. Some of the most enduring of the judgments rendered are quoted here:

. . . It is difficult for a representative democracy to keep up with an authoritarian state in an armament race in peacetime. It can, however, be done. We gained supremacy of the seas by the weight of our naval armament. We can be supreme in the air by the weight of our air power. The United States can build a Military Establishment which will keep up with any nation and be a powerful force for peace.

In our opinion this Military Establishment must be built around the air arm. Of course, an adequate Navy and Ground Force must be maintained. But it is the Air Force and naval aviation on which we must mainly rely. Our military security must be based on air power. . . . Atomic weapons will not long remain our monopoly . . .

This means that the traditional peacetime strategy of the United States must be changed radically. We can no longer count on having our cities and the rest of our mainland untouched in a future war. On the contrary, we must count on our homeland becoming increasingly vulnerable as the weapons increase in destructiveness and the means of delivering them are improved. And we must assume that if future aggressors will have learned anything from World

40

Wars I and II it will be that they must never let United States industrial power get under way; they must destroy it at the outset if they are to win.

The strategy to meet these new conditions is obviously that which we have described above—to have in peacetime a force in being which will protect to the greatest extent possible our air space as well as our water approaches and hold out to anyone who thinks of attacking us the prospect of a counter-attack of the utmost violence. The hope, of course, is that the existence of such a force will do more than win a war; the hope is that by serving notice that war with the United States would be a most unprofitable busines we may persuade the nations to work for peace instead of war.

We have been told by highly qualified persons that other nations may have atomic weapons now. We have been told by equally qualified persons that they will not have them in quantity for 15 years. We cannot rely entirely, therefore, on any one opinion, no matter how expert. Our estimate is based on our composite appraisal of a large number of estimates and of the facts on which they are based. We also have had the benefit of a similar study made by the President's Advisory Commission on Universal Training which used the estimate made that other powers would have atomic weapons sometime between 1951 and 1957.

. . . If other nations develop the means of direct assault on the United States by supersonic piloted aircraft, the threat to this country will be serious, even though these vehicles are not equipped with atomic or comparable weapons. Similarly, if other nations develop atomic weapons in quantity, or some other weapon of comparable destructiveness, the threat to this country will be great even though these nations have only the present means of delivery at their disposition. The addition of supersonic transpolar or transoceanic guided missiles would intensify the damage that could be done by an atomic attack. Should all these

41

developments exist at the same time, the situation would be very grave indeed.

From these sharply conflicting views—those of Dr. Bush and the Finletter Commission—it can be seen that the birth pains of a nuclear strategy were indeed severe. During the course of this great debate the Air Force, being responsible for the air defense of the United States, obviously paid heed to those who believed that Soviet progress in nuclear and other technological areas would be rapid. As the Finletter report stated, the stakes were too high to gamble on the validity of the more conservative estimates.

Today America faces the same gamble and the same controversy regarding ballistic missile defense, the importance of very high-yield nuclear weapons, and the utility of space for military operations. There are great differences of judgment but, unfortunately, the government seems to be gambling on the judgment of the more conservative of the group who have interest in these problems.

The U.S.S.R. Moves

While the great debate over technology and the militancy of the Communist intent was in progress in the United States, the Soviet powers were not hampered in the semantics of military preparedness. The Chinese mainland was taken over by the Communists, and a massive effort was under way within the U.S.S.R. to improve its technological base and to rebuild from the damage and wreckage of the war.

The initial attempts of the U.S.S.R. toward improving its technological base were concentrated on development of aircraft production, the development of nuclear weapons, and on exploitation of rocket technology. Two B-29 bombers forced down in the Soviet Union were impounded, taken apart, analyzed, and a copy reproduced by the U.S.S.R. became known as the TU-4. On the nuclear side, Russian espionage rings in Canada, the United Kingdom, and the United States made excellent progress and the necessary technological information was soon in Soviet hands. These espionage efforts reduced by many years the time that would have been necessary for solution of these problems through indigenous Soviet efforts. It is probable that the recognition or lack of recognition of these activities caused the wide diversion of opinion among our experts as to when the Soviets would produce their first bomb. Military professionals took into account the probability of espionage while many scientists did not.

The U.S.S.R. was also quick to grasp the potential of ballistic missiles, as demonstrated by the primitive German V-2. As a consequence, while some of America's leading scientists were proving on paper that the ballistic missile would never be a significant weapon for future war, the U.S.S.R. was rapidly moving ahead in hardware development of powerful rocket engines. The Soviet effort in this area resulted in that nation's tremendous initial lead in the development of ballistic missiles and space technology.

The fundamental lesson to be learned from these experiences is that *there is no such thing* as a "technological plateau" beyond which significant progress in weapons development may not be made. Technology does not stand still. Some in our government may believe that it can, but these people live in a world of hopes and dreams. The evidence that Russia does not subscribe to the thesis of technological plateau is becoming bitterly apparent.

Even today, camouflaged as it is in the topsy-turvy world of Congos, Cubas, Vietnams, and our hopes for a change in the eventual objectives of the Communist conspiracy, one essential fact still looms bleakly: the Free World population and this nation's tremendous power base are vulnerable today to the sudden onslaught so feared twenty years ago by far-sighted planners whose advice was largely ignored.

43

Chapter III

EVOLUTION
OF THE UNITED STATES
NATIONAL SECURITY POLICY
(NSC-68)

The equation of U.S. military force levels needed to ensure the peace following World War II began to take shape during the fall of 1949 in the halls of Congress. It did not come about because of peaceful debate, it came in the ominous echo of the "premature" explosion of an atomic device by the Soviet Union.

The shock of the explosion sprang around the world even as some of the most brilliant scientific and engineering minds in the United States were assuring us that it couldn't happen for years, possibly as long as twenty. The event was announced to the world by President Truman, September 23, 1949.

However, even in the face of this announcement, highly placed civilian officials of the Administration's Defense Department tended to minimize the importance of the event by making public statements to the effect that it made no real difference to the National Security strategy of the United States.

Nonetheless, the fact that the U.S.S.R. had broken our

44

atomic monopoly did trigger frantic action in Washington. The implications of the Soviet breakthrough were chilling and were generally agreed to by responsible members of Congress and by the uniformed establishment. There was little doubt in these quarters that in a few years the Soviet Union would be entirely capable of launching a surprise attack on the United States. Simultaneously, the U.S.S.R. could move massive land armies and tactical air forces against Europe and support the forces of the Chinese Communists against Southeast Asia.

The strategic problems facing the United States as a result of the Soviet achievement were only too clear:

1. *Situation Report, Free World—Europe, 1949.*

West Germany was still digging itself out from under the rubble of war. For the most part, its new industrial base was embryonic. Italy was faced with the same difficulties and, in addition, was torn with internal power politics. As a nation it was thin with hunger. France shook with the plague of political indecision and change. Its industrial base and finances were both in delicate balance. England, while pulling herself together in quiet dignity, was financially distraught and beset by colonial demands for freedom. Spain, neutral to all intents and purpose during World War II, was still struggling with the after-effects of its Civil War of the late thirties.

The fact that Russia had not demobilized at the end of World War II made a weakened, war-sickened Free Europe a hostage in the clouding international power situation. Soviet forces-in-being, as well as its logistic forces-in-being during the 1947–1949 period were believed by many thoughtful strategists adequate to overrun Europe. Judgment was that in a prolonged action, the U.S.S.R. would have lost, but at a frightful cost to both belligerents and at the expense of Western Europe, which would have been utterly shattered in the battle. This sobering judgment was made despite consideration of the U.S. atomic capability being applied directly against the Soviet power base.

It is true that this nation had not been entirely static on the political-military front during the 1947–1949 period. As early as 1948, all levels of the Pentagon had approved the basic idea of free world collective security and in 1949, we followed up the Marshall Plan with the Military Aid Program.

2. *Situation Report, Free World—Asia, 1949.*

Physically and financially prostrate from its war losses and struggling to rebuild its industry, Japan would be an easy target for Communist China's massive army. The Philippines were in difficulty and Australia was occupied in assessing its war damage. The other "free" nations of Southeast Asia had little to offer. Nationalist China was the strongest, yet even free China would need help to maintain its independence from communism. And, both France and England were facing serious problems within their Southeast Asia spheres of interest.

The logistic and the manpower advantages of the Communist forces for any engagement in Europe and Asia were, of course, tremendous. The Communists would be operating along interior land lines of communications, while the United States would have the difficult problem of maintaining sea and air lanes of communication for logistic support of military operations.

From the end of World War II, and the hasty demobilization that followed, until the fall of 1949, military support of United States foreign policy rested on a capability for atomic retaliation, and upon little else. It was then, and only then, glaringly apparent to those who dealt with military-political policy matters in our government that both our past military-political doctrine and the efforts made in support of that doctrine were inadequate. Confronted with the imminent loss

46

of our atomic monopoly, this nation would need to make a greatly increased effort to provide against the dangers of Soviet atomic attack or the threat of such an attack.

In short order, an analysis of the security implications of the Soviet atomic explosion was speedily made by members of the National Security Council (contributions were made principally by the White House, Department of State, various elements of the Department of Defense, the Atomic Energy Commission, and the Central Intelligence Agency) and a specifically articulated national security policy was evolved. Known as "NSC-68," the policy was approved in principle by President Truman in April, 1950. The detailed programs to support the new policy were just being developed when the attack on South Korea took place on June 25, 1950. The decision to adopt this policy set the United States on the strategic policy path which it still follows to some degree today.

Four Closed Courses of Action

In light of the Soviet Union's entry into the atomic energy field and the manifest hostility of the Soviet Bloc to the Western World, coupled with the loss of the Chinese mainland to the Communists in 1949, NSC-68 sought to define a long-term strategy which would meet the national security need. Basically, NSC-68 identified and discussed four possible national courses of action, and recommended one of these courses as acceptable.

The four courses of action which were considered were:

1. A do-nothing policy—that is to say, a continuation of the slow-paced national security programs which had been characteristic of the immediate post-World War II years.
2. A policy of isolationism—a "Fortress America" concept which would concentrate upon bulwarking U.S. of-

47

fensive and defensive military strength at home and refusing major political involvement with, or assistance to, other nations of the Free World.

3. Pre-emptive action—advocated by those who believed that the world would become much too dangerous to live in if the Soviet Union were allowed time to develop a nuclear arsenal.

4. A policy of containment, comprising a technique of building an imaginary fence around that part of the world already behind the Iron Curtain and then taking all the necessary political, psychological, economic, and military actions required to contain the Soviet Bloc within its current perimeter.

Without attempting to condemn or to defend the reasoning which went into the decision taken, this is the summary of the Council's joint deliberation and recommendation:

The first alternative, a do-nothing policy, was really never given serious consideration. The terms of the policy were developed, and its consequences analyzed, simply to point up the extent of the danger facing the United States with the insinuation of this latest factor in the international game of "Russian Roulette." The point of the analysis was that we had better begin doing more to defend ourselves than we had been doing since World War II. None of the Council championed the do-nothing policy.

The second alternative, the policy of isolationism, had some advocates, but it was never a serious competitor. It was rejected on the basis of this logic: it would only postpone a decisive collision until after the Soviets had overrun the rest of the world, and the United States stood alone. It was already abundantly clear that the U.S.S.R. had declared war on the social, political, and economic structure of the Free World. Further, it made no moral or material sense for the United States to "stop the world" in which it lived in an effort to turn back the clock to the nineteenth century. Both

48

selfish interest and dedication to principle demanded that the "Fortress America" concept be rejected.

The third possible national course, "pre-emptive action" (preventive war, as it was called in those days), was advocated with much more vigor than either of the two possible solutions previously discussed.

Those advocating a pre-emptive course of action placed their reasoning in this frame of logic: it is clear that the Soviet Union intends to destroy our system of government and our way of life. In a future war, the power of military initiative (with nuclear weapons predominant in the order of battle) may well be decisive. While preventive war may be considered immoral, a much greater immorality would result if we were to allow our enemies to destroy our values and inherit the world. Ultimately we will fight, as we have done in the past, to preserve our way of life. Wouldn't it be in our best interests to confront the enemy before he has nation-killing weapons at his disposal? Therefore, issue an ultimatum, demand a stop to international Communist infiltration and subversion and replace the Iron Curtain with an open door. The ultimatum will, of course, be rejected by the U.S.S.R. At this point we will have established the basic morality of our position and will be free, in fact obligated, to act. A favorable military decision will be assured because the U.S.S.R. does not yet have a nuclear war capability.

The preceding argument, as outlined, was presented and defended by some very dedicated Americans. However, the Administration ruled out this course of action.

Preventive war was vetoed for two basic reasons: one ethical and one military. The ethical issue was expressed in the historic judgment that the United States did not instigate wars, that it is "un-American" to strike the first blow. The military issue was not so clearly a factor because there were differences of view. The military dilemma came as a result of this nation's unilateral demobilization after 1945. The Soviet Union had not demobilized, and there were many who

49

sincerely believed that the Red Army could quickly neutralize and capture Western Europe even if we used our small existing stock of nuclear weapons in a direct attack upon the U.S.S.R. This view was also held by many government officials in the United States as well as in Britain and France.

The decision reached was to accept the policy of containment.

At the time, in April, 1950, that the policy was approved in principle by President Harry S. Truman, the military leadership of the nation was reasonably well satisfied. The Communist threat to the national survival had at last been taken seriously. The policy paper stated, without reservation, that the United States must be ready to fight by July, 1954, the point in time at which the U.S.S.R. was estimated to be able to mount a serious nuclear weapons attack against the United States.

The policy meant a reversal of the "lean years" predicated in the aftermath of World War II. It meant that no matter what happened, our nation would be better prepared to defend itself, its four freedoms, its institutions, its culture, and its way of life.

NSC-68, however, quite properly was a "policy paper." It did not prescribe the strength and composition demanded of our armed forces. It was, therefore, up to the Department of Defense and the military services to translate the document into meaningful military terms.

The initial controversy between the services on how to divide up the resources available eased somewhat, though only temporarily, in June, 1950. In that month the North Korean Communists crossed the 38th parallel, and the Korean War was on. The impact on our defense budget was much more immediate and powerful than the existence of NSC-68. Our defense budget moved from a low of 11,094 billion dollars in 1948 to 38.9 billion dollars in 1952.

Even during this period, however, it was difficult to get the Secretary of Defense (Louis Johnson) off the austere budget path of the immediate postwar years. His office kept on trying to get by on a shoestring, and we could not have conducted the Korean operation without the use of accumulated World War II stocks in the Pacific which we had been able to salvage from the demobilization of 1946–1947.

However, the increase in resources available for defense purposes helped in arriving at force structure goals for the three military departments. All were relieved of the drastic limitations of the past several years, and consequently, each was more tolerant of allocations to the other services. Besides, a real war was on and it was no time for internal power struggles.

If the U.S.S.R. had not seen fit to start the Korean War at the time that they did, I doubt that the force build-up required by NSC-68 would have been possible. True, America knew that the Soviets had exploded an atomic device, but the Soviet Union was a long distance away. And the logic of NSC-68 alone would not have brought about an increase in the defense budget from 11 billion dollars to nearly 40 billion dollars almost overnight, nor would it have been sufficient to persuade the average man in the street that we had to mobilize our Reserves and National Guard. In this respect, Korea was a strategic blunder of the first magnitude on the part of the U.S.S.R.

Every American is interested in the security of the nation and the future opportunity of his children and grandchildren to live in a free world. This being so, I think it imperative that we should all know some of the rationale of the policy of containment and its obligations and its opportunities. I have traced and identified its origin as a defensive reaction to the advances of the Soviets in the field of nuclear energy. I have expressed judgment that the build-up of U.S. military strength required by the policy could not have been obtained without the stark reality of the Korean War. I have explained how the alternative policies—do-nothing, Fortress America, and preventive war—were all rejected. Against this background, thoughtful Americans should understand the implications of the containment theory in terms of specific elements of political and military policy and relationships.

Containment automatically involved the expansion of collective security arrangements, strategic deterrent forces and tactical forces to "contain." I will analyze the broad policy of containment, discuss the implications, obligations, and opportunities which evolved from the various elements of the policy and provide my personal judgments on what we did.

Before breaking down the policy of containment into its theoretical political-military components, however, it is necessary to understand the implications of world events which were taking place during the period of time in which our government adopted the policy. What was happening in Korea was probably most important and deserves special mention.

Implications of the Korean War

Our conduct of the Korean War left much to be desired. As a people the United States didn't seem to have much heart in the operation. Perhaps Americans were weary after the difficult years of World War II and didn't grasp the significance of the Korean problem or the urgency of its solution. At any rate, there was no real effort by U.S. leaders to get the country fired up in national patriotic fervor. The contrast with America's early World War II attitude was great indeed. In the Korean conflict, the nation seemed to want the easiest way out and it accepted, even tacitly encouraged, every compromise which was developed during the years of fighting and negotiations.

On July 27, 1950, our people applauded the announcement that the A-bomb would not be used in the Korean conflict. Things seemed to be going our way at the time but we ignored the subsequent fact that the Communists responded to this announcement, on July 28, by launching a major attack on all fronts. The U.S. public saw nothing wrong in announcing the decision not to use its best weapons. It is possible that this national decision *not* to use our best weapons, and our concomitant decision to so advise the masters of Red China, changed the course of history in Southeast Asia.

The nation saw nothing wrong, on September 27, 1950, when our government announced that the decision would be up to the United Nations as to how far north we would move in Korea. The American public saw nothing wrong on September 29, 1950, when South Korean troops were arbitrarily halted in their northern movement.

Apparently we had lost sight of the requirement for strategic flexibility, because we not only made a decision not to use the A-bomb, but we further compounded the effects of this decision by announcing to the world that the bomb would not be used and that we were going to keep south of the Yalu River. Regardless of the merits of these decisions, we should have kept them to ourselves.

Americans saw nothing wrong in these pronouncements because, apparently, as a nation, we wanted to get out of the Korean War. This national attitude was, of course, not lost upon the enemy. Indecision, lack of objective (failure to establish a single, unified, free Korea as a military objective), fear that Communist China would enter the war—all these things were understood by the opposing strategists.

By September, 1950, the U.S. had actually won the war in Korea, but threw it away precisely in the manner in which this nation threw away the political victories which were possible after our military success in World War II.

The incidents which followed should have been no surprise. On October 1, 1950—fresh on the heels of U.S.-U.N. military success, and fresh on the heels of obvious indecision—General MacArthur called for surrender of the opposing forces. He did this *after* military advantage had been fought for and won. But, also, General MacArthur's mandate came *after* the enemy had been told that the United States would withhold use of the A-bomb and that this nation was undecided as to how far north its forces would carry the operation.

The famous Wake Island Conference between General MacArthur and the President took place October 15, 1950, and at this conference all hands seemed to be congratulating themselves on the outcome in Korea. But the relentless purpose of the Communist forces had again been underestimated.

American indecision—with respect to the use of its best weaponry and in terms of political objectives—had been properly diagnosed by the enemy. On October 27, 1950, the Chinese Communists openly entered the war and in November, the U.S.-U.N. Supreme Commander, General MacArthur, advised the President and the Joint Chiefs of Staff that he had a totally new war on his hands.

It is painful even to review the record of the next seven months of American history. On the one hand, this nation was beginning the buildup of its military forces to achieve the force goals implied by NSC-68 to support the policy of containment. On the other hand, the U.S. was backing out of a direct challenge to all the things which it said this nation stood for. On November 16, 1950, the President assured the Chinese Communists that America had no intention of invading China. In other words, China could invade Korea and engage Americans in combat, but the United States would permit Chinese territory to remain a sanctuary. On January 4, 1951, Seoul was lost again to the enemy. But, in February, astounding as it may seem, the U.S. State Department was debating whether or not U.S. military forces should recross the 38th parallel. In the same month, February, 1951, the Air Force was forced to cancel its mobilization plans and, in March, General MacArthur reported that there could be no victory under the terms which controlled his operations. These terms, which have been well documented before, prevented crossing the Yalu River into Chinese Communist territory for air attack on the supplies and forces which the Chinese Communists were pouring into Korea in great number.

The main value of Air Forces in a war like this one is, of course, the capacity to destroy enemy supplies, bases, and forces before such resources can be moved to the fighting front. The United States had the air power necessary to do this task but it was not allowed to cross the line. This was a political decision, not a military decision. As a compromise, American men on the ground faced artillery fire, mortar fire, and machine-gun fire much of which would not have been there under different ground rules. And our men in the air could fight their hearts out, come to the line of the Yalu River and actually see the enemy planes on the ground across the river, but were not allowed to attack. Such is the impact of political constraint on the conduct of war.

In April, 1951, the Supreme U.S.-U.N. Commander, General MacArthur, was relieved of Command by a unilateral United States action. The Communists promptly responded on April 22, with a major offensive. The troops in the field, land, sea, and air, hung on, severely defeating the Chinese Communists in the end. However on May 15, 1951, the Chairman of the Joint Chiefs of Staff, in commenting on General MacArthur's relief, stated in effect that a confrontation of the Chinese Communists with a land war inside China would have been "the wrong war, at the wrong place, at the wrong time."

Incredible though it may seem in retrospect, with decision in the Korean War not yet attained, the U.S. Army announced on May 18, 1951, that it would start the release of reservists to inactive status. I am certain that this was no self-generated move on the part of the Army.

Concurrently with these actions which affected American conduct of the Korean War, other strange, contradictory, or belated actions were in process. On December 18, 1950, General Eisenhower took over as the first Supreme Commander for NATO. This nation was building in Europe while it was trying to get out of a shooting war in Korea. On February 7, 1951, the U.S. asked the U.S.S.R. to return 672 ships which it had provided under an Allied assistance agreement during World War II. The U.S.S.R., of course, rejected the request, but I've always wondered why this demand by the U.S. was not made much earlier. For example, why was it not made during the period of the Berlin airlift or at the start of the Korean War.

But, when General Ridgeway asked for an armistice on June 30, 1951, an action previously proposed by the Soviets on May 23, 1951, he still found things most difficult.

The record of this period of U.S. history certainly presents a curious anomaly. This nation was laying the foundations for a lasting policy of containment—in a theoretical sense—at the same time that it was backing away from the kind of real challenge that the policy of containment automatically engenders. In the mind of the enemy, the United States was subverting its own policy at the moment of its articulation, because the enemy believes in deeds, not words.

From America's conduct of the Korean War, the Sino-Soviet Bloc had learned three important things: one, the U.S. was not going to use the atomic bomb, even tactically; two, it had no stomach for tangling with the Chinese Communists; and three, this nation never even considered carrying the war back to the U.S.S.R.—the real instigator of the aggression. The homeland of the Sino-Soviet Bloc was therefore secure. The Soviets were free to continue border aggression by proxy, and wholesale subversion of perimeter areas. The United States would either react at the border in question, or it would back away. America had become a "paper tiger." And, unfortunately, these conclusions had to be shared, at least partially, by friend and neutral.

Such was the unhappy foundation upon which this nation would attempt to build an effective policy of containment during the next decade.

PART TWO

THE POLICY OF

Containment,

1950-1960

Chapter IV

CONTAINMENT

The broad policy of containment is to restrict communism within its existing borders, then let it destroy itself through internal corrosion and decay. Now, how is this accomplished? Again, in the broadest sense, the framers of the policy said, "It can only be contrived by constant exertion of political, economic, psychological and, as appropriate, military pressures until the political objective is achieved." This, of course, is still abstract policy only. It was necessary to become far more specific in order to exert these pressures, and the Government did become more specific. In fact, as a nation we did fairly well during the period 1950–1960 in identifying what had to be done—so far as the policy went—and in gearing up the wheels of government to support the policy.

Yet, I believe that future historians may regard America's decision to adopt the policy of containment, in the form in which it was adopted, as a very curious decision indeed. Containment, as adopted, was a passive policy offering no real plan for the ultimate resolution of our conflict with the Sino-Soviet Bloc. It was our formula for peaceful coexistence and inherently defensive. The decision was negative in the sense that we did not face up totally to the challenge. We procrastinated and delayed solution of the problem. We evaded the issue, hoping that the factors inherent in the computation would magically balance, and thus cancel out.

In this regard, I have always held the view that there was another course of action which could have been considered. I call this course "containment plus," because it includes all the elements of containment and adds *initiative*. This course of action would not necessarily have required a calculated and deliberate first nuclear blow against Communist powers. Our government could have taken the basic military posture derived from the policy of containment and added to it a political, technical, economic, and psychological strategy which was as "offensive," in every sense of the word, as is that of the opposing powers. The United States *could* have said:

> The United States does not intend to initiate military conflict, but it will have to begin it if the U.S.S.R. and Communist China persist in their attempts to enslave more of the free world. The United States will be ready to fight. The Communist apparatus is trying to destroy this nation with every trick at its command, therefore, the United States will also use every economic, technical, political, psychological, and subversive method which can be contrived. This nation must refuse to be bound to the dogmatic principles of statesmanship while its enemy lives by the law of the jungle. The stakes to humanity are too high.

Curiously, this reaction, one which I would consider typically American, never developed. Possibly it never developed because the American public at large never had a voice in the matter. Likely it never developed because throughout most of our history, Americans seem to have had a double standard of morality and courage. This double standard seems to be particularly typical of the twentieth century. Having grown up to the stature of a mature nation, we have alternately followed a militant and courageous course when war was forced upon us, and an apathetic or timid course during periods of peace.

In war, up until Korea, this nation always went the limit. In peace, we have usually compromised, vacillated, appeased, and piously hoped that the world would react in the manner in which we wanted the world to react.

In all fairness to the framers of the policy of containment, it must be noted that many of the inherent difficulties were foreseen and documented. Its architects recognized that success could be achieved only over a long period of time. That the nation might tire of the sacrifices necessary for the "long pull" was recognized as one of the dangers of such a policy.

But the greatest weakness lay in our determination to accept the *status quo* and initiate no action which would increase world tensions. What sense does it make to try to avoid world tensions when our government faces a tyranny which openly boasts that its prime objective in life is to destroy us? How does a government avoid world tensions under such circumstances? The answer is that tensions may be avoided only by appeasement in one form or another. The Free World has appeased the Communist world in the following ways:

1. By allowing the enemy time to consolidate his position, eliminating the champions of freedom within the territory he controls and educating a new generation on lies and basic ignorance of the outside world.
2. By avoiding and prohibiting any action which could cause the enemy trouble within while he practices world-wide subversion.
3. By giving him time to build up his economic and military strength.
4. By giving him time to use the open door of the Free

61

World to capitalize on *our* technological advances while he maintains a technological Iron Curtain.

5. By accepting a ban on nuclear testing which does not provide for on-the-spot inspection and enforcement.
6. By allowing the confidence of the Free World in the character and principles of the United States to gradually wither.
7. By continuing "Diplomatic Recognition" of an enemy sworn to destroy the United States.

Such is appeasement, and such was, and is the basic difficulty with our policy of containment. It has done much to damage, if not very nearly destroy, our position, particularly in Asia, Africa, the Near and Middle East, and Latin America. We have deliberately ignored many opportunities and obligations which were natural derivatives of a strong policy of containment and which vitally affected these areas. Two of these obligations and opportunities are worth special mention: "credibility" and "national prestige."

Credibility

Credibility of policy is the answer to the questions: do we believe in the policy ourselves, do the ally and the neutral believe it, *and* does the enemy believe it?

To make the policy of containment credible, three separate actions had to be set into motion: first, develop the necessary military strength; second, support the policy with an unshakeable will; and third, show by physical presence globally "on the spot," that the United States was committed and involved at the *outset of any* aggression. No nation, small or large, likes to be overrun, then liberated at some future date. This process usually makes a battleground of the victim's homeland and ruins the country.

No matter how powerful the United States may be, and this is particularly true of the psychology of the underdeveloped peoples of the world, guns, troops, planes, and fighting ships at bases and ports back in the United States cannot be seen. An organized U.S. military force on the spot, no matter how small, is more of a guarantee that "Uncle Sam is with me," than the most powerful fleet, out of sight over the horizon, or the most powerful Air Force in the world, seven thousand miles away.

This fact of life, historically, of course, has posed a difficult question. How much of a United States force is required at various points on the globe in order that our policy of containment may be given visible credibility?

Obviously, the United States by itself cannot afford to match the Communist powers man for man around the vast Asian perimeter, nor should we be required to. All free nations have a stake in the matter, and this government should naturally expect the bulk of the required manpower to be provided locally. This has generally been the case, and the Free World is not outnumbered nearly so badly as many people believe. Roughly, the Communist powers have about eight million men under arms, and the total for the world outside the Iron Curtain is about six million. Of course, the mobilization potential of the enemy bloc, in terms of raw manpower, is much greater than ours, and this country could be worn down in a protracted struggle of man-to-man confrontation. How then should the requirement for U.S. troops be assessed? What kind of a yardstick can be developed which makes sense?

National Prestige

The answer is not to try to match the enemy man for man, but, in lieu of the numbers game, to match him hazard for hazard. Matching the enemy hazard for hazard requires the creation of a political and military situation that can automatically involve a full commitment of national prestige if the enemy attempts aggression—either overtly or by subversion.

63

The number and type of troops would, of course, vary with the geography, nature, and capability of friendly troops on the spot and the enemy threat. U.S. troops required could be an Infantry Company, a Battalion, a Division, an Air Squadron, or an Air Wing. The composite strength and deployment of these U.S. forces and friendly forces should be such as to insure a stout defense, for at least a week or two, against any overt aggression or enemy-inspired and supported internal assault on the lawful government. U.S. troops should be involved from the outset, and U.S. national prestige automatically committed.

The U.S. forces I am thinking of, particularly in the underdeveloped parts of the world, would not have the capability to win or to hold against enemy reinforcements from outside the area. But these forces would create a pause for political reappraisal, and would allow time for our own reinforcement and subsequent action in event the enemy decided to broaden or escalate the war. More important, the automatic commitment of U.S. prestige would be a powerful factor in deterring enemy action before it started.

I think it interesting to note here that the United States government was invited into Lebanon by its President Chamoun to assist in that nation's defense on July 14, 1958. John Foster Dulles personally asked my view as to the probability of Soviet reaction to such United States support. Speaking for the Joint Chiefs of Staff, I assured him that the Soviets would do no more than wring their hands and deliver verbal protests. We knew this because U.S. military forces could have destroyed the U.S.S.R.—and Russia knew it. However, in moving into Lebanon, the United States was prepared for any circumstances that might develop, including the use of the Strategic Air Force. U.S. Commanders were prepared to take whatever military action was required. This attitude of mind contrasts very sharply with the way the Kennedy Administration entered the war in Vietnam.

The only "back peddling" with respect to Lebanon came about through the intervention of the State Department. When our forces were ordered into Lebanon we reinforced our nuclear-capable air garrisons in Turkey, and we also had enroute all of the nuclear equipment that U.S. ground forces were authorized in their tables of organization and equipment. This equipment included Army short-range rockets with nuclear warheads. When the working levels of the State Department heard this they objected so violently that U.S. military forces were directed not to land or deploy these weapons. As the circumstances developed in Lebanon, we did not have to fight, but, if we had, the absence of these primary weapons from the battlefield, in the hour of need, could have been most serious.

Nevertheless, in the Lebanon operation our government did not announce to the whole world that this was a "limited war" and our government did not use the pet phrases associated with some of the military actions of the past five years. We did not tell the enemy in advance what U.S. strategy and tactics would be. U.S. military forces went in to fight, if necessary, and the enemy backed away. If this nation had advised the enemy beforehand that it would limit or constrain its forces in any way, the outcome might have been different and we might still be fighting a local or limited war in that area.

From 1952 to 1960, the United States did very well in creating our national prestige in NATO Europe. We helped the North Atlantic Alliance create both the political framework and the military strength necessary to give credibility to the policy. Politically, the United States undertook solemn treaty obligations to the effect that an attack on one NATO nation would be considered as an attack on all. We sponsored, and agreed to with the rest of the Alliance, a political directive to NATO military planners that military plans will provide for the defense—not the liberation—of all territory of the

Alliance. And not one square inch of NATO territory has gone behind the Iron Curtain since NATO was established. This fact should be recognized as significant.

In other parts of the world this nation has not done so well with its policy of containment. This is so precisely because America has backed away from a full commitment of her national prestige. Our government has allowed the enemy room to maneuver, and he has taken it.

The trend toward defeat in Asia and Africa started, of course, before the policy of containment was formally articulated. It started with the loss of China behind the Iron Curtain during the period 1945–1949. It continued as the United States backed out of the Korean War, *after* the policy of containment was on the books. It continued with the loss of French Indochina and the partition of "North" and "South" Vietnam, which is a dagger aimed at the heart of Australia. It continues today as the United States loses its base rights in Saudi Arabia and Morocco, on which we spent hundreds of millions of dollars. And, in our own back yard, we fumbled and lost the cause of freedom in Cuba.

A partial answer to these reverses can be found in the political arrangements which we were willing—or unwilling—to support. Politically and militarily, our government fully committed itself in the North Atlantic Treaty Organization. By contrast, the old Baghdad Pact, agreed to in February, 1955, is a classic example of our evading the tenets of a real policy of containment. The Baghdad Pact, a mutual defense alliance of Near East countries, was formed through the efforts of the late John Foster Dulles. Originally, it included Turkey, Pakistan, Iraq, Iran, and the United Kingdom. The United States, despite its efforts in organizing the alliance, was unwilling to commit itself all the way. Although we did participate in the operation of several of the committees, among them the Economic and Military Standing Committees, our actual role was never more than advisory. The pact was not strong due to this nation's reluctance to become involved with it. As a result, Iraq later defected from the organization and the alliance was later recast as the Central Treaty Organization (CENTO).

CENTO was supposed to mean, for that part of the world, what NATO means to Western Europe. At this writing, the United States is still not a full member of CENTO and has made no specific commitment of forces to the defense of the area. There is no command structure and no commander for the area. This problem was a point of contention between the Joint Chiefs of Staff and the State Department during my entire tenure as Chairman. Today the divisive policy regarding U.S. commitments to CENTO obviously provides ample opportunity for Communist intrigue, and we now see such maneuverings on the part of Red China in the Pakistan-India difficulty.

The same vague pattern was repeated in the South East Asia Treaty Organization—SEATO, as it is called. SEATO was formed in September, 1954, again through the efforts of John Foster Dulles. The United States is a full member of SEATO. The other members of the organization are Thailand, the Philippines, Pakistan, Australia, New Zealand, France, and the United Kingdom. But even though the United States is a full member of SEATO, no U.S. forces are specifically committed to the alliance and there is no generally agreed upon political directive to serve as a basis for specific combined military planning for defense of the area as a whole.

Military actions such as are taking place in Vietnam in 1966, as this book goes to press, are belated and costly reactions to enemy pressures. The necessity for such military operations could, in all probability, have been avoided if both North Vietnam and Communist China had known that U.S. national prestige was fully committed and that retaliation against aggression would be swift, sure, and devastating.

If the leadership of North Vietnam and Communist China had believed that such retaliation would be extended to the depth of logistic support provided by agencies outside South

67

Vietnam, that there would be no sanctuaries, and that our government would use any weapon most advantageous to the U.S., there would, in my opinion, be no war in Vietnam today.

What would NATO be without an agreed political directive, a commander (SACEUR) recognized and supported by all nations involved, and a military force committed and at hand? I do not have to write the answer to that question; it is too obvious. That is why I say that we are half in and half out in the areas in which the U.S. is losing. Maybe the American people really want it that way, but I doubt it.

Chapter V

COLLECTIVE SECURITY

The collective security element of the policy had been evolving quite some time before the 1949 explosion of the first Soviet atomic device. But the event added a sense of urgency to the need to forge ahead and to crystallize a fully practicable national plan. Korea, a few months later, inserted a still greater sense of urgency.

Collective security is nothing new. We had a form of collective security in the 1775–1783 War for our independence. France was our ally, assisted by Spain and Holland. And, of course, we had collective security in the form of allies during World War I and World War II. But war differs from peace, particularly to an American who has been taught to "beware of foreign entanglements." Collective security in peacetime, and military alliance in peacetime, could never be considered a significant part of American history. Our refusal to join the League of Nations after World War II is just one example of our traditional suspicion of foreign involvement.

However, the United States did actually embark on a major effort of peacetime collective security in 1947. In June of that year, General George C. Marshall, then Secretary of State, proposed a plan to stimulate European recovery. He suggested that the United States should provide large-scale assistance to help Europe get back on its feet. As the U.S.S.R. was still considered an ally by our statesmen, it was invited to participate. Of course, the Soviets tried to block the plan and soon walked out of the multinational conferences which were called to discuss the matter.

The Soviet representative at these initial meetings on the Marshall Plan was the clever old Bolshevik, V. M. Molotov. He used a very odd argument in his attempt to scuttle the idea. He declared unctuously that such an aid plan would infringe on the sovereignty of the smaller nations. This from the representative of a nation that was in the process of enslaving all of Eastern Europe! With that amazing pronouncement, the U.S.S.R. not only withdrew from the conference, but ordered its satellite states not to participate. The Marshall Plan staggered precariously and then lurched on its way anyhow. Despite the attempted Soviet sabotage, it led to a vast program of European self-help supported by U.S. military and economic aid.

This plan was undoubtedly motivated by feelings of humanity and generosity on the part of the American government and people. In addition, many of our nation's leaders, both in government and in private life, were becoming worried about the continued intransigence and belligerence of our wartime ally, the U.S.S.R., and felt that Europe had to be strengthened financially, industrially, *and* politically to prevent a Communist take-over. My own feelings about the Marshall Plan were mixed at the time. However, when I found out that the Soviets were against it, I must admit that I was swayed to favor the Plan and figured it must be a good thing for the rest of the world, including the United States of America.

A second significant evolutionary step leading toward our policy of collective security occurred totally outside American borders. At Brussels, in March, 1948, under the leadership of

France, England, and Belgium, the Western European Union was born. This coalition, primarily intended to facilitate economic reconstruction in Europe, also prompted the establishment of a military committee which became the nucleus of NATO.

Like the Marshall Plan, the Western European Union was helped along by the postwar belligerence of the Soviet Union. There had been constant difficulty with the Soviets in the four-power administration of Berlin, and all attempts to move ahead with an acceptable German peace treaty had been blocked by unreasonable Soviet demands—demands which if agreed to, would have resulted in Soviet domination of all Europe.

The Western European Union was still in its infancy when, in June, 1948, the Soviets blockaded Berlin. The Berlin Blockade, an attempt to starve West Berlin into submission, was shattered by the Allied airlift. The drama of the blockade and the successful airlift made many more Americans conscious of Europe's problems and made a further involvement in European security affairs more acceptable. Consequently, by the end of 1948, both the United States and Canada were participating in the Western European Union as observers, and combined military planning had been resumed. It was then only a step to NATO, to SEATO, to the Baghdad Pact, and to bilateral security arrangements (outside the framework of the regional alliances) between the United States and more than forty free nations.

The broad policy of collective security always made sense to me. When confronted by a hostile, monolithic organization which openly declares its enmity, the whole Free World should participate in a joint defense effort. We should not allow ourselves to be gobbled up, one at a time. However, I am fully aware that this broad platitude is easier to essay than to accomplish. Among the free nations, many obstacles to full co-operation existed then and still exist today.

Economic rivalries, old and deeply rooted political antagonisms, lack of interest in the other side of the world, slowness in grasping the full measure of the Communist threat, substandard living conditions, and the temptation to do business with the enemy—all of these factors made it extremely difficult to marshal the resources of the Free World behind one integrated master plan for stopping Communist aggression.

The credit for the large measure of success which was achieved in the alignment of the Free World into something of a cohesive force probably belongs more to John Foster Dulles than any other single individual. His genius, courage, dedication, patience, and sensitivity brought about modern-day miracles in the reconciliation of the diverse attitudes and views of the many nations involved. Of course his policies were not always carried out as fully as he would have wished. When one looks back at the mistakes which were made and the half-measures which were taken, there seems to be one common denominator: the failure to completely carry out accepted policies all the way down the line. A strong policy can be laid down by the leaders of our government, but it takes thousands of people working in harmony to make it function. Inept handling or deliberate fumbling by those below the top levels of government can do much to vitiate the finest policy ever conceived. I have seen much of this during my career, particularly during my last seven years of duty in Washington.

Be that as it may, our policy of collective security developed five specific prongs: alliances, combined military planning, credibility, economic and military aid, and reciprocity.

Alliances

Obviously, collective security means alliances with other nations. We have already talked about NATO, SEATO, CENTO, bilateral arrangements outside the framework of regional alliances with more than forty nations, and the

72

Organization of American States for this hemisphere. Considering all the obstacles to be overcome, these alliances and bilateral arrangements provided an adequate political framework for co-ordinated economic and military planning. It is true that the United States was not participating fully in CENTO, and that this nation was not paying enough attention to Latin America. But imperfect though it was, the basic political structure represented a mammoth step forward. It provided the opportunity to do better than our government thus far has managed.

Combined Military Planning

Combined military planning between nations is necessary to support a policy of collective security. This we did very well in NATO up through the year 1960. In the Near and Middle East (CENTO) we were handicapped in military planning by our overcautious State Department and the fact that America was not, and is not, a full member of the pact. The State Department viewpoint always took advantage of this fact to prevent formation of a combined command structure, or even a token commitment of U.S. forces to the pact area. I have spent a great number of very unhappy hours sitting around the table with my military counterparts of the member CENTO nations, unable to take the next obvious step in military planning. It's an odd situation to find oneself on the military committee of an alliance of which your own government is *not* a political member. This was the difficulty, and is still the difficulty, of the U.S. position in CENTO.

Southeast Asia, SEATO, as mentioned earlier, presents a similar problem. Even though the United States is a member of SEATO, its representatives were always heavily circumscribed by political instructions which avoided the outright, predetermined commitment of U.S. forces and U.S. prestige. The same type of handicap, in terms of political caution, restricted much of the opportunity afforded by some of our bilateral arrangements. For example, political pressures usually precluded para-military type offensives which could have been conducted from South Korea into North Korea, from Formosa into the mainland of China, and from South Vietnam into North Vietnam. The United States gave this privilege to the enemy, studiously refusing to cause him the same kind of trouble he was causing us.

It was only when the Soviets pushed "too far" and really high-level decisions had to be made that America toughened its stand. The unflinching decisions which were taken in dispatching troops to Lebanon and our deployment for defense of the Quemoy-Matsu islands are examples. These decisions were taken at the very top level, and the Eisenhower-Dulles team had to make them against all manner of timid and over-cautious advice. The results, of course, speak for themselves. When the enemy was challenged, he drew back. I have the unhappy feeling that President Kennedy labored against the same type of advice as he struggled with such problems as Laos, Vietnam, and Cuba.

Credibility

I discussed credibility when treating with our policy of containment and need say little more about it. I might repeat, however, that credibility in the mind of friend and foe alike is based more upon deeds than upon words. The events which our government has allowed to transpire in Cuba constitute a classic example of how to go about undermining credibility of policy. It is certainly no secret that American policy calls for blocking a Communist take-over of any country not already behind the Iron Curtain, and there are many nations associated with us who have done so at their own very great peril. Our fumbling in Cuba can certainly provide no great reassurance in U.S. guarantees.

Firm action in dealing with Castro, incidentally, was blocked during the last two years of my Chairmanship of the Joint

Chiefs of Staff by State Department representatives. The argument was familiar; reminiscent of the "simple agrarian" argument to which our government adhered while the world watched China disappear behind the Iron Curtain. The argument this time, from the "professionals" in State was, "We have no proof that Castro is a Communist. If we get tough, we may drive him into the arms of the Soviets. Let us wait awhile and see what develops." Well, it developed all right. Significantly, the same approach pulled the rug from under, and doomed to failure, the "recapture" of Cuba, which was finally allowed to proceed in 1961.

Economic and Military Aid

Perhaps the most publicized and certainly the most controversial aspect of our program of collective security comes under the heading of military and economic aid. Much good has been done in this vast program of strengthening the military and economic position of many free nations. For example, the armed strength now opposing the Soviet Bloc could not be supported for a hundred billion dollars a year if it were all provided by the United States and costed out at U.S. troop standards.

However, I could never see any sense in the "giveaway" or "grant" parts of the program. Nobody likes to be a beggar. For those countries obviously unable to repay fairly quickly, the United States could have set up a long-term loan account, at zero interest, if necessary. The country involved would not have felt the animosity engendered by "charity," and on the world monetary scene, according to leading economists, this nation could have built up a balance of credits due, which would have been extremely beneficial as our government faces the current perplexities of the "gold outflow" and a corollary imbalance of foreign exchange.

Also, American aid programs have consistently indicated a naïvely high degree of partiality. It would be entirely rational to most Americans to show partiality to those countries which had the moral courage to stand up and be counted in the conflict with communism. However, government agencies responsible have often taken such countries for granted and actually favored the neutrals whose friendships are of nominal or doubtful value. This defies explanation to a nation which has openly sided with the West, which has voted in the United Nations with the West, and which is directly under the Communist gun.

The situation of Pakistan versus India is a good example, and there are several others. Pakistan defied the U.S.S.R. by joining with CENTO and SEATO.* In Pakistan, America had an ally that would and did fight, yet our nation has given far more economic aid to India than to Pakistan. These vast aid programs continue to propagate in spite of the fact that India refused to condemn the outrageous Soviet actions in Hungary and has many times voted in opposition to the United States on many major political issues before the United Nations. Compassion for the plight of the Indian people is understandable, but withal, the compassionate American has a right to expect better reciprocal treatment on the part of India. But, again, if a firmer line of American aid justification is advocated, political indecision manifests itself anew—"the government better be careful; precipitous action might drive them into the Soviet camp." Personally, I'd take

* Pakistan, of course, had its own reasons for an alliance with the United States. That nation needed help in its continuing quarrel with India over Kashmir. I have believed, from the beginning of that argument, that the Pakistanis had the most justice on their side. They were willing to allow a Kashmir plebiscite to settle the issue. The Indians were not willing, and held onto the area by force. However, regardless of the merits of either claim, Pakistan was willing to get off the neutral fence and become an ally. India preferred U.S. grants and loans with "neutrality" and the privilege at the same time to subvert U.S. policy before the United Nations. U.S. indecision on the matter has gradually forced a once strong ally, Pakistan, into accommodations with the Red Chinese and into a U.N. voting record about the same as that of India.

76

the chance. One friend who *will* be counted is worth ten who *might* be counted.

In our aid programs we have not only sometimes favored a passive neutral over a friend, but we have also given aid to Soviet captive nations who, of course, consistently vote against us in the United Nations. Poland and Yugoslavia are good examples. The excuse for aiding these nations (at the American taxpayers' expense and to the tune of hundreds of millions of dollars) is that we will thereby strengthen their independence of Moscow. We all have every sympathy for the unfortunate people of these two countries, and most of us would support any logical plan to make them genuinely free. However, all that America has accomplished so far with her aid programs is to make it easier for the Communists to control the two countries. Through our very subsidy, America has made it seem as if the Communist system is really working, and that things are improving under a Communist economic theory. As for independence, examine the voting record of both nations in the United Nations. The strategists in the Kremlin must get a huge laugh out of this.

Equally serious is the fact that, from the inception of our many aid programs, we have never had a sufficiently close integration of the economic projects with the military problems in the areas involved. When economic aid finds its way into the construction of public works, such as roads, airfields, and communications systems, it would seem elementary to provide for possible military advantages by correlating the economic development with obvious military need. I certainly would not imply that military consideration should have been a dominant factor in the economic aid program. However, in view of the fact that most specific projects can be processed under several varying methods without altering achievement of the same economic objective, the military problems and plans of the various areas should have received more attention. If the military services had been consulted more seriously in the formulation of our economic aid program, the U.S.

capability to make emergency movement of military forces to various parts of the world, and then to support them locally, would have been greatly improved. Similarly, the self-defense capabilities of locally based forces would have benefited.

Yet, deficiencies in the manner in which our government has conducted its military aid program is probably more the fault of the military than the executive. Our military services have had too much of a tendency to help the other fellow build a military force structure in the U.S. image. Everybody had to have an army, navy, and air force along the American pattern. This tendency was helped along by the fact that, due to the ups and downs in our own force structure, the United States had surplus items of tanks, guns, aircraft, and ships which were still usable and which could be allocated to countries being assisted. It was also cheaper, in terms of unit cost of equipment, for America to run her production lines a little longer than required for our own forces and thereby obtain items for military aid. F-86, F-84, and F-100 aircraft are examples of this type of aid.

The national pride of the various participating countries also played a part. Many of them insisted on having a "balanced military force" of land, sea, and air components. When the United States began participation in the major buildup of NATO military forces, the Joint Chiefs of Staff could see this problem fermenting. General Bradley was then Chairman, and he tried his best to sell the plan that European NATO forces should be adequately "balanced" on a NATO-wide basis rather than on an individual nation basis. It was the belief of the U.S. Joint Chiefs of Staff that each country should provide only what it was best able to provide and that the composite force of all the Nations should be steered toward a proper over-all balance. Such a military structure, of course, would have been cheaper and more effective than for each to try to have a little army, a little navy, a little marine corps, and a little air force. The suggestion found small favor with the NATO group. Nor for that matter, did the U.S.

78

team receive strong U.S. political support for the idea. So as a result, one of the SACEUR's major problems over the past several years has been to attempt to steer the hodgepodge of individual forces into something which resembles an overall NATO balance.

The results of trying to mold the armed forces of the underdeveloped nations into the U.S. military image was, at times, even less satisfactory. Much of the military equipment which the United States has provided to the less developed countries has been too complex and sophisticated for them to maintain or properly use. Everybody, of course, wants the latest model "Cadillac," but it would have been better in terms of usable strength if our military planners could have been more discriminating and more resistant to friendly pressures.

This last thought, "more resistant to friendly pressures," leads into the final major element of the U.S. policy of collective security—the area of the "two-way street," or in more sedate terms, "reciprocity."

Reciprocity

The broad policy of collective security obviously benefits the United States. It also benefits every other associated nation which is trying to preserve its freedom. Obligations devolve on all parties concerned. Many times, these obligations are difficult to meet and issues of individual national interests must sometimes be subordinated for the common good.

Earlier in these pages I referred to the difficulties inherent in a "peacetime" coalition of free nations—the economic rivalries, the ancient political antagonisms, the lack of interest in something happening on the other side of the world, and the preoccupation with immediate national interests. These are powerful divisive influences. The enemy recognizes these factors at work, and exploits them whenever and wherever he can create the opportunity.

79

That the Free World has done reasonably well in meeting these divisive issues is evidenced by such facts as Turkey and Greece belonging to the same alliance; by that same alliance including Norway and Denmark; by the admittance of Western Germany as a full member of NATO; by the affiliation of Australia and New Zealand with Pakistan, Thailand, and the Philippines; by the general solidarity of the Western Hemisphere; by European actions to eliminate barriers to free trade; and by large-scale humanitarian and economic collaboration throughout the Free World. And so, in discussing difficulties in the next few pages, we must not forget the positive accomplishments and actions. The negative side is set out here only to indicate where further progress can be made.

Generally, in terms of accommodating ourselves to international effort, we have found that it is far less difficult to be firm with an enemy than with a friend. The following are examples of the lack of our government's justifiable firmness on the "two-way street":

The United States accepted erosion of the multinational agreement to embargo shipment of strategic material to the U.S.S.R.

The United States accepted the same erosion with respect to Communist China, again permitting trade with the enemy.

The United States accepted, and is continuing to accept, a gradual erosion of world-wide base rights and overflight rights for U.S. forces which may have to be deployed and employed for the common good of the Free World.

The United States accepted the decision of some friendly countries that they would have no part in the basing, deployment, or employment of nuclear weapons. These nations wanted the protection inherent in the U.S. nuclear arsenal, but were unwilling to share the hazard.

The United States accepted from some nations less than a fair contribution to the common defense effort in the form of taxation, armed manpower, period of conscripted service, and training standards.

Under friendly pressures, America has accepted at times, and contrary to the recommendations of the Joint Chiefs of Staff, military arrangements which were fundamentally unsound. (Placing the THOR missile, U.S. developed and U.S. purchased, under unilateral British control instead of under SACEUR is a case in point. It established a precedent which will plague modernization of European-based forces for years to come.)

Now, when I say that our government "accepted" these actions which in the long run are inimical to the Free World's interests, I do not mean that the United States was in a position to dictate or that it should have dictated. One government doesn't "dictate" in a coalition of free nations. But America's powers of persuasion or inducement were in these cases far greater than the results would indicate. U.S. representatives gave in too easily, simply because it is sometimes harder to say "no" to a friend than to an enemy.

Further, the United States failed to meet some of its obligations on the "two-way street" of collective security. One of the most startling and fatal examples of this was our policy on the exchange of nuclear information with our allies.

Nuclear Information

Back in the days when the United States had a nuclear monopoly, the U.S. Congress passed some well-intentioned laws which were meant to keep our nuclear information secret, thus to prevent irresponsible nations from "getting the atomic bomb." Those in the military establishment and in one or two other U.S. agencies knew that this would not stop a determined enemy because the basic scientific facts were internationally known and because we understood military espionage.

But, because of the traitorous activities of the British scientist Klaus Fuch and the activities of the nuclear espionage ring in Canada, we were legitimately distrustful. U.S. Govern-

81

ment officials were also aware of the fact that the French counterpart to our own Atomic Energy Commission was saturated with people of leftwing or definitely Communist viewpoints. Thus there was a very natural reluctance to expose the processes required for development of nuclear weapons even to our most trusted allies. Fundamentally, the laws allowed considerable latitude in the exchange of information with Canada and the United Kingdom because these countries had collaborated in the U.S. atomic energy program. The law was quite rigid, however, in withholding information from other countries.

As the United States progressed along the road of nuclear armament, the provisions of the Atomic Energy Act had to be modified from time to time. Occasional modification of the law was required in order that the military establishment could improve the readiness and reaction time of its forces and transmit data necessary to combined military planning with our allies. The Congress always co-operated on such recommendations from the Executive Department. This is an important point, because the "negativists" who popped up later to block some important steps in U.S. preparedness frequently took refuge in the "Law." This, of course, was a trick to avoid the issue.

The matter came to a head between the Joint Chiefs of Staff and the State Department in 1959 during my tour as Chairman of the Joint Chiefs of Staff. The specific problem at issue between the Departments of State and Defense was the delivery of certain atomic information to the government of France. The United States no longer had an atomic monopoly and knew very well the actual status of Soviet nuclear technology.

The issue was raised when De Gaulle announced that France would develop its own nuclear weapons capability. He believed that the dignity and sovereignity of France was not satisfied by reliance on nuclear arsenals totally controlled by other powers. He wanted to become a member of the "nuclear club." France therefore embarked on a nuclear energy program, but it was years behind United States technology and years behind the Soviet technology. It would cost them hundreds of millions of dollars and many years to find out what the Soviets already knew. The problem was, should the U.S. help the French by telling them what the Soviets already knew, or should America let France do it the hard and costly way?

Members of my staff estimated that if the United States did help the French simply by providing information on nuclear technology and related missile technology already possessed by the Soviet Union, our country could save France about seven years' development time and two billion dollars. That two billion dollars, incidentally, would have gone a long way in providing other material important to NATO.

In looking back at the history, a great many reasons why the United States should have instinctively reacted in a positive way to the French atomic decision are easily seen. France is really the cradle of freedom of the individual. France helped the United States to gain its own independence. France is the only major European nation which the United States has never fought. After all, the United States fought the British more than once, and they burned our Capitol in 1812. If France could not be trusted with the atomic bomb, who could be trusted? Tragically, however, the U.S. policy of yesterday and of today *really* indicates that America can trust a Russian more than a Frenchman. The Russian has the bomb and America won't help the Frenchman.

As is customary on problems of national policy, this issue was subject to intensive study by both the State Department and the Defense Department. The Atomic Energy Commission and the Central Intelligence Agency were also deeply involved. The "planners" of the various agencies had to develop the arguments, pro and con, for consideration by their superiors. In this process, the lines were soon drawn between "Defense" planners and "State" planners. The State planners

83

were of course generally supported by the members of the scientific fraternity who had wiggled their way in as advisors on national policy.

Defense planners took a positive view; State planners took a negative view. The general arguments against helping the French and counterarguments were as follows:

1. *State Argument:* This will lead to the "proliferation" of nuclear weapons. The world is already dangerous enough to live in without adding another country that can start an atomic war. Proliferation of atomic weapons is inherently bad.

Defense Rebuttal: Whether we like it or not, the French are going to develop a nuclear weapons capability. It will take time and money and scientific manpower which could be put to other useful purposes, but France is going to do it. If the United States helps now, it will be consulted regarding future applications, and therefore, will have some voice in what France does with its program. If we don't help, this nation will have absolutely no influence in what France does with its own developments. France can give it to Country X, Y, and Z if they choose; thus the United States courts the very "proliferation" to which it is now opposed.

2. *State Argument:* What about the follow-on? If we help the French, this nation will have to help other countries do the same thing. Where do you stop in the "Nth" country problem?

Defense Rebuttal: America must develop enough political courage to look other friends in the eye and say, "No, the French need it and can handle it; you're not ready for it yet."

3. *State Argument:* The French Atomic Energy Commission is shot through with Communists. Whatever we tell them will go straight to Moscow.

Defense Rebuttal: The French have done well in correcting this situation, maybe with more effectiveness than this government has managed in some departments. However, this argument is beside the point; the United States can control atomic data and give the French only what the Russians already know.

4. *State Argument:* There is no real military requirement to do this. The military requirement can be worked out using U.S. weapons under U.S. custody.

Defense Rebuttal: It is true that the military requirement could be met by using U.S. weapons under U.S. custody and control. However, this is clearly unacceptable to De Gaulle. He wants some power in his own hands which he can use on his own initiative to protect his country. Can you blame him in the light of this nation's vacillation in other parts of the world?

5. *State Argument:* Never-the-less, it is against the Law.

Defense Rebuttal: Congress will permit it if we present a proper case.

So the argument went. I am confident that had John Foster Dulles lived he would have overruled his own planners, as he did on many other occasions. He and I talked about this problem many times.

The consequences of our failure to play ball on the "two-way street" on this issue with France were serious indeed: the withdrawal of the French Fleet from the Mediterranean NATO Command; the refusal of France to join a fully integrated Air Defense System for Europe; withdrawal of ten U.S. air squadrons from French soil; the French attitude on nuclear disarmament which developed, to American embarrassment, in the Ten Power disarmament talks in Geneva in 1960; the 1964 withdrawal of senior French officers from NATO; and the 1966 attitude of De Gaulle toward NATO as a whole.

In addition, the program for the necessary modernization of European-based NATO strike forces has been blocked as a direct result of America's policy toward France. NATO Europe faces a large and constantly growing enemy medium-range ballistic missile force based behind the Iron Curtain. This force is zeroed in on airfields which base NATO light-bomber and fighter-bomber strike forces. The requirement to modernize U.S.-NATO strike forces by substituting mobile medium-range ballistic missiles for some of the aircraft has been recognized and approved by the fourteen nations providing military forces to the alliance. The United States did have a few first generation THOR and JUPITER missiles scattered about Europe, but even these have been withdrawn, and America thus far has been unable to get ahead with a small solid-fueled, second-generation MMRBM (Mobile Medium Range Ballistic Missile) program for Europe. All arrangements which have been proposed have foundered because of our nuclear policy toward France. Nor will the current U.S. proposal for a multinational surface sea-based ballistic missile force solve the problem. It cannot solve it because the proposal is militarily unsound, operationally unworkable, and politically unacceptable to several nations. This grave military deficiency could eventually wreck the NATO political alliance if not corrected.

Chapter VI

STRATEGIC DETERRENCE

The technical and military capability of the United States to create a strategic deterrent force was a very powerful factor in the decision to adopt the policy of containment. This technical and latent military capability offered a solution which was economically feasible. The nation could afford it, and through it would not need to indefinitely maintain large standing armies in peacetime.

Up through 1960, "strategic deterrence" was the real teeth in the policy of containment. Strategic deterrence, until the advent of ballistic missiles, meant only one thing—the U.S. Strategic Air Command: the bombers, the tankers for mid-air refueling, the trained crews, the support structure, the organization, the plan, the will, and the weapons. SAC held the enemies of freedom and democracy at bay for more than a dozen years. Back as far as 1949, Winston Churchill stated that if it were not for the power of the U.S. Strategic Air Command, all Europe would have been overrun and communized.

The Power Factor

The character of SAC is changing today; changing as the bomber force is reduced in numbers and as intercontinental ballistic missiles are phased into the national inventory. SAC will continue to change in weaponry, but its mission will remain the same: to provide the umbrella of stark, naked power without which containment and collective security could not have survived long enough to merit even a single page in the history books. Strategic deterrence in the form of the U.S. Strategic Air Command has been the ever-present factor of force which has allowed us to survive thus far, in spite of all the mistakes which have been made in other areas.

The building of the Strategic Air Command, physically and politically, has not been without difficulty. Fortunately for America, the White House and the Congress, up until recently, have always supported a powerful strategic deterrent when all the arguments were laid before them. But the argument *against* a powerful nuclear force was always there. And all evidence indicates that the argument is gaining in support.

The basis of the influential argument against a powerful strategic deterrent was never a head-on assault, never that we did not need it at all. The argument was generally that the Air Force had "too much," that it had enough to blow up the world ten times over; that all Soviet targets would be "overkilled;" and that some of the resources going into SAC should be diverted to preparing for little wars.

In 1959, I had one encounter at the National Security Council on this subject which I shall never forget. My antagonist in this engagement was a man who believed in "finite deterrence." He made a statement to the effect that the United States was powerless to react to a challenge in any way short of a massive nuclear exchange; that as a result, we had to retreat or bring on a nuclear holocaust.

My counterargument was simply this: "Over the past ten

years, the nation has spent about twenty-five percent of its total national defense budget on the Strategic Air Command. If this twenty-five percent of the U.S. Defense investment in fact represents the only real in-hand combat power, what happened to the other seventy-five percent? Rather than try to tear down the only real combat power which you say this nation possesses, I would think it more appropriate for the government to carefully scrutinize the seventy-five percent which you say is ineffective." Needless to say, my viewpoint prevailed at that meeting. However, the opposing viewpoint is symptomatic; it is dangerous to our security; it is still present; and it is gaining support.

Because of the recognized efficiency and power of the Strategic Air Command many people actually believe that we have spent most of our national defense budget on this force, and not just the twenty-five percent I cited above. Personally, I think the resources spent on SAC should have been more—not less. Be that as it may, the facts are that the Free World is still free today because of SAC—a force which the Communists can comprehend.

The idea of a powerful strategic nuclear deterrent force has been attacked in many different ways. The three most common arguments are: "too much," "finite deterrence," and "nuclear stalemate."

"Too Much"

The armchair strategists who say that U.S. strategic nuclear forces are too strong try to prove their point by adding up all the megatons of firepower in our nuclear weapons arsenal. They equate a bomb or a missile warhead in stockpile to a bomb or a warhead successfully delivered on target. Their mathematics "prove" that the U.S. has enough strategic nuclear strength to decimate the world many times over.

This argument is just as fallacious as would be the process of counting the number of enemy soldiers to be met in an

89

infantry battle and buying one round of ammunition for each enemy soldier. In World War II, America bought enough .30 calibre bullets to kill everybody in the world many times over. America also bought enough .50 calibre bullets to do the same thing. In addition, the nation bought enough .45 calibre bullets, mortar shells, artillery projectiles, TNT bombs, et cetera, to do the same job. The point is that a weapon in arsenal is not a weapon on target.

This fundamental fact is critically important in a realistic assessment of the atomic question. In the event of war, the enemy will prevent a certain amount of our force from getting through to the target. As a further consideration, if the enemy strikes the first blow, the U.S. will have to fight back with what it has left, for much of our arsenal will be "missing."

Nuclear weapons are like .30 calibre bullets. Most .30 calibre bullets never find a human target. In event of a major war, many of the nuclear weapons in stockpile on both sides of the Iron Curtain will never find a target.

Finite Deterrence

Advocating the philosophy of finite deterrence is a sophisticated way of saying, "Let's cut back on our strategic nuclear strength." Finite deterrence is just another way of arriving at the "too much" position.

The proponents of finite deterrence claim that all that is needed is to have enough strategic weapons and strategic delivery capability to knock out the enemy's important population centers—100 to 200 targets. The claim is that this will be just as effective a deterrent to Communist aggression as a much larger force.

Common horse sense is really all that is needed to see through this logic. The argument persists, however, because it plays into the hands of those who would achieve nuclear dis-

90

armament at any cost. The argument, nevertheless, does persist, and it is wrong on three major counts:

1. If this nation did actually tailor its strategic force to this plan, it would be a small force indeed. Whether the force was made up of land-based bombers, land-based ballistic missiles, or sea-based ballistic missiles—or a mixture of all three—it would be a small force. It could be carefully targeted and watched, including the submarine component, and it could be destroyed in the first act of war with a relatively minor effort on the part of the enemy.

2. Such a force would provide absolutely no flexibility for military action or for support of U.S. foreign policy. The enemy would know that the force could never be used in a pre-emptive attack. No matter what the provocation, nor how desperate the situation, the force could be used only in retaliation. It would have to be used only against cities because it would not be large enough to attack the enemy military force structure in-being. Consequently, the enemy would be absolutely certain that he had the advantage of initiative. His own force would be secure, and he could be certain that he could push the United States to the wall before it would start trading city for city. And even if the U.S. did trade city for city, he would win anyhow. He would have left a powerful strategic military force in-being when it was over—the United States would have none—and he would dictate the world order.

3. As a combination of these factors, the enemy would have America "cold" no matter what happened. If America really started to enforce its policy of containment, he could initiate the nuclear war and knock out our small strategic force. If our nation became desperate enough to initiate the nuclear exchange, he might suffer great damage, but could find the cost acceptable for final control of the entire world.

The argument opposing the concept of finite deterrence is generally called the "counterforce concept." Under this concept the number one priority target is the enemy military force which can do the most damage to our side. It takes a large force to support this concept. Such a force, however, provides for both military and diplomatic flexibility. It is large enough to let the enemy know that America could, in fact, knock out a large portion of his own forces if we attacked first, and thereby minimize the damage to our homeland by his counterattack. It is large enough to let the enemy know that, if he attacked first, U.S. residual power would be sufficient to trade him city for city. Instead of "having us" in both ways, under these power terms he "has us" in neither way.

In the endless discussions of this matter, the counterforce plan has been opposed by statements to the effect that the idea won't work because: first, we don't know where the enemy bases his ballistic missiles; and second, even if we did know, what would be the point in shooting at empty holes after he launches his missile force? As to the first point, we did a very good job in targeting the airfields on which enemy bombers are based, and there is no Iron Curtain tight enough to prevent the same thing with respect to missiles. As to the second point, if the Soviets wish to achieve surprise in a nuclear attack on the Free World, it is impossible to launch all missiles simultaneously. It is impossible for both technical and operational reasons. All of the "holes" or missile sites, therefore, will not be empty. However, even if both arguments were right, which they are not, the residual force program in itself is more than adequate justification for a strategic force built to counterforce requirements. If the United States should sometime be trapped into receiving the first nuclear blow, it must have something left to fight back with. Otherwise this nation possesses no real deterrent at all.

Today, when political science strategists chat knowingly about lack of capability under the Eisenhower Administration for "flexible response" and facing either "humiliation" or "annihilation" because of a shortage of "limited war" forces, they speak with utter naïveté. They pay little heed to just what national capacity for flexible response and national capacity for avoiding humiliation or annihilation would be required in the absence of a strategic force—tailored in fact to a counterforce concept.

The action taken in the years before 1961 to build up a powerful strategic force was, in the light of history, proper. But in the light of dominant theory and national actions since the end of 1960, there are many with grave doubt about the future effectiveness of this most essential military capability. Under current policy, the U.S. strategic force is moving toward the inflexibility of a Maginot Line and can become suddenly vulnerable to technological and military achievements of the U.S.S.R.

Nuclear Stalemate

The utopian thought behind the argument of the "nuclear stalemate" is that both sides will get so much power that both will be afraid to use it—and wars can then be fought to decision in the simple, old-fashioned way. Many of the people advocating this philosophy are scientists, and they, at least, should know better. The United States, indeed the world, is going through a technological explosion today of great depth and breadth. Nothing is static, any stalemate which might for a time develop will be very quickly broken. Ways and means of delivering nuclear firepower change. What happens to the theory of nuclear stalemate if the Soviets successfully solve the problem of defense against ballistic missles before we do? Claims and counterclaims of prowess in this anti-missile area are already about.

A true nuclear stalemate means that both sides have weapons and delivery forces, and neither side can defend effectively against the other. This idea is also sometimes called "stable deterrence." The advocates of this theory would reduce emphasis on nuclear weapon development, both defensive and offensive, thus holding at our present level, because this nation already has enough to "blow up the world ten times over." If we follow this course of action, we will be committing suicide because the enemy is not following it. Americans will wake up some fine day and the U.S.S.R. will have the nuclear monopoly. The United States will have bombs and warheads which the military cannot deliver—and the enemy will have bombs and warheads which our military services cannot stop. I doubt that the Soviet Union would be as kind to the world under these circumstances as was the United States when it had the nuclear monopoly.

Since 1948, the Strategic Air Command has represented the bulk of our strategic power, and still does today. Complementing this aerospace force is our U.S. Navy's POLARIS equipped nuclear-powered submarine. POLARIS, like bombers and land-based missiles, has certain unique capabilities, limitations, and vulnerabilities. The United States needs a mixture of all these forces, and it is the proper job of the Joint Chiefs of Staff to determine the correct proportion.

Looking further ahead, there is a clear requirement emerging for long-endurance aircraft armed with ballistic missiles of several thousand miles' range. This is now technologically feasible. Further in the future there will be manned military operations, both offensive and defensive, conducted from space vehicles. Does any of this sound like "nuclear stalemate," "mutual deterrence," or "stable deterrence"?

Changes in the technical configuration of strategic forces and in the means to combat these forces are inevitable. This nation must keep top priority in these areas, otherwise it will lose irretrievable time.

As these technological changes take place, the nation must also modernize its strategic command structure. SAC started out under the Air Force. It eventually came under the Joint Chiefs of Staff where it properly belongs. But the Joint Chiefs of Staff still do not have a single unified strategic command to exercise control over all elements of the military's strategic power. POLARIS, for example, is operated practically on an independent basis. The establishment of a Unified Strategic Command, staffed and commanded on a multi-service basis, as is the case for all other unified commands, is long overdue.

Contemporary Views of a Staff Officer

From the above discussion of the birth of a nuclear strategy and the opposing viewpoints which accompanied its implementation, it should be clear that many obstacles were constantly encountered. The concept of strategic nuclear deterrence to aggression, even though adopted as the fundamental basis for military planning, has been under attack from its inception by various elements within our own country. As mentioned earlier, the controversy with respect to these weapons started immediately after World War II with the divergence of views as to the rate of Soviet progress. Then the "morality" issue was added and a handful of scientists, during the later days of the Truman Administration, attempted to block U.S. development of the H-bomb. The bogey-man of radiation fallout was injected concurrently into the continuing argument, and the issues became more and more confused with the problems of mutual inspection and controls which were developed in the U.S.-U.S.S.R. discussions of nuclear disarmament measures.

The attack on our own nuclear program then moved to the questions of too-much, over-kill, inflexibility, finite deterrence, and the theory of stalemate, stability of the balance of power, and mutual deterrence.

The great debate thus had its roots during the Truman Administration. It grew in depth and breadth during the Eisenhower Administration, it flowered during the Kennedy Administration, and it is continued today by those who advocate unilateral nuclear disarmament. Recollection of an incident from the year 1961 pretty well sums up the continuing issues which were involved.

During the early days of the Kennedy Administration, an

95

Air Force Officer (Brigadier General R.C. Richardson, III), on duty in the Pentagon, headed an office for study and analysis of the long-range problems of national security planning. This office had been established by Air Force Chief of Staff General Thomas D. White (my successor in the job) in February of 1958. Brigadier General Richardson naturally became involved in the problems of nuclear energy, and read practically every day the unclassified diatribe in the public news media authored by those people within our own society whose objective is to weaken or completely eliminate our nuclear forces. Richardson made his own analysis, on an unclassified basis, and sent me a copy for information. As a result of his activities, his office was completely abolished by Department of Defense verbal orders and he was summarily transferred to Europe to "get him out of the way." At the time of this DOD-inspired action there were rumors that his office was being eliminated and he was being transferred because of a security violation involving release of information to the public which the Administration considered to be sensitive. These rumors were absolutely false and Richardson was cleared during the process of official investigation. However, his office was abolished and he was transferred. This action was taken, in my judgment, because he dared to think in terms not popular to some of the key Kennedy appointees within the Department of Defense.

I think that his comments are worth repeating. He was writing on a specific subject, "Deterrence and Related Concepts." This is what he had to say:

Definition of Deterrence

When a nation or individual is persuaded not to take a given action by virtue of the fear of the consequences, we can say that the factors which led to the decision, when taken collectively, constitute the deterrent.

Deterrence when used in connection with national security refers to all military and non-military factors which,

96

when taken together, will present to any potential aggressor convincing evidence that the costs or risks involved in initiating war outweigh his chances of gain under any circumstances he can create.

Deterrence a Cold War Objective

Measures taken to deter an enemy focus on his decision making process. Their purpose is to deter him from initiating war. Obviously, therefore, if war occurs the primary deterrent effort has failed. Deterrence of war, therefore, is a Cold War objective and undertaking. As such, it has *no* valid role in affecting the outcome of war once a war has started, except as it might operate in a secondary and different context to deter the use of some weapon system or the expansion of small wars.

Requirements to Deter or Fight Can Differ

The forces and measures which might deter the initiation of war are not necessarily those best suited to prosecuting a war. A credible or obvious war winning capability under any circumstances provides an optimum deterrent to war. On the other hand, it can be argued that war can be deterred by a military posture which does *not* possess a war winning capability. This is what minimum deterrence offers.

This is a vital point generally misunderstood. For example, the certainty that war will result in heavy population and economic loss—say a hundred cities—is a deterrent. These losses alone, however, can leave the military capability intact and able to win the war. In this case, the deterrent is not absolute since all it does is to place a high price on victory, a price which an enemy might be willing to pay, particularly if he knew that having destroyed these cities we had no further capacity to fight.

Again, a small allied strategic atomic capability has great deterrent power against the U.S.S.R., but no useful war winning capacity. Here the deterrence stems, not from fear of the military capability per se, but from the fact that its use would likely trigger off the U.S. capability under circumstances of our choosing. This is the French concept behind their A effort.

Deterrent measures focus on enemy intentions, not capabilities. They combine military and non-military actions. On the other hand, war winning requires measures that focus on enemy capabilities and depends almost exclusively on military actions. These basic differences make it possible to maintain a credible deterrent posture without concurrently maintaining an effective capability to win a war should it occur.

The Fallacy of Minimum Deterrence

The advocates of minimum deterrence would reduce the U.S. strategic forces to a small, highly protected, retaliatory capability suitable only for city busting. Their goal is to minimize the cost of the strategic effort, or alternately upgrade the worth of missile systems whose characteristics limit their usefulness to engaging area targets. The concept has three weaknesses:

a) It does NOT provide a war-winning capability. Having used up our missiles in destroying his cities, we remain open to equal or worse destruction by his undamaged military forces.

b) It does NOT deter limited aggression. The enemy will realize that we would only initiate an exchange of cities as a last resort, and never in retaliation for acts that did not directly threaten our survival. Thus, it invites limited war by killing massive retaliation—i.e., strategic response against limited aggression.

c) It is NOT a rational military strategy in the atomic age. The destruction of cities as a means of defeating an enemy is a vestige of an era in which the key to victory lay in a nation's industrial potential to support the war effort. In atomic war post D-day production contributes little or nothing to the outcome, hence its destruction can only be rationalized as an act of revenge.

On Mutual Deterrence or Stalemate

The stalemate thesis holds that when a symmetrical strategic capability exists neither side will use these forces for fear of retaliation. This requires, however, 1) equally adequate weapons, 2) equally adequate ability to deliver, 3) equally effective force survival measures and, 4) equally ineffective active defenses. The fallacy of this thesis lies in the unlikelihood that this symmetry can exist over any period of time in the face of technological progress.

Even if the conditions for mutual deterrence prevailed at a given time, the resulting stability in the strategic equation is jeopardized by the very existence of an independent third party capability. The stalemate or mutual deterrence thesis is only valid in a Two Party game, which no longer exists now that the U.S., and soon France and China, own atomic weapons.

The concept of minimum deterrence is an outgrowth of the so-called stalemate or mutual deterrence idea, which as we have seen is in itself fallacious. By combining the arguments that general war will never intentionally occur, since both sides will fear retaliation, with the argument that if general war did occur, even through accident, the U.S. strategic capability will always be hit first (which assumes an enemy first strike counter force capability) one arrives at minimum deterrence as an adequate strategy on the assumption that a counter force capability is useless if the enemy birds have flown the coop.

On Stable Deterrence

This thesis holds that war by accident is the greatest threat. It assumes the existence and validity of a condition of mutual deterrence or stalemate, and seeks to obtain further economies at the expense of the strategic effort by eliminating readiness to respond as a survival measure. This is little more than a conceptual rationalization to eliminate air alert, airborne dispersal of weapons, automatic response to warning, and hence the need for BMEW's satellite warning systems, etc.

99

Stable deterrence ignores entirely the war-winning requirement and would protect only minimum deterrent forces by hardening, ground mobility, or submarine bases with the argument that even our minimum deterrent forces should not retaliate until after deliberation, and no force should be maintained so ready to respond as to risk inadvertent reaction.

Deterrence and Military Programs

The primary, and only valid, military objective is and remains readiness to defend the nation successfully in war. The military cannot properly accept force programs or concepts that gamble our survival on our ability to prevent war, i.e. deterrence—alone, and that admit defeat, or at minimum, mutual destruction should deterrence fail.

Deterrence is a valid national Cold War objective to which the military posture contributes. Deterrence requirements cannot be allowed to govern the military posture, which must always be optimized for the prosecution of war.

Military policies, plans and programs while contributing toward influencing enemy *intentions* (deterrence) must aim primarily toward coping with enemy military *capabilities*. This means enemy forces or that which makes them effective.

Concepts of minimum deterrence, stalemate, mutual deterrence, stable deterrence, etc. are little more than rationalizations for reducing the cost of national defense, or elements thereof, by gambling on enemy intentions and the ability to prevent general atomic war at the expense of accepting defeat or annihilation if the gamble fails.

We must be careful, henceforth, not to be awed by catch phrases and parrot these in military planning. We don't build forces for deterrence or even deterrent forces. We build forces for national defense—to fight. Their deterrent effect is only a peacetime by-product of their war waging capability. Failure to clearly recognize this fact has led too many people to assume deterrent and war-winning force postures as synonymous, and then to accept *reduc-*

tions in the war winning capability based on arguments
for a lesser requirement in the deterrent capability.*

It is always dangerous for a military man, even though he is an expert on the subject, to become involved in such matters on an unclassified basis. He can be transferred, forced into retirement, or passed over for promotion without having a chance to defend himself. In this respect, nuclear policy matters have imposed an unusually heavy burden on many officers and undoubtedly will continue to do so for many years to come. The officer on active duty who knows the truth is usually "boxed-in" and "muzzled" by security restrictions or "policy"—while the antinuclear amateur, with no continuing responsibility of any kind, writes books, magazine and newspaper articles, makes speeches, and continues to flood the public media with guesswork, opinion, distortion, and half-truth—all aimed at one objective: U.S. nuclear disarmament at any price. In this observation I am *not* referring to the legitimate newspaperman or journalist who has an obligation to report, in a free press, the world as he sees it. I am referring to the vociferous minority of antinuclear intellectuals scattered throughout our society.

In assessing for themselves these problems of monumental importance, Americans might help to find the truth if they were to ask a simple question: "Now, let's see, with respect to Dr. Blank's views on the matter, what is this man's real responsibility for the military security of the United States? If he is wrong, what responsibility does he carry?" In our free and open society we should, of course, not attempt to "muzzle" these people—even to the degree that the active military establishment is muzzled. However, we might look on their activities with as much careful suspicion as the average American looks at the objectives of the misguided youth who burns his draft card.

* As this book goes to press, General Richardson is back on duty in the United States.

Chapter VII

LIMITED WAR

I know of no term in the political-military lexicon which can equal "limited war" for creating confusion in the public mind. Its meaning has been a subject of analysis and debate by politicians and scientists for the past fifteen years, yet still remains elusive. The lack of a satisfactory definition causes bitter differences within the various agencies of government.

Earlier in these pages I summarized the events leading to, and concerning our conduct of the Korean War. I explained how our government attempted to evade the issue of that limited war at the very time that this nation was adopting a basic policy which would inevitably bring us into peripheral collisions with Communist governments. That is, peripheral collisions *had* to occur if the government attempted to enforce its announced policy of containment. This remarkable contradiction between the words which the State Department uttered and the action subsequently taken probably represents the first and greatest "confusion" which has since been associated on a vast scale with the concept of limited war.

I have never liked the term because of its thinly veiled

weakness and the uncertainty of national interest which it implies—and which in fact are its genesis. Nevertheless, I must discuss the concept and its history because millions of words have been written on the subject, most of them by people in our foreign policy group lost in the maze of their own creation.

The term "limited war" in itself is a new term for the United States of America.

It is true that limitations on the scope of armed conflict, imposed by a sort of mutual consent on the part of the belligerents, has historical foundation in both Europe and Asia. Space does not permit me to discuss the technique of the Oriental warlord, nor does the purpose of this book require it. However, European history *is* pertinent.

The end of the bloody religious wars and the Thirty Years' War in 1648 introduced a period of almost a hundred and fifty years during which European states deliberately avoided all-out conflicts. During this period of history, Europe's many masters played a kind of political-military chess game, always trying to keep their armies intact, always trying to gain concessions from the opposition, and always trying to live to fight another day if circumstances seemed to indicate retreat. This opportunistic attitude and approach to warfare, apparently totally devoid of basic principle, ended, of course, with the close of the eighteenth century and the Napoleonic wars. From that time—shortly before the turn of the nineteenth century and up until the time of the Korean War —European military action and United States military action developed a different character. The medieval period was past, governments were stronger and better organized, objectives and principles were more clearly defined, and war became more total in character.

The late date of our birth as a nation spared us, though not our ancestors, of the pragmatic philosophy of limited war during the one hundred and fifty years of European history between 1650–1800. In our own War of Independence, we went all out to win our freedom. The new united states were unencumbered by the jealousies, the commitments, the economic and political problems, and opportunities of the Old World. Americans stood on principle, and Americans fought for principle.

As a consequence, I do not recall that the United States ever applied the term limited war to the many limited military engagements which it conducted throughout the period of its growth to maturity as a nation. In the old days, war was war and peace was peace. Our nation did not ask its political leaders for a definition, "Is this a 'limited war,' or a 'general war,' or a 'total war'?" When the nation was at war, Americans were at war, and Americans did what was necessary to win.

The United States fought its first war as a new nation against the pirates of Tripoli during the period 1801–1815. Did our President call it a limited war? Indeed not! This nation was fighting for freedom of the seas, and it did what was necessary. Was the British assault in 1812–1814 a limited war? No! The country did not do too well in that effort, and the British burned our Capitol—but Americans fought, adhered to principle, and maintained their dignity and freedom as a nation. Were the Mexican or the Spanish-American wars limited wars? Even though Mexico or Spain were something less than a total threat to our survival, our government considered itself at war and did what was necessary to totally win.

The meaning of historical events can be twisted, just as the truth can be twisted, and there are undoubtedly many historians who would disagree with my reaction to these precedents of our times. My only counter to a different—and incidentally, always weaker—interpretation is that during my forty-four years in uniform I was always proud to wear it because of my understanding of the fact that the United States stood on principle, not on opportunism. I never heard of limited war before 1950. The term came into the general vocabulary as the nation developed an articulate political and scientific minority who greatly fear a general war.

What Does It Mean?

One of the very confusing things about limited war is that no two people have the same definition of the term. For the better part of two of the years during my tenure as Chairman of the Joint Chiefs of Staff, we had a paper before us, intermittently, which attempted to define the term, limited war. The Joint Chiefs of Staff met on this paper often. The discussions which flared and flickered were beneficial and enlightening, but never could the JCS agree on definition of limited war. After two years of exploration, the Staff finally voided the paper by deleting its definitions and talking about the substance of the problem. We were in the realm of idle philosophy when we talked conceptually about limited war.*

Limited war means many different things; it depends on the frame of reference. To some "students," limited war means a war in which nuclear weapons are not used. To others it means a war in which nuclear weapons might be used tactically but not strategically. To others it means a war limited to a particular geographical area. To others it means a war limited in political or military objective. To others it means that the war is fought by proxy—that is, the Communist powers get somebody else to put peace to the torch, as was the case in Korea, Laos, South Vietnam, Cuba, and the Congo. To others it is anything short of a transpolar nuclear exchange between the U.S.S.R. and the United States. To still others it is any war our nation might fight against anybody but the Soviet Union.

All of these definitions can be defended with vigor because all are, indeed, characterized by a common denominator—a *limitation.* But what sense does this academic debate really

* The Joint Chiefs of Staff finally agreed on a limited war definition in principle, which can be found in Appendix B.

make to an American who would like to see his form of government survive and flourish? None, in my judgment.

Much of the theorizing and philosophizing on this subject is really far more destructive than just "making no sense." Much of it telegraphs a signal of weakness of purpose, of indecision, to the enemy. It tells him that a significant segment of the American population is concerning itself with ways and means to avoid a showdown with the dynamic force of communism, a force which has openly and consistently dedicated itself to our national destruction. If I were a dedicated strategist on the other side, I would be inclined to become even more aggressive.

There have been many special interest groups involved in this limited war debate. Without condemning any agency or interest, it is important that all Americans understand these special interests and their parochial attitudes.

There are at least seven different types, or groups, of people who have led the way in propounding a philosophy of limited war. There are undoubtedly more than seven, but let's confine ourselves to the seven which exert the most influence on the conduct of U.S. foreign policy. The first six of these categories probably comprise less than one percent of our population, but they make nine-tenths of the noise.

The Scientist with the Bad Conscience

First there is the scientist with the bad conscience. As a theoretical physicist, or mathematician, or director of a research project, he has made a contribution to science and technology which has increased the terrible power of modern weaponry. He believes that science should serve mankind, not destroy it. He feels that scientists, being responsible for modern technology, have a special responsibility to help control it. Instinctively, he believes that our nation should stop nuclear weapons testing, stop the production of nuclear material for weapons, transfer present nuclear weapons materials

106

back to "peaceful" purposes, limit the membership in the atomic club, and eventually arrive at world nuclear disarmament—with or without inspection, controls, and insured compliance on the part of all concerned.

Naturally, this type of person likes the sound of the term, limited war. It offers, he hopes, a way out. "Little people," civilian soldiers by the millions, if necessary, can do the fighting and dying by bayonet and bullet in limited war, but the intelligentsia will have the traditional personal safety of a bombproof job.

This type of scientist almost blocked development of the H-bomb by the United States at the very time that the U.S.S.R. was feverishly developing the weapon. This same coalition of men was chiefly responsible for the self-imposed United States moratorium on nuclear testing, without mutual inspection, during the period 1958–1961. And curiously enough, people of this mentality shy away from squarely facing such real limited-war problems as those presented by the earlier situations in Laos and Cuba, and today, Vietnam.

No one can challenge the genuine motivation of this group. They really believe that science should serve man, not destroy him, and all Americans would agree to this. However, this humanitarian viewpoint does not universally prevail in the international jungle in which we live, and the physical scientist (who becomes a political scientist by extrapolation of genius from one field of human knowledge to another) is capable of great blunders. He carefully uses the scientific method in his own area of scientific competence, but totally abandons the scientific approach when pontificating in an unfamiliar area. As a consequence, he carries an intellectual bias into the debate on political-military issues. He is an expert, for example, on nuclear physics, but he speaks as an expert on foreign policy. Unfortunately, few people have had the courage in recent years to challenge the competence of these self-styled experts—experts who excel in their own area, but who are uninitiated in the field of political-military reality. These peo-

107

ple are a great hazard to the survival of our nation. Fortunately, not many of our scientists have this frame of mind, but those who have are the most active in propagating their views.

Lower Level "State"

The second group that has a vested interest in the philosophy of limited war resides in the U.S. State Department. They reside generally, and over a period of time, at the second, third, and lower levels of responsibility. Limited war in this clique is an interesting and hopeful derivative of the concept of *status quo*.

As late as June, 1960, I was absolutely astounded and shocked to hear a presentation of this philosophy by a man who was high up the ladder of professional practitioners of the art of diplomacy. He was at Undersecretary level, as a matter of fact.

This official explained how America had come to grow fat, dumb, and happy. He took us back to the Industrial Revolution and the founding days of our republic. He explained how our nation had grown materially prosperous, and how Americans knew that they had the best possible arrangement for free government. Because the nation was satisfied with its material prosperity and because we liked our form of government, this man reasoned that Americans wanted no change. Therefore, Americans were a *status quo* people. He held the view that, lacking in drive and objectives, as we have been for several years, the genius was largely gone out of us— that our people openly courted mediocrity. He doubted very much that there was any individual, or group of individuals, left in America who could today create such deathless documents as the Declaration of Independence and the Constitution of the United States.

This picture of today's American shocked me on two counts: first, this man's thesis was exactly that preached by those advocating a soft line. He believed, philosophically, that we were over the hill—decadent, lacking in dynamism, drive, genius, and old-fashioned American virtues. Second, this man influenced U.S. foreign policy. If this was his mental image of an American, what kind of advice was he going to give when the problems were tough and the chips were down?

Well, as a matter of fact, he was kind enough to explain the natural course of events as he saw them. Lacking any dynamic drive and purpose, Americans were always to be on the defensive. The Communist enemy would always have the initiative. This nation would always be responding to Communist thrusts and would be fighting a gradually retreating, rear-guard action. At the end of this road, of course, lies defeat.

It seems inconceivable that a highly placed American could make such a speech. Maybe he made it because he wanted to shock somebody into action, but I doubt it. He and his kind usually lined up against any firm course of U.S. action which was suggested in connection with the cries of the last decade. The possibility of accepting limited wars is always more appealing to this group than taking a firm stand which involves the risk of general war. And paradoxically, when the chips are down, they usually try to shy away from their own brainchild, limited war. This is nice diplomacy, but in my judgment, it is a sure way to ultimate loss of our freedom.

The Moralist

The third type of person who instinctively likes the sound of the words "limited war" is the moralist. This type is found across the board; his habitat is not confined to any particular skill, profession, or governmental agency.

This chap believes that it is all right, if you have to fight, to disembowel a man with a bayonet, blow off his face with a hand grenade, shoot him full of holes with a .45 pistol or a rifle, starve and freeze him in filthy trench, and make an

109

animal of him through years of exposure to privation, danger, and destruction. On the other hand, he is oposed to strategic bombing of any kind, and particularly opposed to nuclear weapons and any instrument connected with their possible delivery. These weapons—these pieces of hardware—are immoral in his judgment.

This type of mentality does not recognize that the basic immorality lies in the causes of war and not in the instruments of war—those which can carry the battlefield into everyone's back yard—possibly even his own. If we must have a war, he would like to live in a world in which someone else puts on a uniform to serve his country in some far-off corner of the earth, without disruption of his own comfortable environment. He likes the sound of the term "limited war." Someone else will be involved.

The Political Scientist

The fourth group who have exerted considerable influence in the national debate on limited war are the political scientists with pacifistic tendencies. They usually live, grow, and preach in university environments. They generally have a better historical perspective than the physical scientists turned statesmen, but they normally come out with the same judgments. Because they are more qualified in the field of foreign affairs than the natural scientist, they have a better grasp of the power relationships among nations. But they are also somewhat moralistic. Little "blow-ups" are better than big "blow-ups" in their judgment, and our foreign policy should place our nation in a better position to accept an unending series of little "blow-ups," as opposed to adopting a policy which could escalate suddenly into general war.

There are two obvious difficulties with this approach: first, if America were to go as far as the pacifistic political scientists would like to go in preparing to meet contingencies all over the world with conventional (non-nuclear) weapons, the cost in manpower, resources, and dollars would require a condition of semi-mobilization and wartime controls. The defense budget would be doubled at least. The nation would have to become a garrison state, the same as the U.S.S.R. and Red China, in order to pay the bill. Second, this concept would allow the Communists to wear the Free World down, little by little, until the country would eventually have to make the ultimate decision anyhow. This decision would have to be one of surrender or general nuclear war. Hence, this intellectual approach merely defers the problem awhile; it evades the issue while the enemy becomes stronger. The ultimate cost of possible U.S. success, in terms of blood and resources, goes up, while the probability of our ultimate success simultaneously goes down.

The Defeatist

There is a fifth kind of mentality associated with the concept of limited war, the defeatist. This chap believes that "no one can win a nuclear war," that the end of civilization as the world knows it, would be the certain aftermath. The same judgments were rendered, of course, with the advent of the crossbow and gunpowder.

Certainly, wars of all kinds and in all ages have exacted a toll which humanity could have avoided if all peoples and all nations had been truly civilized—if they had been willing to live by law instead of by force. In that sense, nobody can win an atomic war—but only in that sense.

The greatest danger in the concept that no one can win a nuclear war is the effect which such convictions can have and are having on U.S. defense programs. Those who hold to this conviction usually think in terms of "mutual suicide" that is, a massive delivery of nuclear weapons by both sides. This faction believes that such attacks cannot be stopped and that a transpolar exchange would be the inevitable result. But what if the enemy does not believe this and solves the problems of

111

ballistic missile defense and antisubmarine warfare before we do? In that event, our nation will have a nuclear war which the opposition *will win*—or the United States will be black-mailed into virtual surrender. Unfortunately, the conviction that no one can win a nuclear war does much to pull the force, drive, and sense of urgency from American research and development programs and it also adversely affects U.S. force structure in-being.

There is no question that a nuclear war can be "won," as wars of the past have been won—by the side which is best prepared to fight it. This preparation of which I speak includes as top-priority items civil defense measures as well as military offensive and defensive power. The tenacious attitude, incidentally, of Americans in refusing to recognize and heed civil defense measures is just about as idiotic as would be the action of an infantryman facing certain rifle fire and refusing to get into a foxhole.

Nevertheless, the defeatists believe that no one can win a nuclear war, that civilization will be destroyed; hence, the human urge to fight must somehow be channeled into limited, non-nuclear wars. This approach is a different way of arriving at the same weak answer. If ever the belief that "no one can win a nuclear war" becomes completely dominant and controlling in U.S. national policy, the enemy will know it. The enemy will know that America will go to any lengths to avoid nuclear war, and then by virtue of his geographic and demographic advantages, he will be in position to destroy us.

The Unilateral Disarmer

A sixth type of mind that instinctively perks up at the term, limited war, is the unilateral disarmer. The cults, sects, odd-ball groups and intellectuals associated in some way with this school of thought really run the gamut of humanity. Representation here includes the "illiterate," some forms of the "religious," the opportunist, the do-gooder, some college professors, and some scientists.

The illiterate, to my mind, is represented by the "Ban the Bomb" marchers who frequently converge on London. There are a number of the same type in this country. A second example is found in some forms of the religious. These pacifistic cults live in prosperity and security and under a condition of religious freedom because other people have died to give them a safe haven. But the intellectuals associated with the basic philosophy of unilateral disarmament are much more dangerous. They speak in terms and on subjects with which the man in the street is not too familiar. They have a step formula worked out which is intended to achieve nuclear disarmament by this country, whether or not the Communist powers do likewise. The plan is as follows:

1. The nation will stop the testing of nuclear weapons whether or not we have the proper assurances that the Communists agree to follow suit. They have already accomplished this.
2. The nation will reduce the nuclear-weapons production program. They have already accomplished this.
3. America will stop entirely the production of nuclear material for weapons use.
4. The nation will close its nuclear production facilities one by one.
5. The nation will transfer nuclear weapons materials back to "peaceful" uses.
6. The nation will start getting rid of anything that can deliver a nuclear weapon, whether aircraft or missile.
7. Having progressively retired all nuclear weapons and means of delivery, the country will have achieved nuclear disarmament.
8. Having set such an example for the world, America will have "reduced world tensions," and then in righteous

113

triumph call upon the Communist world to follow our example.

In the meantime, the nation should be ready for limited wars.

Military Interest in the Term "Limited War"

Certainly no responsible military leader of any service, land, sea, or air, could be grouped with the types I have described here. However, there have been differences of military viewpoint on the subject of limited war, and the seventh category of people having special interest in this subject, the military professional, must be discussed. This aspect of the subject needs careful and objective analysis because the differences in military viewpoint have been more of degree than of the merit of limited war. And treatment of this important subject would be incomplete if the special and natural interest which each military service has in the term, limited war, were passed over.

As a starting point, a realistic view of war provides a common ground for all services. The dedication, patriotism, and performance of one service is no better or worse than that of any other. The same kind of American boys go into each service, and the same kind of men remain to make the defense of their nation a lifetime work.

Accepting this as a fundamental fact, which it is, we are all only mortal, and we see the total task of military preparedness through the eyes of our own experience. Even so, if national resources for defense purposes had been more readily obtainable over the past fifteen years, I doubt that there would have been much of a difference of service viewpoint on the subject of limited war. It was the shortage of resources, and how these limited resources were to be divided up, that really caused service interest in the idle philosophy of limited war.

114

The Air Force, quite naturally, took a dim view of the term from the beginning of the national debate in the late nineteen forties. Limited war meant conventional, non-nuclear forces, and Air Force planners feared that a diversion of resources to such activities would cripple the Strategic Air Command. For exactly the same reason, in reverse, some Navy, Army, and Marine planners gave enthusiastic acceptance to the term. Considering the total military task and mission, many felt that too much of available resources were going into Air Defensive and Air Offensive Systems at the expense of their own service. The philosophy of limited war offered a convenient bandwagon, the music was pleasing, and some got on it.

Their motivation was perfectly natural and there is no quarrel with their intent. The military services *were* spread too thin, and are still spread too thin in certain areas. However, those in uniform who are enamored with the limited war thesis are in bed with some very strange company. There were—and are—other ways and means available to bolster an argument for stronger land forces and stronger sea forces. It was not necessary for dedicated military men to become associated with the philosophy of weakness as represented by the six types of mentalities dissected previously in these pages. The simple arguments which I laid out in discussing containment, collective security, credibility, and commitment of national prestige are an adequate military justification for larger conventional force structures. Furthermore, these arguments point the way toward a meaningful and balanced military effort as opposed to a blind hodgepodge created to support the meaningless term, limited war.

Unfortunately the schism which developed in military ranks over this term has done much to support the timid and fearful in the formulation and conduct of national affairs. The intellectual theoretician, the scientist turned statesman, the moralist, the defeatist, and the nuclear disarmer have all gained in stature and influence. And even some dedicated

115

military men will have to go down in history as associated with a patently specious and superficial judgment on limited war.

In this chapter, I have talked about the origin of the term, the difficulties inherent in its definition, and some of the natural attitudes involved in this great debate. Now that the attitudes of the participants have been drawn, let's examine some of the more specific arguments which have been used to lend credence to the theory of limited war.

The most popular of these seemingly fail-safe arguments is that limited wars are now more probable because (*and this is important*) because the U.S. and the U.S.S.R. have now reached a condition of nuclear stalemate. Each side now has in hand tremendous nation-killing power (so the argument goes), and neither dares to use it; hence limited war is more probable. The critical fact to remember about this argument is that it is the nuclear balance of terror which makes limited war "more probable."

This argument is so obviously fallacious that it is astonishing it survived its verbal birth. Even recent history, if history is to be considered as any kind of guide to human affairs, defeats it. Looking back only a few years:

The Korean War was probably a limited war by anybody's definition. It was limited in terms of geography, weaponry, participants, and political objective. The Korean War is the only limited war this nation has fought since the end of World War II.* And yet no so-called nuclear stalemate existed. But America had a limited war anyway.

The United States had a limited war in Korea at the time that its atomic monopoly was *supreme*. It is true that the Soviets had exploded an atomic device a few short months before Korea. But the Soviets had no atomic warfare capa-

---

* The action in Vietnam is currently described not as a limited war, but as a "counter-insurgency operation."

bility at the time of Korea. The U.S.S.R. had no stockpile of weapons and it had no delivery force worth the name. They knew it, we knew it, and they knew that we knew it. No atomic stalemate existed. Yet the U.S. and the U.S.S.R. (by proxy) fought a limited war under a condition of atomic imbalance between two ideological gladiators.

If it was not an atomic stalemate which caused the Korean War, what was it?

The answer is obvious, and it is again provided by history. The United States conducted a limited war in Korea simply because American policy led the Soviets to believe that our nation would not fight to defend South Korea. When our government did elect to fight, the decision was made against the use of atomic weapons. In retrospect I have often thought that had we dropped one A-bomb on a tactical target during the Korean War, thereby advising the Chinese Communists to stay on their own side of the border, there might have been no Chinese invasion and no second phase to that war, and Korea today might be a united, independent country: Furthermore, Dien Bien Phu might not have happened, nor would Vietnam have been partitioned in 1954.

Therefore political attitude, not a nuclear stalemate, brought on the Korean limited war and the subsequent Communist take-over of French Indochina. Furthermore, political constraint on weaponry served to broaden and prolong the Korean War. Political constraint was also felt in other ways which served no purpose other than to make the enemy bolder. For example, the establishment of the sanctuary across the Yalu River was nothing more than a hopeful token of appeasement, but that sanctuary simultaneously sapped away the real power of our Air Force and very nearly saw the loss of our Army and Marines when the Chinese Reds attacked. And even without nuclear weapons, U.N. Forces would have done great damage to Chinese air and land forces—if there had been no sanctuary.

Looking back, the Korean War can serve a useful purpose

in meeting the U.S. foreign policy challenges of today and tomorrow. If we believe that limited wars are somehow related to an atomic stalemate and are more probable now because an atomic stalemate does exist, our Government may be inclined to tamper with or weaken U.S. nuclear posture in order to be better prepared to fight the little war. Nothing could be more fatal, in my judgment, to the security interests of the nation. This is the Unholy Grail of the story. Here again, the limited war concept plays into the hands of the pacifists, the appeasers, the antinuclear fraternity, and the unilateral disarmers. They would finance the little war forces by reducing the nation's nuclear forces. Now, I am all for strengthening our forward deployments as necessary to match the enemy, hazard for hazard, and insure full commitment of U.S. prestige. But if our nation is going to do it, let's pay for it and not tear it from the sinew of the strategic nuclear forces.

Rather than buying the argument that the probability of limited war is related to nuclear power relationships, those who would appease the Red Bear would do well to look at the history of mankind. Over the period of the last 400 years, history shows that the odds have been even that at least one war of some kind would break out every year. These wars had nothing to do with nuclear power relationships. They were rooted in the nature of man.

A corollary argument, and one which must be disposed of, is that our military forces, because they are muscle-bound, lack military capability to handle these "more probable" limited engagements.

The argument has been that the military lacks the capability for flexible response; that as a result, the United States must face either humiliation or annihilation. Here we have either/or again. This argument is not in the best interest of the United States for two reasons: first, it is not true. Second, the implication of facing annihilation is a reflection of the defeatist attitude that no one can win a nuclear war. If the enemy thinks that America thinks it faces annihilation, he will naturally push our country to the wall.

118

You can bet your bottom dollar that the Sino-Soviet Bloc does not share the view that no one can win a nuclear war. But it is precisely what they want America to believe. They do not believe it, and they are preparing to win it. Those aren't firecrackers and sparklers that the Soviets drag through Moscow's Red Square on May Day each year.

As to the accuracy of the statement that, under the Eisenhower Administration, United States military forces lacked capability for flexible response, what about our aircraft carriers, our marine forces, and our bombardment forces that can carry conventional weapons, or nuclear weapons, against any kind of a target—be it strategic or tactical?

U.S. military forces have had the capacity for flexible response all along. No sane man believes in driving a tack with a sledge-hammer. The nation has not had to. What this nation has lacked has been the political nerve at times to use what it has had.

Now I do believe, as I have said before, that our military land and sea forces did need numerical strengthening in forward areas, not for the purpose of building up our capability to win a non-nuclear war, but for the purpose of on-the-spot commitment of national prestige. The concepts are vastly different.

The United States can continue on down the present limited-war garden path, spending additional billions on material for flexible response and not improving its international position one iota. If our nation increases its military force structure by two, three times, even four times the strength it has now, but avoids military deployment and political commitment of prestige, it would accomplish exactly nothing. All four Services, Army, Navy, Marine Corps, and Air Force—large and small—are greatly handicapped unless this government is willing to use, promptly and effectively, the weaponry most suitable to the military situation, and to avoid an appearance of weakness by informing an enemy, in advance, on any self-imposed constraints on the scope and depth of our own military intentions.

119

The argument that our country lacks capability for flexible response is also always rooted in the two big "IFs." The argument has merit and foundation *if* we accept certain arbitrary restrictions *before* we assess our strengths and capabilities. If America accepts political restraints which provide for sanctuaries—and if we accept political restraints which deny our military services the use of nuclear weapons, even tactically—then the nation's limited war capability as of today is indeed limited.

On the other hand, if the enemy knows beforehand that the United States will extend a peripheral war just as deep as its enemy's logistic support, that there will be no sanctuary for those fighting by proxy, and that the United States will use the weaponry most suitable to its military task, then American limited war capability today is fantastically great and has been so for several years. It is greater than any general war capability which the United States has ever produced in the past, including that of World War II.

This statement is true even if the power of the nation's strategic weapons systems are excluded and we examine only the power structure which could be brought to bear in a conflict short of a transpolar nuclear exchange. United States limited war capability, as of today, is purely a function of political decision.

All wars of civilized experience have really been limited. Any war which stops short, in objective, of total annihilation of the enemy population is limited. World War I, therefore, was limited; World War II was also limited. The limitations are recorded in familiar history. This being so, the academic interest in limited war troubles me. It may be symptomatic of a growing attitude of national weakness because, by contrast, Americans never asked what kind of a war they were fighting in years gone by. War was war and once engaged, America fought it to win.

Chapter VIII

MILITARY POLICY
IN SUPPORT OF
CONTAINMENT
(1950-1960)

United States military policy of the decade 1950-1960 continued, of course, to be influenced by economic considerations, but not to the extent of the preceding five-year period. I am no expert in the field of economics, few men in uniform are. At the same time, it is often difficult to find "experts" in the field of economics who agree even among themselves.

I do recall that the total national defense budget, running from twelve to fourteen billion dollars a year in the lean days following World War II, was considered excessive by some economic experts. Those experts declared emphatically that such sums were all the nation could stand—more would bankrupt the country. The same thing was said a few years later at about a forty-billion-dollar level. I don't *know* the answer to what level the military budget should hold, but I do know that when one is wearing a uniform and is in a responsible position, strict attention is paid to what your government tells you in respect to the impact of military requirements on the national economy.

Each year the military departments bring in a statement of

121

programs, people, and dollars necessary to meet their requirements for the next fiscal year and a projection of longer term requirements. And each year requirements, when totaled up, exceed resources which seem to be available. After the Department of Defense, the National Security Council, the White House, and the Congress have reviewed the various programs, a national defense budget is hammered out within which the military departments must operate. The problem is always how best to use the manpower and dollars made available within the limits set by legislative and executive action.

The conflicting demands for the resources available can be broken down into two broad categories: one, the requirement for forces-in-being, and two, the requirement for research and development. Each of these broad categories can be further subdivided into components which compete with one another for resources of one kind or another. A common denominator in looking at both areas, the problem of today and the problem of tomorrow, is weaponry—how much conventional, how much nuclear, and how much of other types.

The organization which we establish to solve these problems is also a vital part of our national military policy. Accordingly, I shall discuss the military policy in support of the containment theory for the period of 1950–1960 under four general headings as follows:

1. Force-in-Being
2. Weaponry
3. Organization
4. Research and Development

Force-in-Being

Resources for forces-in-being are the dollars, facilities, and manpower to be allocated for what the military services know they can build in the next two-to-four year period, based on the proven technology of the day. Under the basic national security policy, between 1950–1960 national defense had three major obligations to meet, or contribute to, with U.S. military forces. First, the Department of Defense had to build a strategic nuclear deterrent force—how big was always a subject of debate. Second, it had to build a North American air defense force—how big was also always a subject of debate. And third, the Department had to build "theater" type forces for overseas deployment, together with their back-up in the United States, their sea and air communications, and their logistic base. Again, how much was always a subject of debate. One overseas area competed in its requirement for resources with another, and the whole package competed with how much was spent on strategic deterrence and air defense.

There is no mathematical formula which may be used in solving the problem of forces-in-being. It is ruthlessly stalked by building hundreds of strategic, tactical, and logistic studies and conducting endless war games in an effort to grasp the magnitude of the various and endless military equations. But the final decision is one of human judgment.

The task of building and maintaining force-in-being is not new to military planners. It troubled Genghis Khan and Alexander the Great as well. However, something more recent, and yet sufficiently distant to have historical impact, can be found in the works of Admiral Alfred T. Mahan. This brilliant naval officer had this to say about war three quarters of a century ago:

> The problem of preparation for war in modern times is both extensive and complicated. As in the construction of the individual ship, where the attempt to reconcile conflicting requirements has resulted, according to a common expression, in a compromise, the most dubious of all military solutions—giving something to all, and all to none—so preparation for war involves many conditions, often contradictory one to another, at times almost irreconcilable. To satisfy all of these passes the ingenuity of the national

123

Treasury, powerless to give the whole of what is demanded by the representatives of the different elements, which, in duly ordered proportion, constitute a complete scheme of national military policy, whether for offense or defense. Unable to satisfy all, and too often equally unable to say frankly, "this one is chief; to it you others must yield, except so far as you contribute to its greatest efficiency," either the pendulum of the government's will swings from one extreme to the other or, in the attempt to be fair all round, all alike receive less than they ask, and for their theoretical completeness require. In other words, the contents of the national purse are distributed, instead of being concentrated upon a leading conception, adopted after due deliberation and maintained with conviction.

The creation of material for war, under modern conditions, requires a length of time which does not permit the postponement of it to the hour of impending hostilities.

War, at the time this was written, was rather simple by our present standards. Wars were still fought in two dimensions; both naval and land forces had to get fairly close to each other in order to fight at all. Powered flight, which would add a third-dimensional aspect to war's order of battle, was yet to be invented and exploited. The slow methods of travel and difficult logistical support provided a large degree of security for an isolated nation such as ours.

Yet Mahan still found: That the preparation for war was extensive and complicated. That there were competing requirements working against each other. That compromise solutions gave unsatisfactory military results. That the budget did not go around in peacetime, and was split so that no force was sufficiently supplied. That preparation could not be delayed until the hour of impending hostilities.

I can visualize the super-eloquence of Mahan's prose on this subject if his problem had been complicated by three dimensions instead of two—by supersonic speeds instead of ten or twenty knots—and by weapons which make those of his time look like firecrackers.

In assessing the competing requirements for force-in-being during the 1950–1960 time period, I always leaned strongly to the side of the strategic deterrent force. I felt then, and am certain today, that this one striking power must be strong. The military services pursuing any other goal may well so dissipate their resources as to become weak everywhere—and strong nowhere. Naval forces and ground force divisions are both extremely necessary to the defense of the United States. In fact, more, rather than less, would be useful today. However, at times I had to differ with my colleagues on priorities. If the services couldn't have everything, one had to sacrifice to the strength of another.

Air defense of North America has always been a knotty issue and daily is getting more tangled in costly, sophisticated complexity. Air defense means more than fighter interceptors and surface-to-air missiles. It also means warning systems and vastly complicated electronic systems for control of the combatant forces. The SAGE* System, the DEW† Line, the BMEWS** radar, the AEW‡ net, the radar picket ships were all a part of the Air Defense System for North America. Lengthy negotiations, treaties, costs, jurisdictional problems, all had to be worked out, of course, in collaboration with the governments of Canada, Iceland, and England.

Materially speaking, if the military services had no other requirement for defense resources than the air defense of

* SAGE: Semi-Automatic Ground Environment; an electronic system of sensors, computers, communication links, and control centers which is established to control fighter aircraft and air defense missiles.
† DEW Line: Distant Early Warning Line; a radar system across Canada designed to detect the approach of enemy bombers.
** BMEWS: Ballistic Missile Early Warning System; powerful radar based in Alaska, Greenland, and England which can detect a Soviet-launched ballistic missile in flight and transmit a warning signal.
‡ AEW: Airborne Early Warning; aircraft on patrol, generally over the seas, which have radar to detect an approaching bomber attack.

North America, it could easily spend fifty billion dollars a year on this one effort. However, resources having a finite limit, air defense had to take its place in line—and it was generally standing behind strategic deterrence.

Much has been written on these pages concerning the necessity for overseas deployments of U.S. Forces—and some indication of the U.S. military manpower actually needed to secure the peace at various points on the globe. But one of the things which must be considered in overseas deployments is that it costs far more to station U.S. Forces overseas than it does to station the same forces at home. When troops are stationed in an overseas area there is automatically built-in a huge transportation problem in shuttling people, supplies, and equipment back and forth. What is more, very costly foreign base facilities often have to be constructed which are already available in the United States.

Another factor, of course, is the requirement for a U.S.-based support structure of back-up units. An American soldier, sailor, or airman can't remain overseas away from home, family and friends indefinitely. There must be supporting organizations in the United States to provide trained replacements. Fortunately the Zone of Interior (Z.I.) support structure is not only useful as an overseas replacement pool, but it also constitutes the bulk of the nation's strategic reserve.

An explanation of the many operational, technical, administrative, political, and morale problems of maintaining overseas deployments in peacetime would, of itself, fill volumes. But to satisfy the purposes of this book, only two observations need be made here.

First, the problems are common to all Services. The Navy, like the Army and Air Force, needs overseas bases for efficient operations; and second, considering any possible trouble area on the globe and assuming a major enemy effort at that particular locale, development of very large military requirements for that area can easily be made.

Obviously, to burden the economy of the U.S. and that of

the Free World with very large forces in a dozen or more places where trouble may or may not start would be unwise, to say the least. The problem then, is one of providing relatively small forces in the potential trouble spots, and simultaneously maintaining mobile reinforcements at home which may quickly be moved into place if necessary.

A relatively small force on station in any troubled area should be adequate to guarantee a full commitment of U.S. national prestige. This America has not done in some parts of the world, and in other parts I'm afraid we may have overdone it.

For example, looking toward NATO, there is no significant difference between three U.S. divisions on station and five divisions, or seven divisions. Three divisions are a guarantee of U.S. commitment just the same as are seven. Actually, looking only at Army forces for the moment, in NATO Europe the United States has maintained about five U.S. divisions and several units of regimental combat team size, plus scores of thousands of dependents of military personnel.

With this observation, I do not mean that U.S. force reductions in Europe should be taken without compensating moves because such an action could be interpreted by friend and foe alike as an indication of U.S. surrender in Berlin or as a prelude to abandonment of NATO. However, in the latter part of the decade 1950–60, the Army had to go through a thinning out process of its U.S. overseas forces. The Army was forced to do this because its tactical or theater type forces had to stand in line with strategic forces and air defense forces for resources. In this thinning-out process through the exercise of firm diplomacy, the United States could have reduced its Army forces in Europe somewhat—and found the resources, under the same budget, for full commitment of U.S. prestige in some other critically important parts of the world. The President felt that European Army commitments could be increased with reduction in U.S. participation thereby providing for an even stronger alliance. The State Department and the

127

NATO Commander voiced strong objections and the plan never went forward. The opposition view was based on two arguments:

1. The United States can't afford to show less visible interest in Europe; it will wreck the Alliance.

2. The Government has gone as far in committing the United States in other parts of the world as the American people will support.

This very brief resumé of the problems of forces-in-being has been presented here only to indicate that its rational solution was no easy task. Human judgment had to provide the leavening influence. Suffice it to say that over a ten-year period, the composite of human judgment gave enough priority to strategic deterrence to allocate to that mission roughly twenty-five percent of the total dollars available for U.S. forces. The remaining seventy-five percent was spread over theater forces and other essential tasks. The ratios of that decade are in the process of drastic change at this writing. The current preoccupation with limited war seems destined to effect even more drastic changes. The soundness of military and administration judgments applied in the coming months in allocation of resources may well determine the future fate of mankind.

Weaponry

Over the decade in question, military policy on weaponry evolved in a very logical manner. The United States had tremendous commitments to fulfill and its resources were limited. It was, therefore, necessary to make each fighting unit—land, sea, or air—as effective and powerful as technology would permit. Our government elected to use the most effective form of firepower which was available. This was nuclear energy.

Rapid advances in nuclear technology allowed us to produce weapons of all categories for warfare on land, at sea, and in the air. Thus, the military services raised the firepower potential of the individual soldier, sailor, marine, and airman by factors of thousands. This seemed to be a good idea because the enemy could always field many more troops than could the U.S. for hand-to-hand primitive combat.

Consequently, the force-in-being was tailored for use of, and reliance on, nuclear weapons. The force for tomorrow, in the research and development stage, was also tailored for the use of nuclear firepower. Conventional TNT and .30-calibre type firepower was retained, but the specific military directive for defense of NATO Europe provided for the use of nuclear weapons from the outset of war; and U.S. military planning for a major confrontation in any other part of the world was also predicated on the use of nuclear weapons. Therefore, over a ten-year period our total U.S. force structure was methodically tailored to the use of nuclear weapons. There really was no other way in which the military services could have even partially met the demands of U.S. national policy.

Today, the confusion of the debate on counter-insurgency (COIN) and limited war tends to obscure sight of this fundamental shift in the power equation. Those charged with national defense during the decade of the fifties developed a military force structure under one set of ground rules—the use of nuclear weapons. That force structure was re-evaluated during the early days of the Kennedy Administration under the assumption that nuclear weapons would not be employed.

Organization

The dull subject of "organization" is a vital part of military policy. Earlier, when discussing the 1946–1950 birth pains of a nuclear strategy, I reviewed significant organizational changes of the immediate postwar years, and indicated the trend toward greater centralization of authority over the military departments.

The evolutionary pattern leading toward greater centralization of control of the entire United States Military Establishment under a civilian Secretary of Defense continued during the ten years following the basic Act of 1947, and the modifications of 1949. The reorganization plans of 1953 and of 1958, and the Department of Defense Reorganization Act of 1958 culminated in the defense structure of today. The specific provisions of these plans and acts (all leading to greater centralization) were constantly added to through the investment of greater executive authority in the Secretary of Defense.

The 1953 Plan abolished the Munitions Board, the Research and Development Board, the Defense Supply Management Agency, and the Directorate of Installations and transferred the functions of these agencies to the Secretary of Defense. This reorganization plan also authorized six additional high-level civilian positions as "Assistant Secretaries of Defense."

The Reorganization Act of 1958, which followed the Reorganization Plan of 1958, amended the declaration of Congressional policy by vesting "in the field of research and engineering . . . overall direction and control in the Secretary of Defense." What this paragraph means, translated into ordinary language, is that the future military strategy of the United States can be controlled by a civilian *transient* political appointee. His judgment can determine what military hardware will be in the future U.S. inventory of weapons. And, of course, the nature of the hardware in-hand will have a dominant effect upon the military strategy and tactics which may be chosen at any point in time.

The Secretary of Defense does, of course, consult with the Joint Chiefs of Staff and the military services in arriving at his decisions. However, his judgment is overriding. For example, he can block development by the Air Force of a follow-on bomber to the B-52, and the development by the Navy of a nuclear-powered aircraft carrier, if he so chooses.

Under the Reorganization Act of 1958, the Secretary of Defense was also given broader powers to transfer, reassign, abolish, or consolidate the combatant functions of the military services. He could initiate such actions, under the new rules, if he advised Congress and gave them thirty calendar days of continuous session to review his actions. If Congress does not act in opposition to the proposals of the Secretary of Defense within this time period, such proposals then become law.

Under the 1958 Act, the Secretary of Defense was also given authority to assign or reassign to one or more military departments the development and operational use of new weapons or weapons systems. This, of course, is a powerful lever with which to whip a reluctant service into conformity with a predetermined political position. In addition, the 1958 Act authorized the Secretary of Defense to "provide for the carrying out of any supply or service activity common to more than one military department by a single agency or such other organizational entities as he deems appropriate."

During the period of time in which the Reorganization Act of 1958 was being worked out, I was Chairman of the Joint Chiefs of Staff and worked very closely with Secretary of Defense Neil McElroy, the Joint Chiefs, the military services, the major field commands which were affected, and the members of Congress who had primary interest in the organization of the Defense Department. Faced by plans for even further centralization, I agreed to the modifications which were embodied in the Reorganization Act of 1958. In retrospect, I think that I made a mistake with respect to some of these issues.

The task was to create a defense structure with the power of decision in regard to matters on which there were differing judgments from a military viewpoint. While the Joint Chiefs of Staff normally agreed on most matters, it was necessary that a higher authority be given the power and the responsibility to make immediate decision on controversial subjects.

During the years which preceded the reorganization of 1958, the Joint Chiefs of Staff were agreed on more than ninety percent of the basic problems which came before them.

131

However, the ten-percent area of disagreement was important and it was always accorded full attention by the nation's press. There was no newsworthy circumstance when the Joint Chiefs of Staff agreed, but it always made the front page when they disagreed. For example, during the year 1958, the Joint Chiefs of Staff processed on their agenda more than a thousand items and developed a basic difference of view on less than twenty of these items.

The problem probably can be best expressed by reference to a specific dollar problem. At one time, during this period, the Secretary of Defense asked the Joint Chiefs of Staff how they would divide up and spend for national security purposes a budget of thirty-eight billion dollars if this were in fact imposed as a ceiling on the budget. The Joint Chiefs of Staff, after a couple of weeks, reported back to the Secretary of Defense that they were in unanimous agreement as to how to spend thirty-four of the thirty-eight billion dollars, but were unable to agree on how the last four billion dollars should be spent. The problem was that each service felt that it needed the additional four billion, because of its own defense responsibilities, and could not voluntarily give it away to another military department.

What this means is that the responsible military authorities had agreed on about ninety percent of the problem and had referred to higher authority the hard decisions on the remaining ten percent of the problem.

During the formulation of the provisions of the Reorganization Act of 1958, I knew that all Secretary McElroy wanted was the firm authority to make those decisions, after listening to the arguments of all concerned, related to that part of military force structure on which the professional military establishment could not agree. Secretary McElroy was not hunting for authority to do the entire military job of force-structure requirements. He simply wanted authority, and I thought that he should have it, to make decision on competing requirements, all of which could not be obtained. Therefore,

I viewed the Reorganization Act of 1958, at the time of enactment, as an instrument that would insure prompt decision on the more difficult parts of the annual defense budget, but I did not visualize that the Act would be used, in later years, to pre-empt professional military advice across the board.

Secretary of Defense McElroy was succeeded by Mr. Thomas S. Gates, who held the same views as his predecessor. Secretary Gates worked very closely with the Joint Chiefs of Staff and did not intrude his own judgments into military matters on which there was a unified and harmonious Joint Chiefs of Staff position. His job, as he saw it, was responsibility for the orderly business administration of the Department of Defense and authority to recommend the course of action to the National Security Council and to the President on those matters involving differing judgments of the responsible people of the military departments.

If I could have foreseen that the powers given to the Secretary of Defense would have been used differently by those who were to follow, I would have strongly recommended that greater safeguards be written into the modifications of the 1947 Act. The law still says that the Joint Chiefs of Staff are the principal military advisors to the National Security Council and to the President, but as a matter of fact it does not seem to be working that way at the present time. Secretary McNamara, who succeeded Secretary Gates, now seems to have the last word—even when the uniformed professional establishment is unanimously opposed to his views.

Research and Development

When an enemy has the initiative, he has many obvious advantages. And he also has some advantages which are not so obvious. One of these advantages is the power to determine *when* there will be war; when, not in the narrow and obvious sense of timing a surprise attack, but when in terms of a technological generation of weapons.

133

For example, the Soviets safely minimized the buildup of a large force of subsonic bombardment aircraft while concentrating on the development of ballistic missiles. From our policy announcements, it was clear that America would not initiate nuclear war. All the Soviets had to do was build up enough of a bombardment force to represent a hazard to the United States if *they* initiated the war. A much greater effort could then be spent on ballistic missiles.

The United States, on the other hand, has had no assurance at all as to when the Soviets might or might not attack. U.S. military forces had to be ready to fight the war of the today and the tomorrow and at the same time find resources to prepare for the day *after* tomorrow.

The Soviets therefore have always had a double-edged initiative. On today's front their leaders can choose the time and place for probing and the exertion of erosive local pressures. In a broader time frame, they can choose a peak period of relative strength.

The entire area of military research and development has been, and remains, an extremely unpredictable and at times frustrating enterprise. Results and time schedules for military research and development cannot be predicted accurately simply because of the time element needed to ferret new knowledge and techniques of process and manufacture. It would not be "research and development" if scientists and engineers knew all the answers before the start of a project.

Two very striking characteristics are common to all efforts to advance the frontiers of human knowledge and bring into being new technologies and new military weapons systems. The first is that technological progress is almost always underestimated when looking ahead ten years. The second characteristic is that we have always tended to overestimate what could be done within the next two or three years. When the nation's industry is working to meet a tight schedule in the production of a new missile, ship, or aircraft, there always seems to develop some short-term slippages inevitably resulting in a six months to two years lag behind the original prediction as to when the new hardware would be in the combat inventory. However, in reviewing the previous ten years, we find that we are much farther advanced than the most optimistic of the technical planners had thought possible.

There is another major factor associated with research and development which has been brought into sharp focus in the last few years. This is the philosophical approach to technological progress. Posed as a question one might ask: "What are the advantages of high-risk, bold technological effort as opposed to a more conservative and incremental building-block approach to the orderly solutions of scientific and technological problems?" Dr. Edward Teller once told me of the significance of these two approaches in connection with a statement made by Dr. Enrico Fermi. As I recall, laboratory officials briefing Dr. Fermi were congratulating themselves on the fact that most of the atomic tests which had just been completed had been accomplished as planned and had attained results almost precisely as predicted. Fermi's reaction, paraphrased, was, "If this is so, you are failing in your job. You are not bold enough, you are moving ahead by inches, and you would be doing better if some of your experiments were failures from which you could learn something new."

As a general observation, the Executive Department, during the 1950–1960 decade, was forward-looking in support of research and development for military purposes. Likewise, the Congress was generous and understood the importance of preparing for the future. Overall research and development budgets were generally satisfactory and the government provided adequate subsidies for privately undertaken research and development.

Against this background of Executive and Congressional support were three major policy obstacles to overcome in the research and development effort. These obstacles are represented by the following examples:

1. The anti-nuclear fraternity of scientists, it will be recalled, tried to stop U.S. development of the H-bomb

back in 1948–1950. They have persisted since that time in every possible way to achieve U.S. nuclear disarmament. The 1958–1961 uninspected moratorium on nuclear testing was a direct result of their handiwork and specifically against the advice of the Joint Chiefs of Staff. Fortunately, not the entire scientific world was involved in the plot. Such stalwarts as Dr. Edward Teller helped those charged with the National defense to preserve what measure of sanity they did manage to preserve during this continuing debate.

2. Some of our scientists, supported by the familiar pacifist group in government, attempted to slow the entry of United States military men into space. So far I believe they have had a fair measure of success.

3. A barrier to full multi-national co-operation in military research and development was erected. I remember so vividly that it was not an American who pioneered the Jet Engine, discovered Radar, and built the first ballistic missile. Yet, then and now, our restrictive policies on exchange of technical information with allies have prevented full collaboration with European genius. The full collaboration—the necessary collaboration—has been barred by the timid mind; the mind which believes that the world is already too dangerous to live in. As a concrete example of what could be done, I would like to see an allied co-operative effort in research on the problem of ballistic-missile defense. Maybe the combined genius of the Free World could solve the problem before the U.S.S.R. does.

These three examples are only indicative of the basic problem which had thousands of specific derivations.

However, of the three major research and development dilemmas of the 1950–1960 period—nuclear energy for military purposes, military man in space, and collaboration with allies in research and development—the problems involved

136

with respect to nuclear armaments and the testing of nuclear weapons are probably the most significant for that time period.

The uninspected moratorium was a gentlemen's agreement that both powers would refrain from testing as long as the "other" prohibited such testing. The United States government, of course, abided by the gentlemen's agreement. It did not perform the time-consuming and extremely expensive preparations for a future resumption of nuclear-weapons testing, nor did the U.S. even maintain those capabilities which we already had; they faded into obsolescence.

The Soviets, on the other hand, worked feverishly during the three-year lull (1958–1961) to ready experiments, to install the necessary measurement and recording devices, and to train the massive technical forces which were necessary for the actual testing.

It seems to me that the United States got itself trapped into the uninspected nuclear moratorium of 1958–1961 because some nebulous thing called "world public opinion" demanded a stop to nuclear-weapons testing. Concurrently, the same advisors insisted that the military risk to the United States, if the government stopped testing, was negligible.

According to their story, technologically, the nation already knew enough, and had enough nuclear strength. This judgment on military risk was not made by the Joint Chiefs of Staff who have the responsibility under existing law for providing military advice to the President, to the National Security Council, and the Secretary of Defense. This "military" judgment was made by persons who had no statutory responsibility, who were itinerants on the scene, and who will not be accountable when the full disaster of their advice may become apparent.

But, fundamentally, the American is a character who wants to be liked. This being so, the arguments with respect to reducing the U.S. lead in nuclear technology became the more persuasive. There was, of course, a vast segment of world public opinion, skillfully fostered and controlled by the Soviet

Union, against nuclear-weapons testing. The hazards of radiation from fallout were greatly overplayed by both the American press and by the Kremlin. Consequently, wanting to be loved instead of respected, Americans generally went along with world public opinion and came to accept the 1958 moratorium without the slightest guarantee that the Soviets would keep faith.

The progressive erosion and degeneration of the national position regarding the moratorium is a classic example of what can be done to a nation by a handful of influential pseudo-intellectuals. America started out with a very strong position. To wit, that she would keep on with a nuclear-testing program until there was an agreement in effect, and *working*, which allowed inspection and verification on both sides. Of course, even if such an agreement to stop nuclear-weapons testing had been accomplished, it still would have taken two to three years to install technical control machinery to mutually inspect and enforce the arrangements.

Initially, our government had said: "We are free to test until the inspection and control mechanism is actually working." As the pressure of world opinion built up (under careful Soviet tutelage and as our own United States group of anti-nuclear weapons people became more vociferous) the government started backing away from its original position. The United States backed off to a position in which it said: "U.S. testing will stop the minute an agreement is signed or agreed to in some form, and this nation will trust the good faith of the U.S.S.R. to go ahead with installation of an effective inspection and control system." The United States, of course, stopped and the Soviets did not.

During the next few months, following the tacit agreement of 1958, this nation was maneuvered into endless meetings with the U.S.S.R. to detail the technical characteristics of a detection system. How many stations, of what type and location, were necessary in order to detect a clandestine nuclear explosion? U.S. scientists and negotiators usually went into these meetings with hastily prepared data and hopes. Consistently they came back with nothing but a compromised and weakened U.S. position for the next round of discussions.

Full and specific documentation of these events in terms of names of individuals, dates, and issues is not yet permitted under security regulations. But I can declare without any fear of honest rebuttal that my general summation of this gradual deterioration of this nation's position of strength and principle is absolutely accurate.

In 1961, Russia, by unilateral action, abrogated the "gentlemen's agreement." This action was precisely what every responsible U.S. military leader expected that they would do. With the move, the U.S.S.R. accomplished a series of nuclear tests of great sophistication, technological depth, and vast military significance. The Soviet tests startlingly advanced their nuclear capability in the field of very high-yield nuclear weapons. Considering the scope of the testing program, it is only reasonable to assume that Soviet military scientists made precise measurements of the physical effects of various types of weapons, including the effects of thermal blast and radiation, as well as the effects of nuclear detonations on various kinds of electronic and communications systems.

This nation was not prepared to resume an effective and sophisticated nuclear-weapons testing program. Thereby, America gave the Soviets at least three *free* years of nuclear progress, relative to her own struggling nuclear technology. During the time of the moratorium, we lost our Pacific bases for nuclear testing, lost the trained nuclear technical teams, lost the motivation in nuclear laboratories, and lost the capacity for producing meaningful and up-to-date plans. Consequently, I am convinced that the decision to accept the uninspected nuclear-test moratorium in 1958 was a great strategic mistake and there have been no new developments since that time that would change my views. I hope that history will prove me wrong.

During the decade preceding the Soviet nuclear tests of 1961, Air Force strategic-planning levels had fought valiantly for the development of very high-yield nuclear weapons, but always lost in the final decision. The arguments of overkill, cost/effectiveness, and political unacceptability of such weapons always won out. Then, in the fall of 1961, the nation was confronted with the absolute fact that the Soviets had gone ahead of us in this field and had developed such weapons.

Those vocal few from the political and scientific echelons who defeated the military pursuit of very high-yield nuclear weapons ignored—even when the problems were visibly brought to their attention—three basic elements of the equation.

Military Tactics

Military tactics has a place in the world of intercontinental ballistic missiles exactly as it has a place in the world of infantry land battles. As an example, it would be much easier to co-ordinate a surprise massive attack with two hundred very large-yield ballistic missiles than it would be to co-ordinate an attack of two thousand smaller-yield ballistic missiles. It would also be easier to perform the initial bomb damage assessment, after attack, on a few aiming points than on a large number of aiming points. The command and control problem would also be greatly simplified for a numerically smaller force. There are many other problems of tactics applicable to ballistic missiles which are of such classified nature that they may not be discussed here. As a generalization, however, the entire area of military tactics was ignored in the judgments of those who rendered negative verdicts regarding the development of a very high-yield nuclear weapons system by the United States.

Technical Implications

There are tremendous differences in the dynamics, geometry, and kinematics of defensive *versus* offensive systems. These diverse systems vary in warhead yield and the particular

140

effect of the weapon to be used. When operating any kind of an attack vehicle and a defensive vehicle in the lower, sensible atmosphere, certain technical characteristics are governing. These same technical characteristics do not govern when operating offensive and defensive missile systems above the sensible atmosphere in, or in the near vacuum of space. Volumes can be devoted to this one subject. All that time permits here, however, is to indicate that geometric-, kinematic-, and weapons-effects relationships do make a great difference in assessing the importance of very high-yield weapons against the characteristics of lower-yield weapons.

Acquisition of New Scientific Data

Throughout the history of nuclear weapons tests, scientists have continued to encounter new and hitherto unexplainable phenomena. The significant potential of the acquisition of new scientific data from experimentation with very high-yield weapons was given only scant consideration by those people who blocked the military's very high-yield weapons program. Electronics experts, for example, have fleetingly noted some possible effects of nuclear detonations on communications and other electronic systems. However, thus far they have not had the opportunity for the testing necessary to acquire the empirical data needed for full understanding of the scientific principles involved.

Even after the Soviet tests in the fall of 1961, the same dogged arguments continued persistently to deny a high-yield weapons program for the United States. The Nuclear Test Ban Treaty which followed, uninspected and unenforceable, still prevents the military services from moving ahead with necessary experimentation. Today, even though there is reason to believe the Soviet Union has developed a very efficient high-yield weapons system, oddly enough, the prospects for obtaining such a system for the United States arsenal of weapons remain dim indeed. They are dim because of the constraints which were imposed by the moratorium and followed by the

141

Nuclear Test Ban Treaty under the Kennedy Administration.

Closely related to the problem of nuclear-weapons testing for research and development purposes was the testing of our ballistic missiles to full-scale nuclear detonation. I fought several battles on this issue while I was Chairman of the Joint Chiefs of Staff and lost them all. I held the old-fashioned view that even weapons as simple as a bolt-action rifle had to be proof-fired before being handed to the combat troops. To me, it was incredible that our government could seriously plan deployment of something as complicated as a ballistic missile force—upon which our survival as a nation might depend—without having fully tested the system. Arguments were that testing ballistic missiles did not require a full-scale nuclear detonation at the end of the flight of the warhead. It was unfortunately argued that electronic techniques, telemetry, and so forth could provide all the data that was necessary. I personally was confident that the Soviet Union was testing its ballistic missiles to full-scale proof of the warhead under conditions of re-entry into the atmosphere. U.S. military forces meanwhile were not, because of the dominant national pre-occupation toward complete elimination of nuclear-weapons testing.

During the course of the lengthy debate on this subject, President Dwight Eisenhower approved the re-establishment of Camp Cook (later renamed Vandenberg Air Force Base), a World War II Army base in California. This base was ordered into being primarily to include the capability of testing *fully operational* missiles along a range over the vast expanse of the Pacific Ocean in an area devoid of shipping. The President had approved development of this new base because the Canaveral range was not suitable for such tests due to various island populations, heavy shipping, and air travel.

At the time, I considered approval of the new missile-testing facility a victory for "our side," because finally the Air Force could prove the validity of the U.S. missile arsenal. As

142

I studied the complications involved in these modern systems —the tremendous deceleration loads on the warhead; the tremendous build-up of heat on the warhead, generated by atmospheric friction; the aerodynamic shock waves produced, and the secondary shock waves which might be introduced; the obscure phenomenon of trans-sonic and hypersonic effects, and the effects of "plasma" and ionization—I felt that some empirical data was required from the actual testing of these complete weapons.

However, the battle for operational testing was lost and ATLAS, TITAN I, TITAN II, MINUTEMAN and POLARIS, all went into deployment without validating the weapon system as a whole through at least one shot involving a full-scale nuclear detonation. Some well-known scientists felt that such testing was unnecessary.

With the exception of this kind of a handicap, the United States did well during the 1950–1960 decade in recognizing the importance of research and development to its future survival; research and development, standing in line with force-in-being, fared generally well in its claim on national resources.

Research and development is never an easy task, either technically or in providing organization and procedures necessary for its expeditious conduct. During the decade 1950–1960, the United States nevertheless maintained an excellent overall "Batting Average" in the fields of both aircraft and missile development. Regrettably, we did not move as rapidly as possible in the development of powerful rockets; in laying the foundation for military space technology; or, in pressing the development of nuclear technology. However, the nation in that decade of decision did proceed adequately in an orderly development of manned aircraft and in providing the organizational machinery which would respond effectively once the government made up its collective mind as to what it wanted its military services to do.

143

Chapter IX

IMPORTANT
NATIONAL DEFENSE DECISIONS
TRUMAN AND EISENHOWER

In the preceding pages, I have written my analysis of the evolution of the policy of containment and the application of that policy during the period 1950–1960. The policy of containment automatically involved the problems of collective security, strategic deterrence, limited war, and specific military policy. In view of the foregoing, I think it appropriate to offer a summary from a military viewpoint, of my reactions to some of the more important decisions of the Truman and Eisenhower administrations.

The basic policy, known as NSC-68 and adopted by President Truman in 1950, provided a solid though debatable foundation for this nation's foreign policy through the Eisenhower Administration and until January, 1961. During those eleven years, our national security policy did indeed receive general bipartisan support. However, the impact of the views and leadership of the two Presidents and their chief advisors in implementation of the policy is important. Needless to say, I look at the high points of this period with a military bias because of my military responsibility for supporting the national policy. Politicians, psychologists, sociologists, and economists may disagree with my judgment.

Both the administrations of President Truman and President Eisenhower supported the concept that the superior technological capability America then possessed should be exploited for our national security purposes. Neither one believed that it was in the best interest of America or the Free World for the U.S. to get bogged down, with its own manpower, in a major war on the land mass of Asia. Both Administrations recognized the deep-seated menace of communism, but both appeared to believe that the best road toward solution of the problem lay in initial constraint and patience, with ultimate reliance on a superior military technology, superior tactics, and superior strategy.

Both Administrations supported the concept of containment—enforced by a massive nuclear capability to destroy the power base of communism. Both supported the principle of collective security to include the establishment of regional alliances, bilateral security agreements, and aid to friendly countries attempting to ward off the subversive and overt blows of imperialistic communism.

Specific Actions of the Truman Administration

In my judgment, the Truman Administration made six great decisions to effect, to build toward, and to maintain the military security of the United States. Those decisions were:

1. To drop the atomic bomb during the last days of World War II.
2. To provide American leadership and resources during the late forties and early fifties to prevent a Communist take-over of Greece, Turkey, Italy, and the entire eastern end of the Mediterranean Sea.
3. To support the Marshall Plan for aid to free nations struggling for survival in the aftermath of World War II,

145

and particularly, to support full United States commitment to the North Atlantic Treaty Organization.
4. To fight in Korea, after a series of actions had convinced the U.S.S.R. and Red China that South Korea was theirs for the taking.
5. To build the H-bomb in the face of powerful opposition from a part of the "intellectual" and scientific community.
6. To build up U.S. strategic nuclear forces—both as a deterrent to Communist aggression and as a war-winning capability in U.S. hands.

On the negative side, the Truman Administration did not fully achieve World War II political objectives in postwar Europe, and in the Far East his Administration was in power during the loss of China to communism. This loss fostered the embittered and embattled circumstances that made possible a Korean War and the problems of Southeast Asia today. And the choice was made that this nation should not use its best weapons in the Korean War.

In contrast, President Truman's decision to drop the atomic bomb during the latter days of World War II has been a subject of much discussion. It has been attacked on the basis that the war was already won and that dropping the bomb was therefore unnecessary. I was there at the time, in command of the 20th Air Force that had the operational responsibility for dispatching the mission. I will always believe that President Truman's decision was correct because the Japanese home army was still intact and could have inflicted tremendous losses on our forces in the Operation Olympic invasion which had been planned. We all knew that Japanese industry had been destroyed, that most of her shipping was at the bottom of the sea, and that her army, air force, and navy air force had been defeated. However, none of us really knew how much final resistance would be undertaken by the

146

Japanese ground forces, which were the final defenses of the home islands. Consequently, from a military standpoint, President Truman's decision was eminently sound.

If our strategy had not contemplated a surface invasion of the Japanese home islands, the decision to drop the bomb could be reasonably questioned. However, the full impact of the air attacks on Japan and the consequences to Japan of the loss of her combatant navy and her merchant marine apparently had not been fully understood by U.S. policy makers, and they still insisted on an old-fashioned across-the-beach invasion. In the face of this decision, the bomb had to be dropped.

Specific Actions of the Eisenhower Administration

Like the Truman Administration, the years under President Eisenhower, from a military viewpoint, had their share of pluses and minuses.

In terms of specific issues, on the positive side of the equation, the Eisenhower Administration never wavered in giving priority to the build-up of nuclear striking forces which could, in fact, provide a massive deterrent to Communist aggression and a war-winning capability if general war were thrust upon us. This build-up required the development and procurement of both long range nuclear bombers and intercontinental ballistic missiles during the same time period—an outstanding accomplishment. The Administration fully supported the general theory of collective security to include the establishment of Free World regional alliances and bilateral agreements which could not be accommodated under such alliances. It also supported a vigorous military and economic aid program to assist the nations of the Free World in their fight against communism.

NATO was strengthened, SEATO and CENTO came into being as a result of the foresight of the Eisenhower-Dulles

147

team, and more than forty bilateral mutual security treaties were negotiated. All these actions undoubtedly gave strength and staying power to our allies.

With respect to specific crises—the defense of the Quemoy-Matsu Islands off the coast of Red China was firmly and successfully handled, and the Soviet bluff to take over in Lebanon was called. As a consequence, Lebanon is free today.

With respect to over-all management of the defense establishment, the Administration of President Eisenhower also did well. The Administration resisted the establishment of a separate governmental agency to work for disarmament as its only purpose in life; it resisted over-centralization and detailed control of professional military activities; it respected and solicited professional military advice on military matters, and it encouraged the full interchange of pertinent views at National Security Council level.*

On the negative side, still speaking from a military viewpoint, the Eisenhower Administration failed to make full commitment of United States national prestige in Asia and the Near and Middle East. The developing problems of Africa and South America were likewise accorded insufficient attention. In addition, there was a tendency to allow a gradual erosion of U.S. military posture through partial accommodation to those American pressure groups who were working for unilateral disarmament, the abolition of nuclear weapons, and the denial of the medium of space for military operations.

The armchair strategists, the do-gooders, and the appeasers thereby achieved a toe hold during the latter days of the Eisenhower Administration. They moved rapidly to exploit this toe hold with the change of Administration in January of 1961.

---

* Author's Note: A disaster such as occurred at the Bay of Pigs could not have occurred under the national security planning procedures in use during the Eisenhower Administration.

PART THREE

THE POLICY OF

Containment,

1961-1964

Chapter X

TRENDS DURING THE PERIOD
1961-1964

During the ten-year period from 1950 through 1960, the United States had a specifically articulated basic national security policy. This was a written document analyzed in great depth and reissued every year. However, annual modification of the basic document did not change the basic premise or the basic direction indelibly written into the original document NSC-68.

The principal contributors to the formulation of the document each year were the Offices of the Secretary of Defense, Secretary of State, Joint Chiefs of Staff, Central Intelligence Agency, Atomic Energy Commission, and Secretary of the Treasury. Each year the document was delivered to the National Security Council for review and final recommendation to the President. During this process, the uniformed chief of each military service "had his day at court." If he disagreed with any provisions of the document, or with the views of the National Security Council, the President became the final arbiter and resolved such differences as might arise. Following approval by the President, the document became

151

the basis for political-military planning for the coming year. The document thus provided essential guide lines to insure a cohesive national effort in political, economic, and military affairs. While not required by law, the basic policy document served a very useful purpose.

Since 1961, the government of the United States has, to my knowledge, had no such document. Strange as it may seem, there is apparently no formal annually updated document to provide guidance in the conduct of national affairs. Therefore, what can be said of the basic national security policies and the military policies of the Kennedy Administration must be gleaned from fragmented statements of high-placed public officials, from testimony before the Congress, and from an interpretation of the specific actions which were taken by that Administration.

As an immediate aftermath to Mr. Kennedy's inauguration, it appeared to me that many of the new faces elevated to high governmental position were strongly influenced by a belief that America now had a "co-operative" enemy. These people also seemed to me to have overemphasized the siren song of peace and prosperity for all.

The virtues of peace and prosperity cannot be challenged philosophically or intellectually. However, rational Americans cannot doubt that our own War for Independence was justified; neither can thinking Americans question the necessity for opposing the aggressive purpose of the Kaiser in World War I, nor the collision with Hitler, Mussolini, and Tojo of World War II.

The aggressive actions of the totalitarian systems which lead to these wars, like the ruthless invasion of South Korea by a Moscow-inspired North Korea, exist as a matter of fact. The danger of the Kennedy years seemed to me to lie in the tendency of many government officials to ignore international lawlessness or, if recognizing it, to assume that such lawlessness would disappear of its own accord.

Before moving on to the national security policies evolved under the Kennedy Administration, objectivity requires that I recognize that these policies had their roots during the latter years of the Eisenhower Administration. Some few energetic intellectuals were making progress even during the latter part of President Eisenhower's Administration in undermining the resolution of this great nation with respect to key elements of our basic defense strategy. This erosion accounts, in my judgment, for the three-year uninspected nuclear test ban moratorium, approved by President Eisenhower in 1958, and violated by the U.S.S.R. in the fall of 1961. It accounts for the emphasis of the United States space program on "space for peaceful purposes," and for some concern over the activities of the now institutionalized Disarmament Agency.

Limited war came into vogue during the administrations of Presidents Truman and Eisenhower. But COIN—counterinsurgency—came along under the Kennedy Administration. The military services were specifically directed by the Secretary of Defense during the Kennedy Administration not to use the words "limited war" in connection with operations such as those then under way in Southeast Asia. The services were directed instead to use the term "counter-insurgency." While the concept of limited war seems to repudiate a full commitment of U.S. prestige and resources in an armed conflict, the concept of COIN backs away even further.

It is interesting to note the difference between the definitions of war as used by the U.S.S.R. and those used by the United States. This government talks about cold war, counter-insurgency operations, limited war, and general war, while the Soviets talk about wars of national liberation, local wars, and general war. Our counter-insurgency operations are, of course, aimed at neutralization of what the Communists call "wars of national liberation." The Soviets' local war definition somewhat approximates our own limited war definition. Their

153

terminology, however, does *not* imply limiting the war through limiting the use of special types of weaponry; it limits the war in a geographical sense.

In fact, the Defense Department has had so much brain power whirling away on the semantics of this problem that a series of formal definitions finally evolved and were approved by the Joint Chiefs of Staff after my retirement from active service. A three-page document attempts to spell out for our men in uniform what kind of a war they may face. This Glossary of Terms defines general war, limited war, cold war, civic action, counter-guerrilla warfare, counterinsurgency, covert operations, insurgency, paramilitary forces, paramilitary operations, psychological warfare, unconventional warfare, evasion and escape, and guerrilla warfare. Fortunately, war was easier to understand when I was involved. However, I have included this Glossary of Terms and definitions as an appendix for the information of those who might be interested in the sophistication and finesse with which control and motivation of our military establishment is now monitored.*

Basic Military Policy

The basic military policy of the Kennedy Administration appeared to me to embody the following major elements:

1. A desire for maintaining stability of the power balance which existed between the Communist world and the Free World.
2. A desire to exercise, at White House level, a precisely controlled military response to any circumstance which might develop.
3. A desire for the establishment of a series of negotiating thresholds in the event of a limited or a general war situation.

* *See* Appendix B

4. A desire for the establishment of war termination capabilities, to include the necessary communications system with the enemy.
5. A desire to pursue disarmament negotiations, even in the face of steadfast Soviet refusal to permit mutual inspection and verification.

Characteristics of Military Forces

In consonance with these fundamental policy objectives, it appeared that the Kennedy Administration philosophy required the military force structure to possess the following general characteristics:

1. Flexibility.
2. Survivability.
3. Multiple Option Capability.
4. Strong capability in the lower levels of intensity of conflict.
5. Parity—rather than superiority—with the enemy forces with respect to weapons appropriate to the higher levels of conflict.
6. Highly effective military systems arrived at on a theoretical cost/effectiveness basis.

Aspects of Military Force to Be Avoided

Consistent with these objectives and force characteristics, it can be deducted that military planning in the Kennedy Administration sought to avoid:

1. Escalation of the level of intensity of any armed action which might take place.
2. Proliferation of nuclear weapons.
3. The use of nuclear weapons, if at all possible, in consonance with the firebreak theory.

155

4. Destabilization of power relationships then in effect.
5. Creation of any new United States weapons systems which might be considered provocative by the enemy.
6. Deployments, programs, and force structure which would contribute to the gold flow problem.

Areas of Concern

Although not explicitly stated as an authoritative governmental position, implicit in the program as a whole were some troublesome trends and factors. Considering each one of the national and military objectives of the Kennedy period (deduced in the absence of a governmental statement on national and military objectives), it is difficult to find specific fault. The sum total, I fear, adds up to a defense of mediocrity and passiveness. Therefore, the problem is *what is left unsaid, or unimplied*.

As a simplified statement of the nature of the problem and the impact of 1961–1964 trends, it was difficult to find the concept "win" in the sum total of the policies. It was also difficult to find initiative on the part of the United States government. The government still seemed to be reacting to enemy thrusts, as opposed to conducting a positive program of its own to put teeth into our policy of containment.

Chapter XI

SPECIFIC ELEMENTS OF
MILITARY POLICY

1961-1964

The foregoing chapter reviewed the general political-military policy trends which became evident under the Administration of President Kennedy. I discussed general trends, the basic military policy which seemed to be in effect, the characteristics of military forces desired, the aspects of military force to be avoided, and the general underlying assumption.

I must be more specific, however, in analyzing a policy which was never written, but which became a living heritage to the next President, Lyndon B. Johnson.

Accordingly, this chapter examines specific elements of basic national security policy which appear to me to be part and parcel of the direction in which we, as a nation, moved under the Kennedy Administration. Issues to be discussed are: escalation, proliferation, the firebreak theory, a co-operative enemy, stability of the balance of power, controlled response, crisis management, damage limitation, negotiating threshold, war termination capabilities, arms control, multiple option capability, survivability, research and development policy, prestige of the military establishment, and Defense Department organization, post-1960.

157

All of these subjects were discussed publicly and all of these terms were used, more or less at random, by highly placed appointees of the Kennedy Administration. I believe that the composite fabric created by these ideas and theories was, in fact, our unwritten basic national security policy of that period of time. Therefore, I will discuss what I think was intended by each term, and provide my own reaction from a military viewpoint as to the significance of application of the particular concept.

Escalation

Some young political and military sophists, steeped in textbook analysis and joining government in increasing number —making studies, writing papers, and advising on politico-military policy—developed an almost violent attitude toward the subjects of escalation, proliferation, and the firebreak theory.

The term escalation has developed over the last few years to describe, generally, a circumstance in which a war confined to a small area, or confined to the use of conventional weapons, might be expanded to include operations in a greater geographical area or to utilization of weapons of greater power. Escalation has been feared by most of the planners in the State Department as a series of progressive steps which might ultimately result in a full-scale nuclear war between the United States and the Communist powers. Therefore, the general attitude of the State Department has been to take such political and economic action, during any crisis, which might result in holding any given conflict to the lowest level of intensity and attempting to negotiate a settlement of the issue before expansion of the armed conflict.

This fundamental objective, or desire to avoid expansion of a limited war, cannot be criticized on a purely theoretical basis. Certainly, all civilized people would like to see the political issues of the war settled, in a fair and honorable manner, without resort to massive slaughter on either side. However, the specific danger in the practice of the theory of controlling escalation lies in the accommodations which the government seems inevitably to make in attempting to prevent the expansion of military operations into larger dimensions. We have had a consistent tendency to vacillate, compromise, and lose a little ground—a piece at a time—because of the fear of escalation.

In the real power world in which we all live, the opportunity to escalate the level of intensity of conflict would have provided advantages to the United States and disadvantages to the enemy. This nation could in fact, escalate, on the basis of its own decision, in terms which all existing enemies, during the past twenty years, could not hope to match. In other words, America could have used escalation as a tool of diplomatic policy—with no serious threat to the country —whereas, in many cases, the enemy was in no such position. It is a curious anomaly that, under the apparent terms of the military policies of the Kennedy Administration, the capacity to escalate and the will to escalate were stated as essential to the successful implementation of the policy and yet, at the same time, the Administration was afraid to use this particular tool as a vital instrument of United States policy.

Proliferation

During the last few years, along with the introduction of escalation into our defense vocabulary, the term proliferation has taken on new military significance. The single word "proliferation" is now generally understood to mean the development of nuclear weapons, and the means to control and deliver these nuclear weapons by nations which do not now possess such capability. Proliferation of nuclear weapons capability has generally been opposed by the Department of State and opposed because, in the judgment of many of these sincere people, the present dangerous world would

159

become much more dangerous if more and more fingers were added to the nuclear trigger.

This question of proliferation, and our general national attitude toward it, is indeed a difficult problem. Certainly, we would prefer a world which had disarmed completely, in a world of law and order. However, there is no such world and, starting with the Baruch Plan of 1947, all U.S. efforts to effect nuclear disarmament have failed—failed simply because the U.S.S.R. (and now Red China) would not accept mutual inspection to verify such disarmament.

On the Free World side of the fence, the problems associated with obtaining an effective means for insuring nuclear disarmament and the spread of nuclear weapons to additional countries became complicated by the attitude of the French Government. France refused to sign the Limited (and uninspected) Test Ban Treaty which was negotiated under the Kennedy Administration. France has gone on its own way to develop an independent nuclear capability. This course of action requires testing by France, in the atmosphere, which would not have been necessary to repeat if we had provided France information which both we and the Soviets already possessed. Ironically, those who have argued against nuclear-weapons testing because of contamination of the atmosphere have generally been against giving France nuclear information—and have thereby helped to bring about more of the very thing to which they object.

In the continuing international debate on the control of testing and the proliferation of nuclear weapons, my instinctive sympathies have been in favor of the French attitude. After all, the United States refused to back the French viewpoint during the Suez crisis of 1956, and I can understand the attitude of a French patriot who does not want to be totally dependent on the judgment of another nation in matters involving the survival of France. If France had not gone ahead with its own program, it would now be behind even Red China in weapons technology. On balance, I doubt that this would have been good for the Free World. In our reflection on this grave issue, we should remember that the national policy with respect to France is not the sole responsibility of the Kennedy Administration. It was debated continuously during the Eisenhower Administration and became set policy with the change of Presidents.

The whole of the NATO alliance was shaken by America's failure to make a reasonable accommodation to the desires of De Gaulle with respect to this problem. And, because of rigid application of the U.S. political attitude toward proliferation, the nuclear strike forces of NATO Europe are today one technological generation behind the deployed forces of the U.S.S.R. which directly confront the NATO military establishment. The U.S.S.R. has a force of intermediate-range ballistic missiles in place and targeted on vital Western European military installations, including those installations basing U.S. forces. NATO could have had such a force-in-being today if the U.S. government had seen fit to recognize what seems to me to be legitimate French self-respect and French self-interest.

During the period 1957-1959, under the direction of Mr. E. H. Meili (who was then Assistant Secretary General of NATO for Production and Logistics), a plan was worked out which would have been acceptable to the French. This plan (called the Meili Plan) would have put the bulk of Allied nuclear forces (both aircraft and missiles) under the command of the Supreme Commander Allied Powers Europe, SACEUR, an American officer, but would have allowed something on the order of ten percent of the force to be under French government control. This plan was reasonable and workable, from my viewpoint as Chairman of the Joint Chiefs of Staff, but it foundered because of the resistance of the U.S. State Department.

The Firebreak Theory

Those who advocate the firebreak theory hold that there is a political "firebreak" between the use of conventional

161

munitions and the use of even one small tactical nuclear weapon—that the use of even one small tactical nuclear weapon on a military target, anywhere in the world, would escalate into general nuclear war.

This theory has seemed to most military realists as founded purely on a fear psychosis. Responsible military planners have never believed that the U.S.S.R. would risk its own destruction because of U.S. delivery of a few tactical nuclear weapons on military targets in North Vietnam, in North Korea, in Red China, or in any other peripheral area subject to Communist aggression by proxy.

This fear psychosis, however, has been so strong that it has forced the United States government into playing a political-military game which is tailored to the greatest strengths of the world-wide Communist movement and to this nation's greatest weaknesses. Obviously, it is much easier for Red China, North Korea, and North Vietnam to arm millions of men with conventional munitions than to arm them with the more advanced weapons of war; and it is much cheaper to support a Viet Cong guerrilla with a rifle than to support an American soldier with a rifle. We might question the basic morality of the decision to withhold our best weapons while sending our young men to die in hand-to-hand combat on terms dictated by an enemy.

The emergence of Red China as a nuclear power will probably test the firebreak theory in the not too distant future. The question must be asked: If the Red Chinese were to drop a nuclear bomb on a U.S. aircraft carrier, or on a garrison of Chiang Kai-shek's forces on Formosa, would the United States automatically attack the U.S.S.R.? I doubt it. I think that this nation would react with a heavy nuclear attack on Red China—not the U.S.S.R. Under these circumstances, limited nuclear war would occur, and the use of a few nuclear weapons would not mean a general transpolar nuclear exchange. These circumstances, however, probably would mean general nuclear war if the U.S.S.R. had achieved such superiority in attack and defense capabilities that it was certain that U.S. nuclear forces could not survive a surprise attack and retaliate against the Soviet homeland.

When thinking about the problems of nuclear weapons, these points should be kept in mind: First, regardless of ill-advised statements to the contrary, highly suitable targets for the use of tactical nuclear weapons do exist in guerrilla warfare; and second, regardless of ill-advised statements to the contrary, even a few nuclear weapons in Red Chinese hands could be disastrous to the Free World.

Currently, there is talk deprecating the importance of a *few* nuclear bombs in Red Chinese hands and citing the time that is needed for Red China to develop an effective delivery system. Americans should soberly remember that the *second* atomic explosion in world history was over Hiroshima. This nation needed *only one* test before dropping its first bomb.

If the United States should adhere to the firebreak theory and Red China should not, what is to deter the use by Red China of nuclear weapons, even on a small scale, to blackmail all Southeast Asia into the Communist camp?

A Co-operative Enemy

The concept of a co-operative enemy seems to be derived from the assumption that a nuclear balance of terror exists, and that a condition of stable deterrence is the only answer to survival on both sides of the Iron Curtain. The premise is that the enemy, recognizing these facts, will assume a co-operative attitude and work with America in solving the problems of the world. This basic premise is in error on three counts.

First, it denies the fundamental nature of communism and Communist intent to dominate the world; it ignores the Communist Manifesto, the history of the Communist movement, and the clearly stated objectives of contemporary Communist leadership; it presumes co-operation on the part of an enemy dedicated to our destruction.

Second, the concept of mutual deterrence, upon which the

163

premise is based, degrades the character of the Western World—in that the term mutual deterrence explicitly indicates that both sides are being deterred. This is difficult to rationalize when it is recognized that one government has announced its intention to destroy the other, and the opposing ideology wishes only to deter in terms of preserving its own values and institutions. Where is the "mutuality" in this equation?

Third, the premise, founded upon the concept of perpetual mutual deterrence, also denies the inexorable progress of science and technology.

Stability of the Balance of Power

A natural corollary to the assumption of mutual deterrence and a co-operative enemy is the feeling that America should strive for stability in opposing military power capabilities. The consequences of these interrelated ideas, under the most optimistic assumption, places the population and the industrial base of the United States and the Free World in a condition of perpetual hostage to the U.S.S.R. Later, the Free World undoubtedly will also have to add China to the same category. In other words, we, as free people, can no longer control our own destiny; the national survival depends upon the will and judgment of an enemy. Thus, the normal self-defensive reactions of a free people have been denied by the assumption and the premise.

The totality of this chain of logic found firm foundation in the views of various influential people of the Kennedy Administration. Not long after the violation by the U.S.S.R. of the 1958 nuclear-testing moratorium, a close advisor to the White House on nuclear matters, Dr. Hans Bethe, made a statement to the effect that the progress of the U.S.S.R. in nuclear-weapons technology was good for the Western World because it contributed to stability and reduced Soviet fears of an attack by the United States. This type of reasoning, I believe, must appear to most Americans as upside down as the whole of Communist philosophy.

Another bit of reasoning most Americans must find difficult to follow is the 1961-1962 judgment of Dr. Jerome Wiesner (then the top scientific advisor to the White House) that the development of military anti-satellite weapons systems would be provocative and would trigger the Soviets into a counteraction in space which they would otherwise forego. Dr. Wiesner, now out of government, is Dean of Science at the Massachusetts Institute of Technology. But, along with colleagues of like views, he is still pushing the theory of stability of the balance of power. According to the public press he recently headed a committee, established by President Johnson in October, 1964, to "Search and explore and canvass and thoroughly discuss every conceivable approach and avenue of cooperation that could lead to peace."

In the left column below I have listed some recommendations of the Committee (paraphrased for brevity) which appeared in the public press, and in the right-hand column I have made by own comment on the military significance of the recommendation.

Wiesner Committee Recommendation	Author's Comment
1. An uninspected three-year moratorium during which both the U.S. and the U.S.S.R. would agree not to install defenses against ballistic missiles.	1. We had a similar uninspected moratorium on nuclear weapons testing between 1958-1961. The Soviets violated the agreement and thereby gained at least three years of free development time in nuclear technology while the U.S. practically stood still. What the recommendation means to me is simply this: "If you take measures to defend your own soil, this is destabilizing. Trust the

2. Eliminate the concept of an Allied nuclear force for defense of Western Europe.

U.S.S.R. and completely ignore, in the meantime, the nuclear technology which is growing in Communist China."

2. There is in-being a nuclear force consisting of both aircraft and medium-range ballistic missiles based on Soviet (not Satellite) soil and aimed directly at the vital targets of Western Europe. This force would not necessarily be dismantled. Even if it were—and both sides had no nuclear weapons—Soviet forces, in a conventional invasion, could probably advance as far as the English Channel within thirty days.

3. A total ban on nuclear testing together with a new American "flexibility" with respect to the question of mutual inspection.

3. What the term "new flexibility" amounts to is abandonment of mutual inspection; again, trust the U.S.S.R. and ignore the growing Chinese Communist threat.

4. A total stop to the production of nuclear materials for weapons purposes.

4. Again, no doubt, to be accepted without adequate inspection and guarantees.

Even though the Wiesner report of 1965 follows his tenure as Science Advisor to the President, it is clearly indicative of the kind of advice which was being provided to President Kennedy and is still being provided to President Johnson.

Unfortunately for America, in my judgment, the minority pacifistic element within the scientific community has not been alone in arguing for the concept of stability. A former Assistant Secretary of Defense for Research and Development pragmatically stated in September, 1962 (while in office) that the United States was very far-sighted in 1907

166

in its endeavor with other nations to bar aerial bombardment in advance of its development, and that we are far-sighted now in trying to "evolve policies that hopefully will avoid the development of war-making weapons and machinery in space." This viewpoint might be rationalized if coming from the Department of State but not, to the average American, from a highly placed official of the Department of Defense—the Department responsible for our military security.

In the same vein was the judgment by a top executive in the U.S. Disarmament Agency, that development of a 100-megaton weapons system by the United States would be unacceptable from a disarmament negotiating viewpoint. This judgment, of course, has been accompanied during the past several years by the steady deterioration of this nation's early and virtually impregnable negotiating position on disarmament. As a result of this philosophy, the Disarmament Agency *is now* advocating arrangements which were *proposed by the Soviets*, and rejected by the United States only a few short years ago.

In consonance with the concept of stability, the power drive by the Kennedy Administration to obtain the uninspected limited nuclear-test ban treaty with the U.S.S.R. was engineered in a most unusual fashion. This action was accomplished in such a manner that scores of nations had approved the treaty before the U.S. Congress was allowed to act upon it. For the most part, and against their better judgment, America's senior military officials concurred in the action, *after the fact*, on the basis of political rather than military considerations. It is indeed an odd commentary on the state of national affairs when America's top military advisors must render judgment on the basis of political rather than military reasons, and when some of the politicians in Congress object to the treaty on the basis of military reasons.

The concept of stability has also influenced the debate with respect to civil defense measures, fallout shelters, and the development of a new bomber. Some "authorities" have considered these actions as destabilizing and provocative; and the 100-megaton system was good for the Soviets to have, but had no place in this nation's sophisticated weapons arsenal.

Controlled Response

There can be no question that the military establishment should be totally responsive to civilian control and direction. The President of the United States is Commander-in-Chief of the Armed Forces and is responsible to the nation for the conduct of military operations. This is as it should be and no responsible man in uniform disputes this premise.

The current philosophy of controlled response, however, has brought to very high executive levels the management of military operational details which in previous military history have been delegated to operational commanders. It is not so much this philosophy which is troublesome to the professional military establishment as is ineffectual detailed management which has evolved over the last few years. This detailed management was particularly evident in the crisis which occurred at the Bay of Pigs invasion of Cuba. It was evident in the problem of removal of Soviet missiles from Cuban soil in the aftermath of the bold gamble by the Soviet Union to fully arm at the threshold of the Western Hemisphere.

Ineffectual and detailed control of military operations by political officials is probably best illustrated by Hitler's conduct during World War II. Adolf Hitler, operating on the basis of egotism and intuition, frequently ignored or abrogated the advice of his professional military staff in determining tactics as well as strategic objectives. The consequences are a matter of history.

The present detailed control of military operations by transient nonprofessionals extend beyond deployments, employment of forces, and tactics. Today, it involves the determination of military research and development programs and the selection of weapons systems which will dictate U.S. basic defense strategy for many years to come. This growing tendency to override professional military advice leads inevitably to a future culminating not only in episodes repetitive of the Bay of Pigs but, also very possibly, to inept decisions on long lead time military hardware.

Controlled response cannot be criticized in terms of its objectives nor in terms of the constitutionality of the philosophy. But of deep concern to the military professional is the degree to which transient nonprofessionals become involved in the actual fulfillment of military policy. Perhaps, in oversimplification, they do not believe that squads or companies should be commanded out of the White House. And they do not believe that specific ship deployments in the conduct of an authorized military directive should be determined by the Secretary of Defense. In the same vein, research and development decisions vitally affecting the force structure and capability of our future power base should not be determined by transient nonprofessionals who are overriding the consensus of military judgment. The case of the still highly controversial TFX (F-111) fighter bomber and the delay in approval of the nuclear-powered aircraft carrier are specific examples.

Three additional and interrelated terms, having direct meaning in the management of this nation's basic national security affairs, have come into being during the past few years. These terms are "crisis management," "damage limitation," and "negotiating thresholds." On a purely philosophical basis, none of these terms may be effectively criticized. However, they may convey an impression of U.S. indecision to the Communist world. If, indeed, these terms do translate into this kind of meaning for our opponents, then they inspire and encourage further subversion and limited wars throughout the underdeveloped areas of the world.

Crisis Management

Crisis management is the establishment of governmental machinery to effectively manage the affairs of the nation during periods of international tension. The difficulty of the

169

practice of crisis management, as the nation observed it with the abortive Bay of Pigs invasion and again in the deployment of Soviet ballistic missiles to Cuba, lay in the corollary practice of the management of news relayed to the American public and to the world at large. Certainly, no thoughtful American can deny the legitimacy of managing national affairs properly under conditions of international tension, but it is difficult for the average American to rationalize the necessity for the management of the news about what is actually transpiring in this restive world.

Damage Limitation

The term damage limitation means simply that U.S. military forces should apply power in such manner as to avoid unnecessary destruction of civilian life and property. Textually, it means that this nation will go out of its way to limit damage on both sides of the fence in the event of armed conflict— either limited or general. The fundamental difficulty in the American definition is that it telegraphs, in advance, a message to the enemy that he can take risks of rather large magnitude without having to pay the full price for his aggression.

Negotiating Thresholds

The desire for capability to establish a series of negotiating thresholds that might be useful in terminating a war short of a nuclear holocaust cannot be attacked in terms of its objective. However, when these thresholds are established and their values are telegraphed *in advance* to the enemy, then that enemy has a distinct advantage. Fully knowledgeable in the intent and purpose of established thresholds, he becomes certain in his counter strategy. He can push the Communist effort inch by inch and then, when the American will stiffens, he can stop, pull back or withdraw with impunity and with no damage to his objective. The philosophy thus presents a continual invitation to vicious probing and lethal subversion.

War Termination Capabilities

The war termination capability suggests that the United States government should insure that its lines of communication to the enemy are kept open so that any future war can be promptly terminated when both sides believe that such action would be in their national interest. Again, this element of policy is unassailable in terms of fundamental logic. However, it telegraphs to the enemy the fact that America does not necessarily have a policy to "win," but may be ready to back off at any time convenient to enemy desires.

Arms Control

Disarmament and arms control is a very complicated problem. The United States government has been through many cycles of negotiations with the Communists on disarmament and arms control during the past fourteen years. In the aftermath of World War II, America entered into negotiations with a fixed set of arms control principles. These principles have gradually eroded over the years. Initially, the national position on the matter embodied three major elements:

First, that the Soviets should demonstrate their sincerity by political action to eliminate the Iron Curtain and by permitting political self-determination to the captive Eastern European satellite states.

Second, that a "package deal" is required, simultaneously providing for both conventional and nuclear disarmament.

Third, that mutual arms inspection and verification by both sides are required. Inspection and verification were, and are, considered most important from a security standpoint

171

because we know from the historical record of more than fifty violations of solemn treaties and covenants entered into by the U.S.S.R. In addition, American statesmen were well aware of the oft written and repeated Communist premise that treaties were "scraps of paper" to be torn up or ignored at any time that they became inconvenient to the Communist cause.

Over the years the American government seems to have lost sight of these three fundamental positions on its arms control policy. It no longer insists that the Communist powers demonstrate their peaceful intentions by an elimination of the Iron Curtain or by freeing their enslaved satellites. America no longer insists on a "package deal" involving phased and simultaneous reduction of both conventional and nuclear armaments. In fact, the United States has taken the first steps toward nuclear disarmament, through the test ban treaty, with no agreement on the reduction of conventional forces. In addition, we no longer insist on mutual agreements for inspection and verification with respect to nuclear-weapons testing. The United States has also unilaterally decided on a national space program oriented toward "peaceful purposes." It has also accepted the removal of Soviet missiles from Cuba without on-site inspection—which had been previously demanded.

In addition to what has been noted here, our government may also have authorized something far more dangerous to the nation's long-term national security posture. The government has now established a separate Disarmament Agency and has given it a charter focused unalterably on arms control and disarmament. The pressure to establish such an agency, or agencies, within other departments became very strong during the latter part of the Eisenhower Administration. For example, there were proposals from the disarmament enthusiasts to establish a separate disarmament shop under the Secretary of Defense. The Department's planning for arms control at that time was under the supervision of the civilian Assistant Secretary of Defense for International Security Affairs. From a military standpoint, I felt that the responsibility should remain in that office because the impact of arms-control negotiations could be soundly integrated into the other aspects of security planning. During President Eisenhower's Administration, the military services successfully resisted pressures to establish separate arms-control agencies. The dangers inherent in the present institutionalized arrangement, initiated during President Kennedy's Administration, is that the agency has only one mission—arms control and disarmament. It has no over-all responsibility for national security. Therefore, it can much more effectively accomplish a piecemeal, unilateral disarmament of the United States than it could if merged under the ultimately responsible officials of the Departments of State and Defense.

Flexibility and Multiple Option Capability

The objectives of flexibility and multiple option capability are as old as the art of warfare itself. However, some specific actions which have been taken in recent years by the government seem to mitigate against the stated policy. For example, America is moving toward a time frame in which her reliance for strategic forces will be placed almost completely on a ballistic-missile force. Ballistic missiles, inherently, are not really flexible in terms of application, nor do they provide very many tactical options.

The land-based ballistic-missile force has many of the characteristics of a Maginot Line. The force can be pretargeted by the enemy, and it can be applied effectively only against an identified and precisely located target system. That part of the ballistic-missile force which is at sea—the POLARIS force —has the current advantage of concealment and mobility, but it represents a very small number of aiming points to a desperate and determined enemy. If this nation builds and deploys forty-one POLARIS-type submarines, it must expect

173

that, at any point in time, a sizeable fraction of these craft would be in harbor and, therefore, easy targets to a surprise attack. The balance of the force may be at sea. Any significant improvement in antisubmarine warfare capability by enemy forces need only focus on those submarines at sea and representing mobile aiming points.

The U.S. ballistic-missile force also has the other very important characteristic of inflexibility. We have published so many pictures and other data on missiles that the Soviets should have no difficulty calculating the probable warhead yield and concluding therefrom that to be effective the re-entry vehicle carrying the nuclear weapon must penetrate into the sensible atmosphere before detonation.

This characteristic of our ballistic-missile force makes the problem of ballistic-missile defense much easier for the enemy. On the other hand, a 100-plus megaton ballistic missile need not make a deep penetration into the sensible atmosphere. It may be detonated with devastating effects many miles above the surface of the earth. Nevertheless, our government has entered into agreements (the uninspected nuclear test ban treaty) which inhibit the U.S. military development of a superballistic-missile offensive system, while the Soviets seem already to have it.

U.S. civilian military planners also seem to be ignoring the inherent flexibility of aircraft in the development of future strategic military systems. There is no adequate bomber program for replacement of the B-47, the B-52, and the B-58 fleet. Other recent actions, such as the cancellation of the air-launched ballistic missile SKYBOLT program, seem to be working against the philosophy of flexibility and multiple options.

Though an element of political-military policy under the Kennedy Administration was an announced desire for flexibility and multiple options, its actions appeared to be creating a strategic force structure grossly rigid in all important respects.

174

Survivability

The desire for survivability and, hopefully, "invulnerability," of military forces is ancient in military history. The objective is sound. The history of war, however, has taught us that there is no such thing as complete invulnerability of a military system. What man has been able to create he has been able to destroy, by-pass, or neutralize through technical innovation and/or military tactics. The current emphasis on *survivability* has resulted in the buried silos which house the U.S. land-based ballistic-missile force, and in ballistic-missile-carrying submarines. The basic concepts of mutual deterrence and parity are intimately linked to these two weapons systems. Our government has made an assumption that enough of these forces would survive a surprise attack to be able to deal a crippling blow to any aggressor. This can be a very dangerous assumption. Technology does not stand still and, furthermore, the military and their scientific colleagues know that all the effects of large-yield nuclear weapons are not yet clearly understood. The U.S.S.R. probably has a better understanding of these weapons than does this nation— simply because the Soviets have conducted so many more nuclear tests with very high-yield weapons. The concept of mutual deterrence and stability of the balance of power could conceivably be upset overnight. A combination of technological achievement on the part of the enemy in the field of very high-yield weapons, antisubmarine warfare, and in the field of ballistic-missile defense against U.S. re-entry vehicles could combine to place this nation at the mercy of Russia.

From the military perspective, and from a knowledge of military history, the entire theory of mutual deterrence ignores the lessons of the past. *Technology does not stand still.* Gross military power curves may cross and be equal— at some fleeting moment of time. But to assume that this

175

relationship of parity could exist indefinitely seems, to most military professionals, to be wishful thinking. One side or the other will upset the balance of power sooner or later.

Research and Development Policy

When the first primitive airplane flew in 1903 at Kitty Hawk, it was not possible for any who witnessed the flight to predict the development of a supersonic B-58 bomber or the hydrogen bomb of this decade. It is also impossible at this moment in history to predict the significance of military operations in space ten, twenty, or fifty years into the future.

In the early days of aviation there were many people, including even most of those concerned with aviation technology, who believed that the airplane could never compete with various modes of surface transportation. Some of the knowledgeable people also believed that the airplane would have only limited utility as a weapon of war. The airplane was generally judged to be a fragile instrument which might someday weigh as much as 5,000 pounds and which might have some possible useful military capability in an observation, reconnaissance, or perhaps a communications role—but never as a combat vehicle of significance. Only a few visionaries, such as John Jacob Astor and General Billy Mitchell, dared disagree with this viewpoint.

The nation faces much the same situation today with respect to the possible military value of spacecraft. We are now in the Kitty Hawk era of the Space Age. Again, many influential and knowledgeable people are predicting that spacecraft may possibly satisfy some useful military purposes in observation, reconnaissance, and communications—but never as an important instrument for combat. It may be that these people are right—no one really knows for sure—but my instinct and my experience indicate strongly that they are wrong.

The space problem of today differs from the early prob-

176

lem of aeronautical development. This is true primarily because the costs of research are so high that meaningful space ventures cannot be supported by private initiative nor even by many major foreign powers. In the early days of aviation, individuals could build and fly test models financed out of private funds. Governments could also participate at a very nominal cost. For instance, when the Wright Brothers encountered indifference on the part of the U.S. government they simply moved to France, where they were welcomed. There, at Pau, the Wright Brothers opened up their first flying school. As a result of this migration of United States aeronautical talent to Europe, and because of the interest of European governments in aviation, an anomolous circumstance developed in the air fighting of World War I. Even though the first manned aircraft flight had taken place in the United States at Kitty Hawk, no American pilot flew a U.S.-designed or U.S.-built aircraft in combat in World War I; they flew European models.

The same course of events characterized the pioneering of rocket technology by Dr. Robert Goddard in the United States during the 1920's. This government did not take Dr. Goddard's work seriously; German technologists did take it seriously. As a result, the Nazis had moved into a pre-eminent position in rocketry by World War II. With such examples of the failure to exploit the work of early aeronautical innovators, we should ask ourselves some serious questions regarding the future of America's posture in space technology. With respect to both aeronautics and rocketry, the United States Government lost its lead through general indifference toward the military potential. Later, it hastily caught up. Today with respect to space technology, we enjoy no such initial lead, and still seem to be lagging behind the progress of the U.S.S.R.

The objective of the United States is to maintain peace in space. No nation must achieve a position in space which threatens the security of the United States. We must insure

177

that space is free for the peaceful pursuits of mankind. To do so requires that the military develop an ability to deal with threats that may arise in this medium. The maintenance of peace in space may well depend on the availability of U.S. strength-in-being applicable to this region. In fact, the most lethal threat posed against the United States today is the enemy ballistic missile which would approach the United States *through* space. And, unfortunately, effective defenses against ballistic missiles are not yet available. So, in seeking such defenses, the United States will commit an irrevocable blunder unless it insists upon an immediate and most thorough investigation of the military possibilities afforded by the space region.

Space is no longer the exclusive province of heavenly bodies. Russian spacecraft have traversed the United States many times. In doing so, they passed closer to our inland cities than have any enemy craft ever before in our history, by land or sea or air. Space is a medium that hangs over every square mile of the United States. No other medium provides routes for such rapid access to every part of our country as does space. This new medium is, therefore, a potential new dimension of danger and a threat which this government cannot afford to ignore. Space vehicles may carry weapons not yet perfected and a space vehicle orbiting overhead could be capable of executing an attack in a fraction of the time of an ICBM flight. Moreover, space is a region particularly well-suited to purposes of observation and communications. The wartime advantage to any nation which could have the exclusive use of space for observation and military communications would be enormous.

There can be little doubt that the Soviet Union has military plans for the space region. In a recently translated 1962 publication on military strategy, Marshal of the Soviet Union Sokolovskey has the following to say: "An important problem now is warfare with artificial earth satellites, which can be launched for diverse reasons, even as carriers of nuclear weapons." Marshal Sokolovskey continues: "Soviet military strategy takes into account . . . the use of outer space and aerospace vehicles." Even with the difficulties of translation, the meaning is fairly plain.

The Soviet Union is faced with formidable Free World defenses relative to the mediums of air, sea, and land. But in space, the new medium, they see no evident and applicable Western World defenses. In this new medium the Soviet strategist may well hope to attain strategic ascendancy. But he can only entertain that hope if this nation fails to achieve the timely development of military capabilities for space.

I have essayed some of the military threats from space that are within the foreseeable future. Yet the foreseen dangers associated with enemy dominance of space are probably minor when compared with those none of us can now foresee. When the first aircraft flew, a little more than six decades ago, who foresaw the nuclear bomber? When the first submarine put to sea, who visualized the POLARIS missile submarine able to stay submerged for months? But these, air and sea, are limited mediums with which mankind has centuries of experience. How much less likely, then, are men to foresee the military developments that can emerge in a new medium, space, with which they have relatively no experience? Only with experience will our military forces be able to gain the assurance that is needed to handle the tasks which national security requires.

The space activities of the National Aeronautics and Space Administration have produced and will continue to produce highly important data which is available for application to problems of national security. And, in seeking to identify and advance the development of military capabilities for space, the military establishment wants to take full advantage of the important knowledge NASA acquires. But it is not possible for NASA to develop military capabilities. The reason is simple. A military capability consists of a combination of technical knowledge, military organizations with operational

179

experience, suitable military equipment, tactics, and doctrine. Most of these are factors which can be developed only within a military service.

If Americans should be tempted to believe that the Communists can be dissuaded from developing the military potential of space simply by avoiding it ourselves, we might consider again the lessons of history. The idea of peace without adequate defense has not worked well in the modern world. The United States had no military strength in Southeast Asia before Communist aggression began in that area. There was little evidence of American military power in Korea when the Communists attacked there. When Communist forces invaded and crushed Hungary, they certainly had not been provoked by the presence of powerful military strength.

In contrast, where U.S. military capabilities have been strong and evident and our intent to defend was unmistakable, acceptable peace has been maintained. For example, in the years since the commitment of U.S. forces to the defense of NATO territory, not one inch of Western Europe has been lost to Communist control. A more recent example was the Cuban situation. Only America's existing, in-being military forces permitted President Kennedy to take serious action to prevent the Soviet Union from obtaining a position in Cuba which could threaten the security of the United States. Civil technical knowledge alone could not have done this: ready military capabilities were required. Fortunately, the United States had the needed military capabilities at hand, ready for instant action.

In respect to space, this nation has only a tenuous hold on the flexible military capability for which it strives. The world is living in an age of exploding technology, but new capabilities are still not attained quickly. The United States will learn the military meaning of space in one of two ways: either through exploring the military potential of space ourselves or by observing demonstrations made by its enemies. In the latter case, it could be too late to make use of our belatedly acquired understanding.

180

Therefore, it seems to me that it must become America's immediate objective to develop military capabilities in space which will strengthen the general defense posture of the United States, thus protecting the specific interest of the nation in the space region. To do this, greater knowledge of the military possibilities afforded by space must be gained; military equipment designed to deal with these possibilities must be developed; experience in the application and control of space-oriented military capabilities must be achieved.

In general, the military interest in space *at this time* is within the region bounded by the stationary orbit. The Air Force, for example, must learn to operate on an effective and economical basis both manned and unmanned systems within the near-earth environment. Operational systems to meet some requirements, such as communications, will need to extend out to synchronous orbital distances, and the military eventually will need to be concerned with the possibilities of even deeper space environment. However, the principal U.S. security interests must focus now on insuring that the *near-earth* environment is not dominated by a hostile power.

I consider the need for a comprehensive military space program most prudent in this dangerous world. If this nation is to insure that peace is to be maintained in space, the United States must acquire a range of military capabilities in that region. It should do this with deliberate speed, since our government does not know and cannot predict the time of need.

The failure to initiate a vigorous military space program was symptomatic of the general research and development policy of the early 1960's.

The research and development policy which has evolved since 1960 embodies two characteristics which are extremely troublesome to the professional military establishment. One of these, the "building block" approach to the development of new weapons systems, suggests that the military research efforts may take only small technological risks, thus moving forward by incremental steps to improve the weapons in the

181

U.S. combat arsenal. This procedure has been suspect from the beginning because no such technique has ever been successfully employed in the development of major systems such as aircraft, ballistic missiles, nuclear-powered submarines, or nuclear weapons.

Also in the early 1960's a strong tendency emerged among many high-level scientific advisors to shy away from new weapons and capabilities which could be considered "provocative" or "destabilizing" by the leadership of the Communist conspiracy.

Considered jointly, these two aspects of research and development policy seem to most of the professional military establishment to shackle the progress of this nation's military technology. Inevitably, they simultaneously improve the balance of power for the Soviet Union.

Prestige of the Military Establishment

As a part of United States tradition and law, the military establishment has been separate from politics. The military establishment was, and is supposed to be, free from political pressure. Its service personnel are supposed to remain neutral regarding partisan political matters. Most professional soldiers think that these are sound principles and should be continued.

This same tradition also holds that responsible military leaders may speak freely on national security matters without fear of reprisal. Beginning with General MacArthur, and continuing through the treatment of such military leaders as Generals Lauris Norstad, Curtis LeMay, and Admiral George Anderson, it would seem that the free expression of military judgment on military affairs, by military people, is a dangerous preoccupation.

In addition to the muffling of military people, another impropriety seems to be insinuating itself into the political neutrality of the military establishment. This latter concerns the procurement of major weapon systems with which our military forces are equipped. Prior to 1960, the military

182

establishment had a procedure which was called "source selection" for determining which industrial organization would be awarded contracts for the development and production of major items of defense matériel. This procedure was impregnable to influence. It was completely objective and it was not subject to political pressures. The system gave American industry confidence in the integrity of those in authority and it gave assurance to the fighting forces that the best weapons and other matériel would be obtained.

Our entire system of source selection was breached during the maneuvering which accompanied the award of the TFX (F-111) contract. The questions may be asked, once the integrity of a system has been breached, how far does it go, where will it stop, and how must American industry conduct itself in order to remain competitive and stay alive?

The question may also be asked, when the highly competent technical and operational staffs of the United States Army, Navy and Air Force are overridden by civilian management, what does this do to the military values of integrity? How will such procurements affect U.S. combat teams who may be required to defend this nation with equipment obtained on political merits?

And what about the prestige of those men who have given their entire lives to the defense problems of the country? The detailed direction of military operations of the Cuban invasion; the detailed direction of research and development programs; the explicit decisions on force-structure contrary to military advice; the control of public information; and directives which insulate the uniformed members of the Armed Forces from their counterparts in industry, all add up to a vote of no confidence in the careerists, both military *and civilian,* of the armed forces.

Organization—Post-1960

Earlier in this text, in tracing the evolution of U.S. military policy, I discussed the adoption of the Defense Reorganization Act of 1958. I mentioned the trend during the last years of the Eisenhower Administration toward greater and greater centralization of control of military affairs in the Office of the Secretary of Defense. This trend toward centralized control of military matters has now become so acute that a few more words on the subject are required.

It will be recalled that the 1958 Reorganization Act gave the Secretary of Defense authority to "provide for the carrying out of any supply or service activity common to more than one military department by a single agency or such other organizational entities as he deems appropriate."

In keeping with the powers of the Secretary of Defense to establish centralized agencies to perform defense supply and service functions, we have seen the establishment of the Defense Communications Agency, the Defense Intelligence Agency, the Defense Atomic Support Agency, the Defense Supply Agency, an all-powerful Defense Public Information Office and, soon to be established in all probability, a Defense Legislative and Liaison Office which would further insulate the military services from the U.S. Congress. We have also seen the establishment of ARPA (The Advanced Research Projects Agency) which has authority to choose advanced development projects for actual contracting and implementation by the Department of Defense, acting directly. All of these new agencies report directly to the Secretary of Defense or to him through the Joint Chiefs of Staff. All have assumed responsibilities and prerogatives formerly assigned to the organizations which would have to use the product of the endeavor in war. ARPA, DASA, and the Defense Communications Agency had their beginnings in the last days of the Eisenhower Administration. The other agencies were born under President Kennedy.

The extreme centralization of control of these vital supply and service functions is a matter of real concern to people who have fought one or more wars. It might be claimed that the Defense Supply Agency saves a lot of money by eliminating overlap and duplication and by standardizing military procurement procedures. I will agree with a part of this argument, but if the major savings have been achieved by cutting the logistic heart out of the fighting forces (which I believe to be largely true) the arrangement can become a dangerous snare and a delusion. Likewise, the Defense Communications Agency can be defended, on the grounds of economy, as having eliminated unnecessary world-wide service duplication of communications facilities and activities.

However, any man in a combat situation will always ask for redundancy in his communications systems so that he can maintain control of his forces under conditions of battle damage and the deterioration caused by war activity. The question naturally arises then, how much redundancy and reliability will be left in our world-wide command, control, and communications system under the philosophy of centralization and elimination of duplication and overlapping? The simple question is: Are the dollar savings which may be shown worth the risk which is being taken? What happens if some key communication centers are knocked out in war and there is no alternative system available?

The centralization of control of public information is also a matter of deep concern to the professional military establishment. In general, our United States free press has had a real sense of responsibility, during past wars, and during intervening years, in self-imposing censorship controls to prevent the release of information which would be inimical to the national security. And, in general, the uniformed officers of the military services have used with discretion and propriety their contacts with a free press. This traditional relationship has now degenerated to the point where military officials must make a written report through information channels to the Office of the Secretary of Defense concerning any interview with the press or an agent of any public information media. This inhibits the free expression of military judgment and free intercourse between the armed forces of the United States and the press of the United States.

Then, too, there has developed the centralization of control of military intelligence in a centralized Department of Defense Intelligence Agency. Under the older system, the Army, the Navy, and the Air Force all took independent looks at the fragments of intelligence information gathered by world-wide sources. Frequently there were differences of view with respect to the meaning of the "raw data" which was available. Sometimes the Army estimate proved, in the long run, to be right and sometimes the Navy or the Air Force was right. However, all services looked at these matters freely in light of their individual responsibilities for national security. The question therefore arises as to the impact of the Defense Intelligence Agency on interpretations by the individual services of the data which is under study. It can, of course, be argued that each service still has its own intelligence activity and its own right to appraise the meaning of events, hardware, capabilities, and intentions of enemy forces. Nevertheless, the trend is toward centralization. Since we already have a Central Intelligence Agency, established by the National Security Act of 1947, I wonder why, in addition, we now need a centralized Defense Intelligence Agency.

If I were more inclined to hysteria and gloom with respect to the future health of our military forces, I would take very seriously the comments of one of my former staff officers, who in 1961, made the following observation:

The first thing which a revolutionary coup attempts is to seize control of the communications system, the public information system, and the intelligence system of the government in power which is being overthrown. Even though there has never been an overt coup in this country, it seems to me that our government is creating a very powerful machine, a machine possibly subject to the whim and the control of a single agency. This agency is not now despotic, nor is it interested in the overthrow of the system of government which is America's heritage. However, I worry about the people who will come later and so, I must also worry about this constant erosion of our traditional system of

186

checks and balances and the interference of free communications with the American people.

When Secretary of the Navy, James Forrestal, was appointed as the first Secretary of Defense in September, 1947, he had an immediate staff of less than 100 people. He thought that this staff was fully adequate to meet the requirements of his office. The immediate Office of the Secretary of Defense now numbers somewhere in the neighborhood of 2,450 individuals.

Secretary Forrestal also had reporting directly to his office an additional 250-260 people who comprised the remnants of the World War II Munitions Board and Research and Development Board. In contrast, the Joint Agencies (not counting the immediate office of the Secretary of Defense) which now work directly for the Secretary total about 39,000 souls and include among that number about 1,800 military personnel. The table below illustrates the point:

	1947	As of 30 June 1965	Growth Factor (1947-1965)
Staff of the Secretary of Defense	Less than 100	2,461	About 25 times greater than the 1947 figure.
Other Joint Agencies reporting directly to the Secretary of Def.	About 260	39,327	About 150 times greater than the 1947 figure.
Total	354 People	41,788 People*	About 118 times greater than the 1947 figure.

* This number includes the Defense Supply Agency but does not include the Joint Staff of the JCS, the Defense Atomic Support Agency, the Defense Intelligence Agency, the Defense Communications Agency. These activities, which total about 16,779 people, report to the Secretary of Defense through the Joint Chiefs of Staff. While these groups have one layer of insulation from direct control of the Secretary of Defense, their budgets, manning, and policy direction are extremely susceptible to direct pressure from OSD.

187

When looking at the table above, we should not make the mistake of thinking that "118 times Greater" is a 118-percent growth. Actually, it is an 11,800-percent increase. Putting it another way, if a business man in 1947 had 100 people working directly for him, by the same standards of expansion as that of the Office of the Secretary of Defense, he would now have 11,800 people working for him. This change in numbers probably fairly accurately represents the degree of detailed centralization of management and control which has taken place in our military establishment.

United States law still quite plainly declares that this nation will not have a single military Chief of Staff commanding the armed forces, nor an "overall Armed Forces General Staff." This is probably as it should be, because no one man can master all of the complexities of land warfare, sea warfare, and air warfare. However, America's citizenry should candidly recognize that, while this nation has no military "man on horseback," and no Prussian-type Armed Forces General Staff, a system has evolved in which the nation now has *a single civilian Chief of Staff* in the Secretary of Defense. This single civilian today exercises the total power which our democracy has historically been so reluctant to see fall under any one individual's control. Whether this is good or bad is a matter for historians. My personal views are that it is at least as bad as would be the establishment of a single military Chief of Staff and a single Armed Forces General Staff. It places the future military security of the nation in nonprofessional hands which will be far removed from the scene when the full impact of their decisions, whimsical or otherwise, become apparent.

PART FOUR

Military Analysis

Chapter XII

COST/EFFECTIVENESS

During the years since World War II, a theory of military planning has developed which is now known by the general term cost/effectiveness. This theory of military planning has its roots in what the Army Air Forces called operations analysis during World War II. During that war the Commanding General, Army Air Forces, General H. H. Arnold, recruited and trained a battery of civilian scientists, aided by military professionals, to determine how well the Air Force was doing in the application of military force against the Axis powers. Operations analysts did a useful job because they were able to sit back with no other responsibility and analyze the costs and results of campaigns and individual air attacks which had been made against selected objectives.

The work of the operations analysts dictated neither basic military strategy nor operational tactics, but it was very useful as a *planning tool* to help determine the next series of operations, the tactical objectives which might be identified, and the armament and procedures whereby the military objective might best be neutralized.

191

The operations analyst's function gradually evolved into what the armchair strategist now knows as cost/effectiveness analysis. Cost/effectiveness has become so much a part of military planning, and has received so much attention in the public media, that any American interested in the future security of his country should have an understanding of what is involved.

Because the prosecution of war is an art as well as a science, cost/effectiveness and the principles of war must be considered in the same context for an accurate dimensional perspective of national security planning. Accordingly, I will discuss first the theory of cost/effectiveness and, in the next chapter, the fundamental principles of war as first clearly enunciated in modern military literature by the Prussian military theorist, Clausewitz.

The cost/effectiveness theory really is as old as the history of military operations—a determinative attempt to accomplish an individual, or a whole, military mission at the least possible cost in vital resources. Vital resources may be the number of people available for combat duty, the protection and preservation of established military force and logistic structure, the preservation of basic national resources, or it may reduce itself to a dollar sign. Contemplating all of these possible variations and their inevitable ramifications, cost/effectiveness attempts to get a given job done at the least cost in things which are important to us as soldiers, statesmen, public, and nation. No one can quarrel with the theory.

However, a very real threat to the national interest has developed through the increasingly rigid application of the cost/effectiveness theory to the solution of political-military problems. Operations analysis, the antecedent and precedent of cost/effectiveness, was not the dictator of basic strategy or tactics. Rather, it was but *one* important factor to be considered in making basic military decisions. Cost/effectiveness techniques and procedures constitute a vitally important "input" in solution of today's complex military problems. Unfortunately the procedure appears to have become dominant, to the exclusion of other elements of judgment, in arriving at decisions of military necessity. The fact that cost/effectiveness has assumed virtually absolute dominance in military planning during the years since 1961 appears, to most responsible military officials, to be a potential danger to the future security of the nation.

As specific examples of a cost/effectiveness analysis, let us consider the problems of strategic bombing, and the airlift of troops. In looking at these and other identifiable military missions, the problem first reduces to two basic questions: what is the mission to be performed and how may the job be done in the most economical manner? This procedure is necessary, but fatal trickery may lie in the solution derived from the assumptions made in establishing the framework for the analysis.

All theoretical analyses are based upon what the national defense profession calls "models." A model is a definition of a theoretical circumstance in which the nature of the opposition, both current and projected, is established. Various models, or responses, are "war-gamed" against the theoretical opposition which might exist now or at a predetermined future time.

In the case of a problem such as the airlift of troops and equipment to some point overseas, the model might assume that the U.S. Air Force has operational air bases spaced around the world not farther than 2,500 miles apart; or it might assume that many presently existing air bases might not be available, and that those which could be used would be 5,000 miles apart. In the case of strategic air warfare, it might be assumed to be necessary to destroy only 150 targets or it might be assumed that it would be necessary to destroy 5,000 targets. In both cases, of course, the end results of a cost/effectiveness study would be profoundly influenced by the nature of the assumptions factored into the model.

The process of structuring the assumptions which go into a cost/effectiveness study is therefore the dominant element of solution to the problem. Almost any answer desired may be obtained by juggling the model and juggling the basic assumptions which are the platform for the analysis. The entire process becomes very convincing and sophisticated toward the latter part of an "analysis," because the now glamorous computer technology becomes involved. With automatic mechanical analysis an almost infinite variety of combinations of circumstances and combinations of weapons systems can be played against a given model. In addition, the model can be varied, through the application of computer technology, to determine the "sensitivity" of various assumptions embodied in the model.

Sometimes in war games the analysis of the model itself is given serious attention and an objective effort is made to determine the sensitivity of the assumptions to the results which come out of the computer. In other cases, no such attempt is really made and the results of the war game and the cost/effectiveness study are *dictated by the assumptions* which have, in turn, been *dictated by the bias* of the individual responsible for the study.

This then may inadvertently cause irretrievable danger to the national security because biases of one kind or another are a most human trait. Fundamental biases and judgments are based upon individual experience and upon individual psychological reactions to the world in which we live. In taking the position that the human race is subject to bias, I must also include the scientific fraternity. I have never known an eminent scientist—including those who agree with me as well as those who do not agree with me—to be totally devoid of bias. However, the average scientist assumes that he is a member of a race apart; that he is analytically, irrevocably correct because he utilizes the cold logic of the "scientific approach" to the solution of any problem. However, the record of the last twenty years is filled with scientific judgment which has later proved to be in error, and when this erroneous scientific judgment has been analyzed, we can usually find that the error was rooted in the bias of the individual before he started his analysis.

194

I feel obligated to stress this point, not for the purpose of assessing blame or personal responsibility for mistakes of the past, but rather for the purpose of generating a more thoughtful approach to the unsolved military problems of today.

For example, no one alive today can predict with absolute certainty the importance or unimportance of "military man in space." This is a controversial subject, steeped in bias and emotion as well as in logic and human experience. However, we can draw an historical parallel, in the manner that the parallel affects research and development potential.

I referred earlier to some "scientific" judgments of 1949 which influenced the development of U. S. military posture and which were later proved to be totally wrong. These judgments, as I interpreted them, were as follows:

1. That in all future wars the power of defense would be greater than the power of the offense in a strategic air warfare encounter.

2. That the ballistic missile would never achieve significance as an instrument of war.

3. That it would take the Russians at least twenty years to develop a nuclear weapon—and that maybe they could never do it.

These judgments may have been made because of an instinctive moral objection to strategic bombing and the subjugation of civilian populations to the hazards of war. In such judgment, the morality of war might involve only putting teen-agers and young adults into uniform, calling them soldiers, and allowing them to be blown to bits or eviscerated by a bayonet in some remote part of the world. But it might be considered immoral to bring the war into the front yard and back yard of everyone. Such judgment was reflected in the prosaic ideal of "take the battle back to the battlefield" and leave secure and inviolate that segment of society which has had a traditionally sheltered life.

In arriving at the 1949 judgment that the defense would be ascendant over the offense in any future war, the scientists involved actually performed a very unscientific analysis. In the intellectual model which was created, the World War II B-29 bomber was war-gamed against a ground-to-air missile system, such as the Nike Hercules, and the B-29's were quickly destroyed. The bias and assumptions permitted playing a modern and improved technology (NIKE) of the defense against the technology of an offense (B-29) which was ten years older. The rationale was out of phase technologically. It was probably done because of instinctive revulsion to strategic bombing and in hopes that some way could be found to stop it. The judgment was not founded in fact nor propounded in scientific logic.

The same scientific judgment that the ballistic missile would never be a significant tool of military power was probably arrived at because of a similar bias. The aiming errors *then* predictable for ballistic missiles were linked with the warhead *then* available from obsolete atomic bombs of the Hiroshima and Nagasaki type. A cost analysis study of the ballistic missile under these ground rules would of course show that the ballistic missile was not a practical weapon.

The third judgment, that the U.S.S.R. might not develop an atomic weapon during the twenty years subsequent to 1949, was probably related, again, to the fundamental bias. The analyst *did not wish to believe it,* and, in addition, may have been goaded by some intellectual arrogance. By that I mean that scientists of the United States were so smart that they could develop the bomb in four years, but that no other nation had the capacity to match our intellectual achievements in this technological area.

With fine hindsight, I can truthfully say that the professional military establishment did not subscribe whole-heartedly to these scientific predictions. United States Air Force Intelligence *at the time* believed that the Soviets would probably explode their first bomb about 1950. The device was detonated in mid-September, 1949.

I could summarize my views on cost/effectiveness with the simple statement that operations analysis, cost/effectiveness studies, and war games, are extremely useful elemental tools in the process of arriving at military decisions. However, when the process is allowed to become dominant and the combined expertise of human and technological experiences are submerged and overridden, the technique is a danger and a threat rather than an asset. The results of a cost/effectiveness study are as fallible as the judgment of an individual making basic assumptions defining the "model." An electronic computer provides a convenient method for mathematical probability analyses. *It cannot exercise judgment.* It can rapidly and precisely correlate existing knowledge which has been coded and machined into the electronic sensors of its equipment. *Nothing ever comes out of the computer which has not been programmed in by those who are its "mentors."*

Therefore, it seems to me that these "mathematical" approaches to military problems are not corrupting in themselves, but, rather, that the system can be and has been corrupted by allowing final judgments to be based upon the inevitable bias of some individuals. The final conclusions in establishing cost/effectiveness should be reached in conjunction with other more dynamic methods.

Chapter XIII

PRINCIPLES OF WAR

Cost/effectiveness theories become largely academic once military forces are joined in combat. The opposing forces use what they have, and attempt to devise strategy and tactics to best meet the objectives of the specific battle, campaign and war in which they are involved. The choices of strategy and tactics—the alternatives from which to choose—will, of course, be limited by what *is available* or *will be available* in the time frame of the operation. Earlier decisions, based on whatever judgment or cost/effectiveness technique was used in national security planning, will therefore have a profound impact on the actual course of battle.

I have used the terms battle, campaign, and war. What these terms mean to the military professional follows.

A battle is a unique single circumstance under which opposing military forces collide and fight. One side usually emerges with the least over-all damage. A campaign is a series of related battles. It is often possible to lose a single battle, or several battles, but win a campaign through winning more battles of significance than are lost. A successful campaign is focused on achieving relatively near term objectives while nullifying the relatively near term objectives of the opposing forces. In terms of air warfare, particularly those involving conventional weapons, a single air strike or a single air battle normally will not be decisive. A campaign, involving a series of air strikes or battles, is usually required for decision. This is very pertinent with respect to the circumstances in this nation's conduct of the battles of South Vietnam during the years 1963, 1964, and 1965.

A well-planned and sustained series of air strikes, the summation of which is an air campaign, are inevitably necessary to achieve an effective interdiction or an objective of logistic strangulation. Ordinarily, only transitory damage occurs from sporadic and inconsistent air operations with conventional weapons. Military logic requires that a tactical "cause and effect" decision be taken before such operations are initiated and that a sustained campaign must follow to achieve the desired objective.

Considering then, that a campaign is larger and of greater consequence than a single battle, a war between nations is much larger than a single campaign. A war is the summation of the results of individual campaigns as these campaigns relate to the fundamental strength of a nation. The strength of a nation is measured here in terms of its viable economic and industrial capability, the determination and motivation of its government and population, and in terms of the capacity of its existing military forces-in-being to adequately respond to the national purpose.

If we understand that the procedures and techniques involved in operations analysis, cost/effectiveness, and war gaming studies create a product which, if properly used, is useful in over-all military analysis, we might ask ourselves what, specifically, are the other elements which should be given at least equal weight. It might be easy to evade this question by simply stating that "military judgment" should also be considered. However, it might be more useful to elaborate on the

199

term "military judgment" with the intent to indicate that military judgment is not purely intuitive, but, rather, has its roots in some fundamental logic and experience applicable to most human affairs. I refer to the Principles of War.

I do not intend to repeat a textbook on the nine classic Principles of War as so clearly enunciated by Clausewitz, but I would like to talk about six of these general principles as they have particular application to the problems of today. These principles are the principle of the "Objective," the principle of "Concentration," the principle of "Surprise," the principle of "Flexibility," the principle of "Mobility," and the principle of "Pursuit."

The Principle of the Objective

In military definition, the principle of the Objective means simply that the American government should determine specifically purposeful goals for its military forces. As an example, during World War II, the U.S. government announced a policy of "unconditional surrender" with respect to the Axis powers. This objective has been criticized by some military historians and it has been defended by others. However, the simple facts are that the U.S. government knew what it was trying to do with its military forces. It demanded the unconditional surrender of Italy, Germany, and Japan. Without defending or condemning this objective, the U.S. government had a single purpose, derived from a specifically articulated objective.

On the contrary, a reasonable question can be asked at the present time as to what the U.S. government is really trying to do in its employment of military forces throughout today's world. The government seemed to lose focus, or objective, in Korea when it failed to attack Communist China at the time of its entry into the Korean war. No real purpose of U.S. foreign policy was apparent during the progressive loss of China and the staining spread of the war into Indochina. And today, most of the American public—indeed, the Free World —finds it difficult to identify, in specific terms, what exactly America is trying to do in Laos, Thailand, and North and South Vietnam.

On another rampart of the Free World, this nation seems to have deliberately alienated a formerly stanch ally in Pakistan while simultaneously giving aid and comfort to an Indian government which consistently votes against U.S. objectives in the United Nations. In Europe, the United States has persisted in providing aid, from the pocket of the American taxpayer, to Poland and Yugoslavia, while refusing to provide the government of France, at no cost to itself, nuclear information long in the possession of the U.S.S.R. In 1956, the United States failed to support France and the United Kingdom in the Suez crisis, and indirectly supported Nasser. But, even so, Egypt has aligned itself with the Afro-Asian bloc in opposition to United States policies and even denounced such simple humanitarian operations as the intervention of Belgium and the United States in the Congo, an intervention undertaken to rescue people of many nations from torture and death.

With respect to NATO as a whole, this government has allowed the U.S. military structure to become obsolete in the face of a deployed opposition which exists as a matter of stark reality in the Soviet medium-range ballistic missile force.

Under the circumstances which U.S. State Department policy has allowed to develop over the last twenty years, it is indeed difficult for a military realist to determine the "Objective." What are we really trying to do, as a nation, through the deployment and employment of our military forces? It is axiomatic to the military professional that *objectives* should be defined as the *first purpose* of battle. While the U.S. political administration seems to be involved in a war initiated by the Communists, it remains difficult to identify the objective which would give focus and meaning to the national effort to either defeat or contain communism. Possibly the difficulty has foundation in the fundamental policy of containment. We seem able to justify aid to sworn enemies and failure to support friends on the vague logic that both efforts assist in the containment of the Communist movement.

The Principle of Concentration

In a military sense, the principle of Concentration means that force should be directed to a specific objective, to take that objective rather than be diluted, fragmented, and spread so thinly against many separate objectives that the government becomes weak everywhere and strong nowhere.

In a tactical sense, U.S. military commanders had to relearn the principle of Concentration during the early days of World War II, in Africa. They were parceling U.S. air power out into small pieces that were always overwhelmed by an enemy air force which, *in toto,* was not as strong as our own. U.S. commanders, relearning this lesson in the bitter experience of battle, finally consolidated their air forces and drove first the Luftwaffe and finally the German armies out of Africa.

In the conduct of political-military operations during a Cold War period, concentration of force means much more than just the employment of military forces-in-being. It should also mean concentration of national effort with respect to political and military aid, with respect to research and development, and with respect to specific international commitments. A nation which assumes the advantages inherent in concentration of effort will naturally exploit its own capabilities. Two examples of how this principle works are worth explanation.

The national lethargy following World War II slowed America's nuclear weapons program and its overall military research and development efforts. The nation finally responded in the late forties and early fifties to an obvious threat, and brought a powerful strategic bombardment force into being. Even though we had not used earlier the power inherent in our atomic monopoly, the U.S.S.R. could not ignore the existence of this force. Consequently, a massive air defense system had to be created by the U.S.S.R. This system included, and still includes, high performance jet-fighter aircraft, ground-to-air missiles, and the complex electronic gear required to detect enemy air and missile forces, and to guide and control the defending forces. Every ruble of national effort, scientific and industrial, on the part of the U.S.S.R. which went into this effort could have been spent on offensive and aggressive land, sea, and air military weapons systems if the United States had not built a strategic force. The cost to the U.S.S.R. of its air defensive system was probably on the order of twenty to thirty billion dollars, valued in our monetary terms. The effort, much more importantly, greatly reduced the support of Soviet offensive weapons systems which would have been employed, in consonance with their doctrine, to subjugate the world.

In this particular case, America had a technological initiative and a concentration of national effort which, in combination, put the enemy on the defensive. Russia was compelled to divert a great national effort to self-defense, thus postponing grandiose schemes for control of the world through offensive action.

The pacifists and those who advocate disarmament will, of course, claim that this is just another example of the "arms race," and that the U.S.S.R. could have used the resources spent on their air defense system to improve the standard of living of their people. I agree that they "could have" done so, but I also remember the basic objective of the Communist powers—*to destroy the Western World*. The United States would not have had to build the strategic forces if the Soviets had been willing, following World War II, to abide in a world of law and order. America disarmed following that war; *Russia did not*. America did not seek the territory of other nations, and it conducted no subversive movement aimed at the overthrow of other legitimate governments; *Russia did*. Therefore, if this relationship between governments is an "arms race," let the blame lie where it belongs—on a ruthless system which has already enslaved half the world, and still seeks to enslave the other half.

The classic Principle of War, Concentration of Effort, as demonstrated by the above example, is therefore closely allied with the principle of initiative, which I have introduced and emphasized throughout this book. This relationship leads me to a second specific example of the application of these principles.

During the late forties and fifties, in the face of uncertainty as to whether the United States government would, or would not, exercise the advantage of America's technological lead in military strength, it was necessary for the Soviets to make some hard decisions and to take some political-military gambling chances. One such hard decision, which I have discussed, was to build their air defense system.

However, from the Soviet viewpoint, if this nation had in truth given the initiative to the Communist powers and *would not attack*, America would thereby have allowed Russia time to concentrate its energy on carefully selected offensive striking forces, while safely disregarding other obvious near-term endeavors. The leadership of the U.S.S.R. knew that the U.S. had a tremendous lead in the technology and industry which are required to build a strategic aerial bombardment force. The Russian government knew it could not afford an attempt to catch up in this area while at the same time supporting its massive ground forces, tactical air forces, submarine forces, and bring into being an air defense system. So the Soviets, in a very clever political gambling decision, put only token effort on their bomber force and committed their primary resources to a ballistic missile force which would leapfrog U.S. bombardment forces in terms of surprise attack capabilities.

Many U.S. national intelligence estimates of the 1950–1960 period overestimated the size of the aircraft bombardment force which Russia would produce. These were based on intelligence estimates of Soviet technological know-how, the available Soviet industrial base, and the overall capability to build such forces. These faulty intelligence estimates cannot be rationally criticized by fair-minded people, because military history and experience throughout the ages shows clearly that it is generally safer to depend upon an analysis of an enemy's *capability* rather than his *intentions*. An enemy's intentions can change overnight, but his capabilities cannot.

At the same time that U.S. intelligence sources were overestimating what the Soviets might do in producing a bomber force, they were generally underestimating Russian technological capability to move rapidly in the development of rocket propulsion systems of great power adaptable to both ballistic missiles and space operations. The United States' over-all governmental assessment of enemy technological *capability*— as opposed to *intention*—was frankly, hopelessly wrong. U.S. intelligence sources had shreds of data which indicated Soviet emphasis on large missile systems. And, two years before the Soviet launching of the first man-made earth satellite, the U.S. had an accurate National Security Council analysis of the international repercussions of such an event. However, we, as a nation, refused to take these reports seriously. It was incomprehensible, even to many of our thoughtful leaders, that only twelve years after the end of World War II, a "backward" nation could recover from the wreckage of a war fought on its own territory and be first in space.

The point is that an objective analysis of these events of the past should give all of us reason to believe that *some* of the Principles of War are equally as important as cost/effectiveness studies. If, in the future, the American government continues to give the initiative to the Communists, it automatically licenses the U.S.S.R. to concentrate its energy on selected projects, while safely disregarding consideration of any other possible dangers. Meanwhile, insecure in the knowledge that our enemy could launch a surprise attack, the United States must be prepared to fight today, tomorrow, and the day after tomorrow. This means that America must divide its resources between competing requirements of today with those for tomorrow *and* the day after tomorrow. It means that this citadel

205

of freedom cannot implement the principle of Concentration with maximum effectiveness. The Soviet Bloc, on the other hand, knows that it can safely eliminate today's effort, if it so chooses, and concentrate selectively on the power posture of tomorrow. Communist Russia and Communist China know this. America has told them both that she will not initiate World War III, and that she will fight only when *they* are ready to fight.

The Principle of Surprise

The military Principle of War, Surprise, is, of course, as old as the law of the jungle. Predatory creatures, fish, reptiles, birds, and mammals all rely heavily on the principle of surprise.

In terms of the military history of the past generation, the United States suffered a devastating surprise attack by the Japanese at Pearl Harbor on December 7, 1941. America also reacted to the "surprise" entry of the Chinese Communist forces into the Korean War. England was surprised by the Egyptian closure of the Suez Canal, and the Free World was surprised by the ground blockade of Berlin. Examples of the advantages which accrue to exploitation of the principle of Surprise are numerous in military history and need not be dwelled upon at length. However, in the highly industrialized and mechanized world in which the community of nations live today, the principle of Surprise involves not only political and military action, but more importantly, it involves technological progress.

The United States as a whole was surprised when the Soviets exploded their first nuclear device in the fall of 1949. It was also surprised, as a nation, when in 1957, the Soviets put their first satellite in orbit. Americans were also surprised when the Soviets launched their first spacecraft with a man aboard and the American scientific community was surprised again at the depth and sophistication of the Russian nuclear test series which, in the fall of 1961, violated the three-year moratorium on nuclear testing.

Technological surprise can be more dangerous to the future security of the United States than can tactical military surprise in any battle situation. The future contains the possibility of the application, by the enemy, of the principle of Surprise in at least two critical ways. This nation can suffer a surprise attack by the enemy in which he utilizes weapons systems which have been fairly well identified, or America and its military forces *might* suffer technological surprises which could totally change the balance of power.

Flexibility and Mobility

In a military sense, the terms Flexibility and Mobility mean precisely what they say. A battle circumstance is always fraught with unpredictable events which even the best military or political planner cannot foresee. Therefore, a plan which is so rigid or inflexible that it cannot be altered to take into account the unpredictable occurrences will generally fail. There must be responsiveness, in terms of both force structure and command decision, which will allow advantage to be taken of mistakes made by an enemy, by changes in geographic and weather factors, and by political decisions made by human beings. The principle of Mobility is related closely to the principle of Flexibility in that mobility of force structure provides opportunity to change tactical objectives and react to the developing and changing circumstances of conflict.

The applicability of Flexibility was never more clearly demonstrated than during the conduct of the war against the Axis powers in Europe. The German military establishment was controlled by the transient civilian, Hitler, who consistently overrode the advice of a very competent German General Staff. The effort of the German forces in the air was generally under the direction of Goering, who had become fat, lazy, and morally and mentally incompetent in his job. This combination of inept military leadership, and the "intuition" of Hitler gave the Allies a tremendous advantage in the prosecution of the air war against the Axis powers.

Because of the manner in which the European conflict developed, the appeasement policies of the British and the French leadership, and the late entry of the United States into the war as an overt, participating belligerent, the initiative in the battle was grabbed unceremoniously by the German forces. The early smashing successes of the combined force of Stuka dive bombers and overwhelming panzer tank armor resulted in a very quick attainment of German military objectives in Poland and Czechoslovakia.

These stunning early successes undoubtedly contributed to the basic strategic error which Hitler made in his determination to fight on two fronts simultaneously. In the west he moved enviously toward France, the English Channel, and the United Kingdom itself. To the east, he hungrily tackled the vast territory and latent strength of the great Russian Bear. He had not learned what Napoleon learned of the consequences of a land march toward Stalingrad and Moscow. Having committed this great strategic blunder, he then committed a series of tactical blunders which actually handed the Allied forces the ultimate victory with little difficulty.

The first of these blunders was Hitler's misinterpretation of the results of the Battle of Britain. The Battle of Britain was an air campaign by Germany against the population and industrial base of the United Kingdom. Its intention was to kill the United Kingdom's industrial and moral capability to wage war. On the German side the battle involved hundreds of bombers attacking vital power sources of the United Kingdom. On the English side, it involved the Royal Air Force Fighter Command attempting to shoot down the bombers and neutralize the attack against their own heartland as well as a massive civil-defense effort.

The Royal Air Force Fighter Command was not a very large organization, but it was equipped with a very fine fighter airplane for that period of time—the Spitfire. In the air battles which took place, the Fighter Command did an heroic job, which led to the statement by Sir Winston Churchill that never in the history of man had so much been done by so few for so many.

However, the problems of the Royal Air Force Fighter Command were simplified by Goering's tactical blunders in directing the German bombardment force. For example, during the last great aerial raid on England, the German Air Force flew about 1,200 bombers over industrial targets which were critical to the survival of the British Empire. The German tactical decision in this effort led them to pass these 1,200 bombers over the targets spaced in intervals so that the entire attack required about twelve hours from inception to completion. At the time, the Royal Air Force Fighter Command consisted of little more than a handful of trained pilots and fighter planes. The incredible German tactical decision to stagger the attack, and to use twelve hours for its completion, actually multiplied the strength of the Royal Air Force Fighter Command by a factor of five. This was possible because on that day each Spitfire pilot had the time to fly five missions. He could go up and fight, shoot down enemy bombers, exhaust his fuel range, come back and land, refuel, and take off to attack anew.

It was completely unnecessary for the German High Command to stagger this attack over a twelve-hour period, because each German bomber flew only one mission. The entire force of 1,200 bombers could have been passed over the target in less than one hour. This would have allowed each English Spitfire pilot to fly only one mission instead of five, and it would have reduced the losses to the German bomber forces by at least the same degree.

In analysis, it appears that the German concept of the application of air power during World War II was an artillery, rolling barrage concept of war as opposed to exploitation of the shock effect of massive air operations.

Having suffered a tremendous loss of bombardment aircraft

during this last great maneuver, the German High Command misread the lesson of the battle. The High Command concluded that it was not possible to knock a nation off its feet through aerial bombardment. Goering, sure in the lesson just bitterly learned, stated that "no Allied bombs would fall on the soil of Germany." As a result, the German emphasis on the use of air power shifted to fighter defense. Concurrently, however, other decisions also made by the German High Command resulted in the reduction of fighter aircraft production and the training of combat crews. These factors combined to produce a situation in which the offensive strength went out of the German Air Force, and the defensive strength was not adequate to the task of successfully facing the massive forces which the United States and the British Bomber Command later mounted against the German motherland.

Other tactical blunders, motivated by Hitler's intuition and Goering's incompetence, materially aided the daylight bombing raids of the United States against the sources of German military strength. One such tactical decision on the part of the German High Command was the determination that the German fighter forces should concentrate on destruction of the invading bomber forces, to the exclusion of attack against U.S. fighter aircraft escorting and protecting Allied bombers over German territory.

On a typical bombing trip to Berlin, United States forces had a column of bombers about 400 miles long which had to go all the way to Berlin and back. In terms of self-defensive fire power, the B-17's and B-24's of that day had about twenty seconds of machine-gun fire from their turrets. And the round trip took at least five hours. If the German Fighter Command had attacked the United States fighter forces escorting the bombers as they crossed the English Channel, they would have forced Allied fighters to drop their auxiliary fuel tanks, carried on the wings, and to engage in combat. If Allied fighters had been forced to drop these tanks, they would not have had the range and the endurance necessary to escort

American bombers on the deep penetrations involved. Fighters would have had to go back to base, after an aerial fight, and the bombers, in a 400-mile stream, in and out, would have had only twenty seconds of self-contained fire power to protect themselves. However, the self-imposed tactics of the German fighter forces eliminated this great inherent advantage which they had, and Allied fighter-type aircraft usually were able to make the round trip, protecting the bombers.

Another great tactical blunder of the German Air Force was their failure to neutralize U.S. and English bombardment forces on the ground on English bases. The air forces did the best they could in dispersing aircraft and in building revetments, but most U.S. air forces were nevertheless concentrated in a very small area in East Anglia. They were extremely vulnerable to destruction on the ground. In addition, every major bombing raid against Germany required that the Allied Air Force have an air assembly period over East Anglia and the English Channel. This assembly period sometimes required two or three hours. The bombers were extremely vulnerable during this period of the operation, but the German Tacticians never exploited this opportunity to deal a crushing blow.

As a final example, during the latter days of the war, German technology had created the Messerschmitt 262. This aircraft was a jet-powered machine which could fly about 200 miles faster than anything which the Army Air Force had in combat in Europe at the time. If it had been employed as a fighter airplane to engage U.S. fighters as they crossed the Channel, and with a part of the force reserved for attack of American bombardment formations, it could probably have knocked the 8th Air Force out of the skies and made operation Overlord, the cross-Channel invasion, extremely difficult and costly, if not impossible.

However, the decision of the German High Command was to try to use the airplane principally as a bombardment vehicle. History relates the fallibility of this decision. Through the genius of a few people, the German forces were ahead of the Allied forces in jet engine technology; the Germans built the finest airplane involved in the war, and they lost the air war because they did not know how to use it.

On the other side of the world, the Japanese High Command made similar mistakes. In a strategic sense, probably the greatest blunder of the Japanese government was the decision to join the war against the United States. The Japanese Empire inherently was extremely vulnerable because of its small size, its concentrated industrialization, and its absolute reliance upon sea lines of communication to maintain national strength. But, having made the strategic blunder to join in the war, the Japanese made another strategic blunder in the immediate aftermath of the Pearl Harbor attack. The United States was so disorganized at the time that an immediate Japanese follow-up against the Hawaiian Islands would undoubtedly have resulted in their capture and occupation by the Japanese. If this had happened, American build-up of naval, ground, and air strength in the entire Pacific area would have been extremely difficult. If the United States had not had Hawaii as a base, the air-ferry routes to southeast Asia and Australia would have posed enormous problems. The movement of ground troops and logistic support of fighting forces by our Navy would have multiplied logistic effort many, many times. However, the Japanese did not press their advantage. They failed to exploit the principle of Pursuit and allowed the U.S. a breathing spell during which it regrouped and utilized the island steppingstones of the Pacific to eventually crush Tojo's regime.

Along with these strategic blunders the Japanese also committed tactical and logistic blunders. Probably the most significant of the logistic blunders on the part of the Japanese High Command was their failure to provide an expanded training base for the production of combat pilots.

At the start of the war the average Japanese pilot in front-line combat units, including both the Japanese Naval Air

Arm and the Japanese Army Air Arm, *was much better trained and had more experience in the air than the average American pilot* in comparable units. The average Japanese pilot in front-line combat units at the start of the war had about 500 to 600 hours of cockpit time, whereas the U.S. Army Air Force was sending men into battle with less than half that total flying experience. However, war inevitably exacts a high price in destruction and attrition. So, as the first-line air combat forces of Japan were slowly whittled down, there was no adequate training program to replace the air crews which had been lost.

Toward the termination of the war in the Pacific, the average Japanese pilot had less than 100 hours of cockpit experience. But by late 1944, the tremendous aerial training establishment created in the United States was producing air combat forces at a tremendous rate. The force was constantly growing in size and in terms of the individual experience and training of the air crews. U.S. Navy and Army Air Force pilots were approaching an average of 1,000 hours cockpit experience while the Japanese were rapidly dwindling from 600 hours to sometimes less than 100 hours. This is one of the reasons why, during the last desperate days of World War II, the Japanese Air Force had to resort to Kamikaze tactics.

The recollection of both strategic and tactical mistakes (violations of the Principles of War) made by the Axis powers of World War II also brings to mind blunders on our own part.

From the viewpoint of basic strategy, we entered World War II too late. If America had been fully committed to the defense of Western Europe before Hitler's march to Poland and Czechoslovakia, it is possible that he would never have undertaken it. If America had refused to ship scrap iron to Japan, which later came back at U.S. troops as shrapnel, or if this nation had objected to the Japanese seizure of Shanghai in 1937, that war might have been avoided.

U.S. military forces also committed many tactical mistakes,

such as the fragmentation and penny-packeting of its air power in North Africa during the early days of U.S. overt commitment to the military operations of World War II. And it can be argued that America paid an unnecessarily high price in American treasure in accomplishing the defeat of the Japanese Empire.

As a matter of fact, Japan was so completely reliant upon sea lines of communication that a force of one or two hundred American submarines could have defeated Japan through economic strangulation, that is, a blockade of essential imports. This process would have taken longer than the four years which were involved in the destruction of Japan, but it would have been equally effective.

Actually, what happened was that the United States built three separate military organizations, each of which was capable of defeating the power base of Japan's very small geographic island area. U.S. submarines could have done it by themselves, U.S. strategic air forces could have done it by themselves, and the U.S. Army land invasion, such as planned for Operation Olympic, could have done it. Mutual support, of course, by all branches of the services would have been necessary for any one of these operations to be decisive. The submarine of that day required bases and logistic support, air defense of the bases, and ground defense of the bases. The strategic air forces required bases within range of the enemy, logistic support to these bases which involved Naval fleets of tankers carrying gasoline and oil, air defense of the bases, and ground defense of the bases. An Army land invasion force, such as planned in Operation Olympic, required air support and sea movement of vast numbers of soldiers and great quantities of war supplies in order to be effective.

In other words, regardless of the decision as to the primary instrumentality whereby Japan would be neutralized, all services and arms would have had to be involved in varying degrees. The point of the argument (to the effect that we actually built a military force capable of killing Japan in three

214

different ways) hinges not on the argument of service participation, but on the expenditure of resources which might have been conserved if we had made an early decision with respect to the primary instrumentality, and then provided the necessary land, sea, and air forces to implement that decision.

There is an old cliché that "time is the essence of war." During World War II, America also had a policy which required unconditional surrender on the part of the enemy. These things combined to give the United States the national urge to develop a physical capability to destroy Japan—even without the final use of the atomic bomb—in three different ways. The unnecessary expenditure of resources involved in this three-pronged attack may be criticized by historians and economists. But, in retrospect, the whole operation seems to make more sense than the expenditure of life and resources in Korea, in Laos, and in South Vietnam, with no particular identifiable objective other than to "contain communism." At least, in those days, America built some land, sea, and air forces which had depth and staying power to exploit the principle of flexibility and capitalize on an enemy's mistakes.

Returning to the present time, with respect to the specific defense environment and national vector of the moment, our government has tacitly announced, as a national objective, the desire to be able to fight across the entire spectrum of warfare, from the lowest levels of subversion and counterinsurgency operations to the highest levels of conflict involving a mutual nuclear exchange. This objective, if really carried out, cannot be criticized on any rational military basis. However, the major element of U.S. force structure actually deterring the Communists from putting into operation their announced intention to take over the world is becoming increasingly inflexible and immobile with the passage of time. In terms of the capability for tactical application of strategic nuclear power, and the technical characteristics of such power, the United States is moving toward a position of rigidity and inflexibility which is distinctly at variance with its stated

215

objectives. America is moving toward complete strategic reliance on a Maginot Line of ballistic missiles.

The Principle of Pursuit

In ordinary logic, the principle of Pursuit is not unique to military operations. A trained boxer follows the principle of Pursuit when he has stunned his opponent, has him on the ropes, and tries to knock him out before he can recover his senses. In a broader military tactical sense, the term "pursuit" means that a responsible commander should exploit the disorganization of an enemy and the weakened position of an enemy, before allowing him time to regroup, salve his wounds, rest, resupply, and come back in fighting posture.

It should also be evident that the principle of Pursuit in modern war must apply to technology as well as to the employment of military forces-in-being. The history of the last twenty years would indicate that America has not applied this principle very well in its research and development effort. At the end of World War II the United States had an absolute monopoly on the application of nuclear technology to national security affairs. It was also the leader in aero-dynamic technology, some aspects of propulsion technology, and the various aspects of electronic technology applicable to military affairs. However, America rested on its laurels, assumed a leisurely pace of development, and allowed the U.S.S.R. to overtake her in some areas of nuclear technology and in propulsion technology applicable to very heavy ballistic-missile operations and to operations in space.

Our Government is currently congratulating itself on the presumption that it has closed, or is rapidly closing, these technological gaps. However, can we be certain? This nation had a great lead which it threw away, and America is still confronted with an Iron Curtain. Will the application of the principle of Surprise by the enemy again defeat this nation's neglect of the principle of Pursuit?

216

Persuasive Continuity of the Principles of War

The Principles of War are not taken lightly by the professional man in uniform even though some social scientists and natural scientists behave as though they had never heard of such principles. Accordingly, I am including below two excerpts which show the depth of intellectual interest of the uniformed military establishment in the art of war.

The first is from a group of students in attendance at the Air War College. This passage comes from a student seminar, and was written in 1947:

Consolidation of Seminar Conclusions

I. PROBLEM

To review and re-evaluate the Principles of War in terms of evolutionary advances in warfare.

The objective: to prepare clear and concise statements of the basic principles and to show their relationship to war.

II. FACTORS BEARING ON THE PROBLEM

1. Definitions.

a. *War*—The use of organized force by two human groups pursuing contradictory policies, each group seeking to impose its policy upon the other. It is considered that organized force includes political, economic, psychological, and military components.

b. *Principles of War*—Statements of fundamental rules important to the successful conduct of war. These principles are equally applicable in any operation of organized human effort.

2. Evolutionary advances.

a. The totality of war.

b. Air power.

c. Contraction of Time and Space.

d. Weapons of mass destruction.

III. DISCUSSION

Since at least 500 B.C., soldiers have analyzed military campaigns and written of factors considered important to the successful prosecution of war. For centuries many of those factors have

217

survived subsequent appraisal and have come to be regarded as Principles of War.

While not all recognized writers on war have agreed as to the exact number and wording of these so-called principles, a remarkable similarity and continuity is evident. The oldest military treatise on record, *The Art of War*, written by the Chinese Sun-Tsu about 500 B.C., contains ample evidence that several principles of war were recognized at that time. The principle of the objective is identified in the following passage: "In war let your great object be victory and not a lengthy campaign."* That Sun-Tsu appreciated the importance of mass is illustrated by the following: "We can form a single united body, while the enemy must split up into fractions. Hence there will be a whole pitted against separate parts of a whole, which means that we shall be many to the enemy's few."† The principles of the offensive, movement and surprise are readily identifiable in other passages of this famous military classic. When General Nathan B. Forrest, C.S.A., uttered his ungrammatical but immortal formula for success: "Get thar fustest with the mostest men," he showed keen insight into the importance of concentration and movement.

Although the writings of Napoleon, Clausewitz, and Jomini probably exerted the predominant influence, there is considerable evidence that a British military writer, Major General J.F.C. Fuller, is the father of the currently accepted, modern version of the principles of war or at any rate gave them articulate form and wide publicity.**

The American version of the Principles of War first appeared in War Department Training Regulations 10-5, 1921. They were discussed in Section III of the Air Corps Tactical School text on Air Warfare (March 1, 1936) and again in AAF Memorandum 200-7 (October 1943). They are:

The Principle of the Objective.
The Principle of the Offensive.

---

* Sun-Tsu on *The Art of War*, Chapter II. Translated by Leonel Giles (M.S. Luzac Co., London, 1919).
† Ibid., Chapter VI.
** Charles Andrew Willoughby, *Maneuver in War* (The Military Service Publishing Co., 1939). Page 32.

The Principle of Mass.
The Principle of Economy of Force.
The Principle of Movement.
The Principle of Surprise.
The Principle of Security.
The Principle of Simplicity
The Principle of Cooperation.

It has been said that these nine principles comprise the whole art of war, that they are basic and immutable and are not subject to exception. "These principles have been deducted from the study of military history, the records of which show that the great commanders have ever been guided by them and that success or failure in military operations has depended upon the extent and manner of their application."[*] These statements are difficult to refute, but it should be remembered that the statements of the Principles of War were derived from study of surface operations and written by soldiers with ground warfare in mind. They stem from periods in history when the airplane existed only in the minds of men. They now require analysis in the light of modern war—a period in which air power has reached at least "a stage of full adolescence."[†]

The concept of modern war must be broadened to include not only military operations, but the attainment of all external national objectives in the face of opposition. To stand as basic principles, then, the Principles of War must apply equally to this enlarged concept.

In this study an attempt is made to state and discuss the principles from this viewpoint and in terminology that will be of value in teaching and understanding the subject wherever desired or needed.

Considerable misunderstanding can result from the use of a key word or phrase to denote a principle. Such key words or phrases are subject to diverse interpretations and often fail to convey meaningful thought. An attempt is made here to state

---

[*] Conrad H. Lensa, *Napoleon and Modern War*, (The Military Service Publishing Company, 1943). Page 155.
[†] U.S.S.B.S. "Overall Report, European War," Sept. 30, 1945. Page 1.

the Principles of War in a clear and concise *cause and effect* relationship that embodies an entire thought.

The interrelationships of the various principles become evident upon even the most casual examination. The effects indicated are not solely dependent upon the causes given. They are included primarily to clarify and express the thought desired.

This same group of military students, all of whom came out of the fire of World War II as Colonels, gave their own definition of the Principles of War as follows:

1. Objectives must be recognized, identified and clearly defined in order that every action may effectively contribute to the ultimate aim.
2. The proper selection of means and methods to attain the objectives within the resources and time available produce maximum returns with minimum expenditure of effort.
3. Coordination of effort achieves unified action and direction, with a minimum of complexity.
4. Exploitation of adaptability, mobility and flexibility assures maximum advantage in a changing situation.
5. Timely action based on utilization of all available knowledge achieves maximum effectiveness with minimum cost.
6. Concentration of sufficient effort is required at a decisive time and place to gain a favorable decision.
7. Aggressive action is necessary to secure the initiative and achieve positive results.
8. Deception causes faulty decisions and unprofitable commitments by the enemy.
9. Protective measures to reduce vulnerability must be taken to increase internal and external security.

While the words used in the foregoing passages may not be up to the literary standards of Clausewitz or Fuller, they do indicate an understanding of war not generally shared by the pure theoretician.

My second excerpt on the Principles of War comes from notes on views of the British Joint Chiefs of Staff in London during 1947.

Notes on the Principles of War as Approved by the Joint Chiefs of Staff in London

Introduction

1. The principles of war are not hard and fast laws or rules, such as the laws of natural science where the observance of certain conditions produces an inevitable result or the rules of a game, the breach of which entails a definite penalty.

2. The principles of war have been formulated as the result of reason and experience in war and are intended to provide guidance in the planning and execution of operations of war. They indicate methods of action that have proved successful in the past. Any plan of war-like action should normally conform to the principles of war if it is to achieve the maximum degree of success at minimum cost.

3. All the principles of war are not applicable to all situations at all times and their relative importance varies from time to time and from situation to situation.

4. The greatest degree of success in war is complete victory at the minimum cost. The cost of success is frequently influenced very greatly by observance or non-observance of the principles of war.

Development of the Principles of War

5. The principles of war as we know them today have been developed during the last hundred years. In the period between the two world wars a set of eight principles was formulated and promulgated in service manuals.

6. These principles were reviewed in the light of experience in the war of 1939-1945 and in July, 1947 the Chiefs of Staff Committee approved a set of ten principles for promulgation to al three services as a "guide to conduct." The principles are:

Selection and Maintenance of the Aim
Maintenance of Morale
Offensive Action
Security
Surprise
Concentration of Force
Economy of Effort

Flexibility
Co-operation
Administration

7. The Committee also approved definitions for these principles. These definitions and brief notes on each of the principles follow.

The Selection and Maintenance of the Aim

8. *Definition.* "In the conduct of war as a whole and in every operation of war, it is essential to decide on and clearly to define the aim. When once the aim has been decided on, all effort must be continually directed towards its attainment so long as it is attainable, and every plan or action must be tested by its bearing upon this end."

9. A nation, or a group of allies, will have a main strategic aim. Within this each service will have its own individual aim. These subsidiary aims must not conflict with the main aim but maintenance of the higher aim may, from time to time, necessitate diversions from the various subsidiary aims.

Maintenance of Morale

10. *Definition.* "Success in war depends more on morale than on physical qualities. Numbers, armament, resources or skill cannot compensate for lack of courage, energy, determination and the bold offensive spirit which springs from a national determination to conquer. The development and subsequent maintenance of the qualities of morale, are, therefore, essential to success in war."

11. There are five basic factors without which a high morale cannot exist. These are good leadership, good discipline, comradeship, self-respect, and a strong belief in the justice of our cause.

Offensive Action

12. *Definition.* "Offensive action is the necessary forerunner of victory; it may be delayed, but until the offensive is taken victory is impossible."

13. Offensive action is the only way to gain and retain the

222

initiative, and with it liberty of action. It tends to force a defensive attitude on the enemy, to raise the morale of our own forces and to lower that of the enemy.

Security

14. *Definition.* "A sufficient degree of security is essential in order to obtain freedom of action to launch a bold offensive in pursuit of the selected aim. This entails adequate defense of vulnerable bases and other interests which are vital to the nation or the armed forces. Security does not imply undue caution and avoidance of all risks, for bold action is essential to success in war; on the contrary, with security provided for, unexpected developments are unlikely to interfere seriously with the pursuit of a vigorous offensive."

15. Great Britain's war potential can be developed and her forces deployed only if we have secure bases in which to develop our resources, and secure lines of communication.

Surprise

16. *Definition.* "Surprise is a most effective and powerful weapon in war, and its morale effect is very great. Every effort must be made to surprise the enemy and to guard against being surprised. By the use of surprise, results out of all proportion to the effort expended can be obtained, and in some operations, when other factors are unfavorable, surprise may be essential to success. Surprise can be achieved strategically, tactically or by exploiting new material. The elements of surprise are secrecy, concealment, deception, originality, audacity, and rapidity."

17. It is little use obtaining surprise unless you are prepared to exploit it. Given time, the enemy will regroup his forces to meet an unexpected attack and will develop countermeasures to new methods and new weapons. The benefits of surprise must be reaped before he does so.

Concentration of Force

18. *Definition.* "To achieve success in war, it is essential to concentrate superior force, moral or material, to that of the enemy at the decisive time and place. Concentration does not necessarily imply a massing of forces, but rather having them so disposed

223

as to be able to unite when and where required to deliver the decisive blow."

19. Air forces have a special ability to concentrate rapidly at any point within range of their bases. Concentration may be in terms of time or space or effect. Thus aircraft may attack a number of targets simultaneously, they may attack one target in waves over a period of time or their efforts may be concentrated to obtain a particular effect, say the disruption of the enemy's transportation system.

Economy of Effort

20. *Definition.* "Economy of effort implies a balanced employment of forces, and a judicious expenditure of all resources with the object of achieving an effective concentration at the decisive time and place."

21. In war there are seldom sufficient resources available to meet all needs. If we are to be able to concentrate superior force when and where it is required, we must not waste any effort. This does not mean keeping aircraft idle on the ground. It means that aircraft must have a definite task to perform whenever they are sent off, that diversions must be reduced to a minimum, and that a thousand aircraft must not be sent to do a job that can be done by two hundred.

Flexibility

22. *Definition.* "Modern war demands a high degree of flexibility to enable pre-arranged plans to be altered to meet changing situations and unexpected developments. By strategical and tactical flexibility, force can be concentrated rapidly and economically at decisive places and times. This entails good training, organization, discipline and staff work, and above all, that rapidity of decision on the part of the commander which ensures that time is never lost."

23. Within range of their bases aircraft are extremely flexible but, with the increase in equipment required to maintain them and to provide the necessary aids, the move of air forces between theatres is becoming increasingly difficult and slow. Air Forces have now reached the stage where a compromise must be made between operational efficiency and strategic flexibility.

224

Co-operation

24. *Definition.* "Co-operation is based on team spirit and entails the coordination of all units so as to achieve the maximum combined effort from the whole. Above all, goodwill and the desire to co-operate are essential at all levels. The increased interdependence of the services on one another and on the civilian war effort has made co-operation between them of vital importance in modern war."

Administration

25. *Definition.* "The administrative arrangements must be designed to give the commanders the maximum freedom of action in carrying out the plan. Every administrative organization must be simple. Every operational commander must have a degree of control over the administrative plan within his sphere of command, corresponding to the scope of his responsibilities for the operational plan."

26. Administrative arrangements, including the resources available and the organization for getting them to the right place at the right time, must be capable of meeting the strain imposed on them by the operational plan. If they are not, they must be made so or, if this is impracticable, the operational plan must be modified.

In the last two chapters, I have attempted to explain cost/effectiveness and the Principles of War. Thoughtful analysis of the meaning of cost/effectiveness and the meaning of the Principles of War should give every American reason to doubt that the theoretical and computerized approach to national security planning currently in vogue is *completely* valid. In this government's current passion for the application of cost/effectiveness techniques, it seems to have forgotten the Principles of War and the lessons of history. Some in our government also seem to have forgotten that technology does not stand still and that the gross power curves of competing nations are bound to change.

Chapter XIV

BASIC POWER FACTORS

Like the Principles of War, basic power factors have many interrelationships. Some analysts would probably prefer to call these factors "sources of national strength." Probably no two well-informed people would use the same terminology or the same matrix as a basis for thoughful appraisal, but there would be a wide area of fundamental agreement. This chapter reduces the subject matter into areas which are useful, in a military sense, in analysis of the complex world in which we live.

During the years immediately following World War II, America's senior military schools (The National War College, The Industrial College, The Air War College, The Naval War College, and The Army War College), were indoctrinating senior military students in political-military affairs by emphasizing the interrelationship of four fundamental elements of national strength. The principal elements which constituted the total U.S. national strength, under the generally sound theory of various curricula of the time, were:

1. The economic strength of the nation.
2. The political strength.
3. The psychological strength.
4. The military strength of the nation.

During the ten years which followed, the influence of an expanding technology as a basic power factor was generally recognized. Its importance merited classification of this element of national power as a separate entity, along with the four already identified. Therefore, in generalizing the theory of national security, most military students of today think of five elements of national power which merit careful study, concentration of effort, and specific correlation with the activities related directly to the other elements of national power. Accordingly, a practical approach to national security planning requires simultaneous consideration of the economic, political, psychological, military, and technological factors which bear on the problem.

When the procedures and techniques of cost/effectiveness and the Principles of War are applied to any problem within this context, a necessity immediately arises for specific definition of the terms of reference. Cost/effectiveness procedures and the Principles of War cannot be applied in a vacuum. They must have some relationship to the real world in which we live; and the real world involves identification of the dominant basic power factors which exist on both sides of the Iron Curtain. Discussion of the more important of these basic power factors follows.

Geography

In a military sense, the geography of the world has overriding importance. There are geographical advantages and disadvantages which the nation inherits by virtue of the shape and climate of its country and the relationship of geographic masses.

227

In the current conflict with the Communist powers, the geography of the world provides a distinct advantage to the U.S.S.R. and to Communist China. The U.S.S.R. has direct access to Eastern and Western Europe through land lines of communication No sea-borne effort, or the protection of sea-borne forces, is required for any military adventure which the Soviets might elect in Eurasia. The Chinese Communists, likewise, have direct land lines of communication to Southeast Asia.

Therefore, in any conflict on the land mass of Eurasia between the United States and the U.S.S.R. and/or China, Free World forces would have to be moved great distances over water (either by ship or air) and would have to be supported logistically through these long air and sea lines of communication. The United States was able to do this in World War II, and could possibly do it again, but this nation must recognize, in military planning, the logistical advantages of the enemy in any war which might involve large numbers of troops and enormous quantities of supplies. This problem of logistical advantage of the enemy on the Eurasian land mass was one of the very impelling reasons which led the United States in 1949 towards an adoption of a nuclear strategy. The great destructive power inherent in nuclear weapons would reduce the requirement for logistical support by a factor not measurable in terms of any previous military experience. As America formulates a strategy for the future, she must bear in mind that the geography of the world has not changed.

In assessing the unchanging power factor explicit in the geographic disposition of oceans and land masses, the works of man nevertheless have been able to influence the *over-all importance* of these fundamental relationships. For example, the concentration of human populations in selected areas on both sides of the Iron Curtain provide an assessment of the vulnerability of these populations to a given number of nuclear weapons. Also the number, disposition, and dispersion of targets of strategic military value on both sides of the Iron Curtain are of tremendous military significance. Such assessments have been made by intelligence systems on both sides of the Curtain. The results of these studies show striking differences with respect to the basic vulnerability characteristics of the opposing major powers. Without revealing classified security planning data it can be stated that the population and industrial base of the United States is much more concentrated than that of the U.S.S.R. and Red China. Conversely, the dispersion of U.S. military forces, of real significance, is much greater than that which exists on the other side of the Iron Curtain. This circumstance might suggest to Soviet strategic planners that it would be easier to destroy the cities and the industry of the United States rather than to attempt to attack U.S. military forces directly. It might also suggest to U.S. strategic planners that America would have an advantage in any nuclear war in which both sides elected to attack military targets only. There are so many imponderables in this equation (both political and military) that no group of planners, on either side of the Iron Curtain, can predict the course of events with certainty. However, the average citizen can take some comfort in knowledge of the fact that relationships of this kind are studied intensively year after year, in the unceasing attempt to find the best solution for safeguarding the security of the United States and the Free World.

Population

Another commonly recognized power factor is the demographic, or population, element. The population of Red China and the U.S.S.R. is very great. China, in particular, can afford to lose scores of millions of people without any material impact on her present power capability. In addition, the present mentality of Red Chinese leadership is such that scores of millions of people are considered expendable.

The population equation, in military terms, means simply that a man-to-man, rifle and bayonet type of war would give another tremendous advantage to the enemy. Not only are

229

the United States and the Free World outnumbered, but we put a value on human life which the enemy does not understand or practice. This demographic element of the problem therefore again influenced the decision of NSC-68 in 1950 to rely upon a superior technology and on nuclear fire power in any major conflict with Communist powers. In formulating Free World strategy for the future, America must also remember that this basic power factor has not materially changed, nor, I dare say, will it shift.

However, the demographic equation is not all in favor of the Communists. There remains the question of quality as opposed to quantity. Our high standards of general education, health and sanitation, the motivation for maintaining a free society, and basic respect for a world of law and order are powerful forces which no dictatorial system has ever been able to match.

In confronting the challenges of the world, we have been poorly led at times, and have started late. But once aroused to the danger, the latent strength of our society has been equal to the challenge. As a corollary to this observation, the military planner worries about a future in which there might be no traditional opportunity for the mobilization of latent psychological and material strength.

The leadership of the nation also comes out of the demographic equation. In the long pull, we get the kind of top leadership which we want. However, top leadership, selected through the functioning of our system of government, has special opportunities and special obligations. It has special opportunities because it knows *all* the secrets, while the general public knows only a few. It has special obligations *to lead*, not follow, because it *does have all the information* available to the government as a whole.

Industrialization

Probably the greatest element of strength of the United States during the World War II period was its industrialization and capacity for massive production. This nation was operating from a *secure* industrial base, and it did produce fantastic quantities of war materials. No nation, or combination of nations, at that period in history could out-produce the United States. America still has a great industrial base, but the rest of the world has not remained stagnant. Frantic efforts are under way both in the U.S.S.R. and China to improve the capacity and efficiency of their industrial base.

In addition, in formulating U.S. basic national security strategy for the future, Americans must also constantly bear in mind that our industrial base is *no longer* invulnerable. This nation must rely as an absolute matter of fact, at any point of time, on the adequacy of the U.S. military forces-in-being which have already been created by a functioning U.S. technology and industry. Therefore, the existence of nuclear fire power works for this nation in two ways, and works against it in one way. Through the existence of nuclear fire power the United States can overcome the geographic and population disadvantages, but, at the same time, the existence of such fire power might render our own superior industrial position meaningless in the actual conduct of nuclear war.

Industrialization concomittantly involves activities which are of great importance in their own right. The development of a powerful industrial base automatically stimulates advances in, and national reliance upon, communications systems, transportation systems, storage and warehousing systems and consumer-distribution systems. Which came first —the chicken or the egg—in the interrelationship of these various activities is beside the point. Actually, they all grew together. But from a military viewpoint, all these activities are a thing of reality, and pose problems of vulnerability in event of war.

The survival of a primitive society, living close to the soil, is not dependent upon mass planting and harvesting of food, mass storage, mass transportation, mass warehousing and distribution, and mass production of material and services. A highly industrialized society is dependent upon these services.

Food at the local grocery stores, automobile fuel at the local pump, gas and electric power to light and heat the house, water in the faucet, and sewage disposal are all a part of the vast industrialization of the United States and much of Europe.

From a military viewpoint, industrialization is therefore a two-edged sword. It has given us a high standard of living and the capability to produce the most modern weapons of war, but it has made us extremely vulnerable as well.

The military planner would not turn the clock back to the days of the Pilgrims; he accepts industrialization as a fact of life. But he is aware of the dangers as well as the advantages of the movement of society away from the soil.

National Resources

The existence of basic national resources such as productive land, petroleum, timber, metals, coal, and other natural resources of power (such as inland waterways which could be damned to produce electric current) need only be mentioned as fundamental elements of national power. The United States and Canada, in fact all of the Western Hemisphere, have been blessed by an abundance of natural resources. Without these resources the United States could never have become a major power in the modern world. However, this is not a one-sided advantage. The existing natural resources of the Communist bloc are also virtually inexhaustible and many of these resources have not yet been exploited. In long-term planning for future security, the real significance of an appreciation of natural resources lies in contemporary measures to conserve these resources in order that future generations will have the same tools with which to work as have had present and past generations.

National Intelligence

A businessman cannot strive in a free enterprise system unless he is aware of the environment in which he conducts

232

his business. He must know his own product, he must know his customer, and he must know the business competition which is attempting to take his customer away from him. A nation is in much the same position. It cannot operate in ignorance of the world which surrounds it. "Intelligence," in the military sense (that is, knowledge of world circumstances and knowledge of the activities of friend and foe alike), is an indispensable element among the power factors which control the destiny of nations.

The intelligence problem of the Free World is difficult because of the Iron Curtain and because of the suppression of freedom of the press in Communist-dominated countries. Conversely, free societies are open societies. They freely provide their opponents with everything up to and sometimes even including their most vital national security information. This is a handicap which the Free World must continue to accept. To do otherwise would defeat the purposes of democracy and the free way of life.

The Free World intelligence mission, then, is to rip the curtain of secrecy which shrouds those nations that have developed a closed society under dictatorial rule. The Free World has already done much to destroy this curtain, but much more needs to be done.

In fact, if the total product of the various national intelligence activities could become complete enough to lay before the world the technical and political secrets locked behind the Iron Curtain, and at the same time devise a means to illuminate those darkened nations with the truth from the Western World, the Iron Curtain would evaporate. Then an open society *would have* to develop in Communist countries. Under the circumstances of enlightened exposure, the Communist conspiracy could not long endure and a universally free world might be brought into being. It is, therefore, the height of folly for Americans to criticize our Federal Bureau of Investigation, our Central Intelligence Agency, and the intelligence agencies of the military services and the Free World in general. Indeed, the United States would do well to

233

put more effort into all forms of intelligence. Such a course might be the one sure method of striking at the Achilles heel of Communist aspirations for world domination.

Force-in-Being

We have already discussed at length the importance of existing force-in-being in a nuclear war. The importance of an adequate existing force, constantly ready to fight, cannot be over-emphasized as an instrument for preserving the peace. However, we should never assess the adequacy of a force-in-being only in terms of its theoretical power to deter war. Deterrence of war is a result of psychological reactions, and attitudes and circumstances of people in authority on the other side of the Iron Curtain. Their minds might work differently than our minds and what we had considered to be an adequate force-in-being for the purpose of deterrence might not be so judged by the leaders of the Communist world. Accordingly, the only criterion by which the adequacy of a force-in-being can be judged is its actual capacity to fight and win a major war if one should be thrust upon us through the failure of deterrence.

Science and Technology

The importance of science and technology and the military research and development programs which emanate from these areas of human interest have been referred to frequently in this text. However, redundancy notwithstanding, any thoughtful analysis of *basic power factors* requires that these elements again be considered. Possibly the importance of this power factor can best be emphasized by asking two simple questions:

1. What basic strategy for the survival of the Free World is available if, in addition to its manpower and geographical advantages, the Communist powers were to develop a military technology superior to our own?

234

2. What is the military significance of U.S. science and technology "on the shelf" which has not been translated into fighting hardware and which is not in the hands of the fighting forces?

Governmental Structure and Procedures

Geography, population, national resources, and military forces-in-being can be tangibly measured. As a result, they are easier to comprehend as elements of national power than the more intangible aspects of power relationships. One such important basic power factor, not susceptible to precise human measurement, is the structure and philosophy of government and the procedures it uses to obtain its national objectives. The governmental structure and procedures of Communist nations versus those of the Free World contrast sharply.

The Communist system has advantages in that, being a totalitarian dictatorship, it can react very quickly to any specific circumstance. It can change its courses of action without popular support or popular understanding of the reasons. A dictatorship can abrogate treaties, change allies, go to war, or immediately focus its energies on any circumstance of the moment which appears to offer advantage to the Communist objective. It has no principle to which it must adhere, and in fact, regards international treaties—in the words of Stalin—as "scraps of paper."

On the other hand, a free society is guided by continuity of principle, respect for the given word, and absolute understanding by the civilian population of the motives and the conduct of the government. This imbalance of political philosophy causes a free society to be much more cumbersome in a changing and dynamic world.

However, the whole-hearted dedication of a people to the purposes of its government can never be achieved under a totalitarian dictatorship, whether the effort be in the field of science, industrial production, agricultural production, or in military affairs. Consequently, the advantages inherent in a democracy far outweigh the short-term tactical advantages which sometimes accrue to a monolithic totalitarian system of government. The United States military problem, therefore, is one of recognizing the potential tactical advantages which might accrue to the Communist system. At the same time, this nation of ours must labor to develop systems, techniques, and procedures which can nullify these advantages, thus ensuring that the American democratic system survives *and* thrives.

Chapter XV

COMMONLY MISUNDERSTOOD
DEFENSE ISSUES

Technology is moving and expanding so rapidly these days that persons of timid instinct and uncertain views consider it to be "dangerous" to be identified as protagonist for any one weapon system—dangerous in the sense that a year later they might be proved to be wrong. Nevertheless, somewhere along the military chain of command, someone must be resolute and say, "Let's try to build this one," otherwise there would be no weapons arsenal for the future. The Army, Navy, and Air Force would always be waiting for the next sure step, the technological advance just beyond. Continually involved in the incremental improvement of existing weapons systems, the military services would always be changing toward perfection in paper studies of new weapons systems. And eventually they would have no effective fighting hardware.

Like a constantly changing technology, political-military relationships also change throughout the world, and it is easier for the timid mind to say, "Let's allow the dust to settle," than it is to make a firm decision.

Being aware of the dangers associated with commenting on specific weapons system projects and issues involving political-military judgment, I have nevertheless felt compelled and obligated to do so throughout this text. After all, it was my obligation to recommend specific action on these problems while on active duty and I see no reason for now avoiding that which, to a military man, is a continuing and lifetime responsibility. Therefore, in this chapter I will give my own views on some commonly misunderstood issues which have not emerged as specific topics in the discussion of the evolution of our basic national security policy.

The subjects which appear to merit additional discussion are: first, the executive control of nuclear weapons; second, the acquisition of new combat aircraft; third, the nuclear-powered aircraft carrier; and fourth, the nature of the Russian military apparatus.

The Control of Nuclear Weapons

This issue was of major importance in public debate during the Presidential election campaign of 1964. Presidential-hopeful Senator Goldwater apparently initiated the argument.

Why this particular security issue was ever interjected into the campaign debates will probably never be generally known. However, from the press treatment of the issue during the campaign, it was obvious that the subject is not too well understood. And, in my judgment, its fundamentals are of such far-reaching importance that the American public must understand the issue of nuclear weapons control and be in position to make their own informed judgments now, and perhaps during the next Presidential campaign.

The issue, as presented in the 1964 Presidential campaign was, in fact, nonexistent. The nation's press, I'm afraid, did not present the issue completely.

I do not subscribe to the cliché that national defense issues are too complex for the American public to understand. The public *can* understand the issues, if the public is told the truth within the limits of actual military and political security requirements as differentiated from political administration tactics.

An understanding of this problem requires a correlative understanding of other actions which have been taken in recent years toward complete centralization of control of many very important defense activities. We have already seen the creation of a centralized Department of Defense Intelligence Agency, the centralization of control of public information, the centralization of control of supply activities, the centralization of control of communications activities, and the centralization of control of nuclear energy matters as they pertain to national defense.

All of these separate actions have implications of great importance for the future. But I think it is extremely important that the now controversial issue of the control of nuclear weapons be understood in the context of the other concurrent actions which have been taking place during the last several years.

In looking at this problem it is necessary to start out with an examination of unclassified facts. The FACTS are as follows:

Fact No. 1. Nuclear weapons *are* extremely powerful. In the absence of a military defensive system and an effective civil defense organization, a highly industrialized nation can be crippled by a surprise attack which would render helpless both its production base and the bulk of its strategic retaliatory forces.

Fact No. 2. There has never been any doubt or argument, since the first nuclear weapon was invented, as to civilian or military control. In the first place, the Atomic Energy Act specifically requires Presidential approval before nuclear weapons are used by this nation. In the second place, the President is also the Commander-in-Chief of the Armed Forces and controls basic decisions to use rifle fire, mortar fire, naval bombardment, et cetera, as well as nuclear fire power.

Fact No. 3. From the beginning of the nuclear age, the

239

professional military establishment has been aware of the possible consequences of an unauthorized, or accidental use of nuclear weapons. The leadership in establishing proper operational, logistic, and technical steps to prevent such accidental or unauthorized use was taken by the professional, uniformed military corps many years before the current crop of pseudo-intellectuals even understood the problem. The means by which we exercised control must remain classified; however, our record, Air Force, Navy, Army, and Marine Corps speaks for itself. We have had no nuclear accidents nor incidents, and we maintained this record for many years before the intellectual refugees from the Nuclear Age became influential in this area of military responsibility. There can be no argument in terms of the military intent, our support of the President and civilian authority, our military innovations to control the problem, nor of the results which we achieved. Our record, that is, *the record of the professional uniformed military establishment*, speaks for itself—in both peace and war.

Fact No. 4. Today, America and its Free World allies still confront a Communist conspiracy which, for over forty years, has been dedicated to an unswerving objective to destroy free institutions, the free way of life, and free republican government. The recently deposed head of the U.S.S.R., Khrushchev, openly swore to bury the Four Freedoms by one means or another. I personally had long conversations with him and his contemporaries in Moscow in June, 1956, and will discuss this trip later. But for the moment, I saw absolutely no evidence that during his tenure as the Communist leader, Khrushchev ever changed or even contemplated a modification of the ultimate objective of the Communist movement in favor of one of "peaceful coexistence." And I have seen no evidence that the present leaders of either Moscow or Peiping wish to abandon the longstanding basic objectives of communism.

Fact No. 5. The United States has deterred a nuclear war

240

so far by confronting the U.S.S.R. and Red China with the uncomfortable assurance of their own destruction if either Europe or the United States were attacked. This assurance, to offer exacting validity, had to have some substance—it had to be real, not a bluff. The Soviet espionage apparatus, operating in our open society, would have known instantly if it were a bluff.

Fact No. 6. If a general war situation were to be brought about through Communist aggression, and if the United States failed to use its nuclear weapons in that war, the two seats of Communist power on the land mass of Asia would have virtually an impregnable manpower and logistic advantage in any military adventure against Western Europe or Southeast Asia. Both Russia and China literally have manpower to burn, and would be willing to burn it for success. They also have interior land lines of communication for logistic support of any military operation in Eurasia. And it is well to remember that U.S. and Free World sea lanes of communication are confronted today with a Soviet submarine force at least five times as great as that of the German U-boat force of World War II.

Fact No. 7. One of the most disturbing aspects confronting the Free World today is that the Soviet governmental apparatus is such that surprise attack on the United States or upon any of its allies could be launched simply on the basis of decision by the Kremlin, for whatever reason, logical or illogical. Indicative of the whimsical attitude of the Red Presidium is that more than fifty solemn covenants and treaties entered into by the Soviet Union have been violated by them during the short span of its existence. Red China, of course, is even more unreliable and unpredictable.

Fact No. 8. The President of the United States cannot personally deliver very many nuclear weapons. Somewhere along the line a trained and ready military organization must be capable of doing the job. This has been necessary in order to preserve the peace of the world in the face of Communist imperialism, and would be necessary to prevent defeat in event of a nuclear attack on the United States by Communist powers. Now, fighting forces, whether infantrymen, sailors on battlecraft at sea, combat aircraft crews, or missilemen, cannot do their jobs if their ammunition is locked up in some far-removed, inaccessible vault. Even conventional, non-nuclear war can move too quickly if one side can't shoot. Nuclear war could, of course, move much more quickly.

The facts stated above cannot be disputed by rational men. However, facts are not all that is involved. Judgment and logic also play a part. As a first step in elementary logic, under the circumstance of the undeniable facts, any responsible Chief Executive must consider what would happen to the nation if he were to be immobilized or incapacitated, or if Washington, D.C., were to disappear as the result of a surprise attack. Could the Chief Executive accept a command and control system which would paralyze the nation's military forces if he were unable to act personally? If he were inclined to accept such a gamble, would Soviet espionage detect it, and strike in certain knowledge that retaliation could not be triggered in time to be militarily useful?

The President does carry the responsibility for such emergency actions as are necessary to protect the nation. He also exercises civilian control over the military establishment. In fact, the nation and its soldiery have fought several wars to preserve this concept, among other American traditions and values.

As I mentioned earlier in this chapter, nuclear weapons are extremely powerful; they are the most powerful weapons that exist today, just as the weapons created from the discovery of dynamite were the most powerful of their time (and thought to be the most powerful that would ever be created). However, man has not yet created anything for which he could not or *would not* assume responsibility and use to further human ends, unless, in panic and irrational fear, he allowed his creation to use and control him.

The problem, then, which does indeed exist and must be approached with the utmost awareness and skill, is how shall the responsibility for control and use of these weapons be assumed? How will the President, upon whose shoulders rests the ultimate decision, elect to exercise his ultimate authority over the control of rifle fire, mortar fire, fire from ships at sea, fire from aircraft, and nuclear fire power, *however delivered?*

In terms of basic logic, it would appear that he has only three options:

1. The President can shut his eyes to the facts and hope that nothing will happen.
2. He can maintain personal (and detailed) control at all times, making no provision for national response in event of massive damage to the seat of government.
3. He can predelegate authority to be exercised under certain grave circumstances.

With respect to the first option in terms of logic, no Chief Executive could be so derelict in his duty. With respect to the second, the Chief Executive would be inviting an enemy attack if the enemy knew that the United States would be paralyzed by the delivery of only one nuclear weapon on the seat of government.

On the basis of just plain common sense, therefore, it would appear that the third option—predelegation of authority to take military action in event of certain circumstances—can be the only valid solution to military fire control. This option might assume, of course, that so long as the President or his successor is alive and the government continues to function, that personal and detailed control would be maintained at White House level. But, if the nation were under attack, and there were no Washington, D.C., left, America could fight back rather than die with its own powerful force immobilized.

Just exactly how the President elects to choose and carry

243

out his option is, of course, his business for legitimate security reasons. A responsible and rational Chief Executive would no more tell a sworn enemy how he would trigger off a retaliatory blow than he would admit that he had no system at all.

The difficulty of executive nuclear-weapons responsibility finds its only basis in the militant and aggressive nature of the Communist mentality. Coexistence to any Communist leader means "coexist on my terms after surrendering your freedom." Even though some individuals of the Communist Presidium might be willing to settle for less than world domination, the Communist apparatus, as a whole, is caught up in a web of its own making. If it curtails subversion and aggression and moves toward a genuine basis for world peace, which must include an open society, it will destroy itself. This fact directly relates the grave problems of a possible general war situation in which nuclear weapons might be employed to "limited war" situations and the possible use of nuclear weapons in such "limited" situations.

Having been thus far deterred from a massive general attack through certain knowledge that they could not win—even in a surprise attack—subversion, guerrilla tactics, and limited wars have been the only outlets in the recent past through which the Communist apparatus could keep moving forward. This does not mean that the danger of general war or a massive surprise attack against the Free World is gone for good. It means that the Communist system knows that it would destroy itself at this moment in history in such an adventure. They are still plotting it, of course, and may someday be in position to attempt it, if they solve the problems of ballistic-missile defense, or anti-submarine warfare before America and its Free World allies do.

Therefore, it seems to me that the United States invites world-wide subversion—Congos, Cubas, and Vietnams and the like—*to be fought on the enemies' terms* if we continue to advise the enemy beforehand that we will *not* use tactical nuclear weapons in such encounters. Furthermore, this nation

244

invites surprise enemy attack and general war if it decides to advise the enemy that its military officials do not have predelegated authority to react under certain circumstances.

It might be accurately stated that one "question mark" and one issue of "basic morality" bear heavily on individual judgments on this problem.

The question might be stated as follows: "Will the use of tactical nuclear weapons, or predelegation of civilian authority to responsible field commanders automatically bring on a general nuclear exchange and the holocaust so feared by those among us who are trying to turn back the technological clock and to back out of the nuclear world?" In my judgment, the answer is emphatically, *No*.

The issue lies in the commitment to combat of young Americans, and the young men of other free nations in military encounter from which we withhold our best weapons. With regard to this most basic issue I inevitably came to the conclusion that the use of tactical nuclear weapons in certain limited war situations and employed selectively and with discretion could truly be in the over-all best interests of humanity and civilization. These weapons, if employed once or twice on the right targets, at the right time, would, in my judgment, stop *current* aggression, and stop *future* subversion and limited wars before they start. After all, in seeking a world of peace, Americans should be vitally interested in deterring limited war as well as general war, because the seeds of general war may sprout from a limited war situation. This great nation cannot deter limited war through a policy of weakness any more than it can deter a general war through elimination of its massive retaliatory capability.

Acquisition of New Combat Aircraft

All of the combat aircraft in the fighting inventory in 1965 were conceived, designed, and initial production funding approved before the start of the Kennedy Administration.

245

Some pertinent statistical details on the composition and origin of today's air fighting forces are given in the table on pages 260–61. The material shown in the table clearly indicates to me that this nation is now rapidly approaching an "airplane gap."

The U.S. Military Aircraft program, particularly in the development and acquisition of major new combat systems, has been dangerously retarded during the past ten years because of two factors: first, the impact of the ballistic missile program; and second, the research and development policies and the system acquisition policies which came into being under the Kennedy Administration, and which still persist as a powerful force as this book goes to press. These policies were conceived and directed chiefly by White House and Department of Defense scientific advisors and are rooted in the sterile logic of cost/effectiveness, the "building-block approach" to new systems, and the maintenance of capability to "exercise later options."

The ballistic missile force (land-based and sea-based) is absolutely necessary to national security. It was expensive— expensive in dollars, in the enormous requirements for technically trained manpower, and in the requirements for advanced technical facilities needed in its development. This drain on the national budget, on the industrial structure, and on the scientific community would have had an adverse impact on aeronautical development under any kind of national policy. In addition, the ballistic missile force was being phased into the United States arsenal of weapons to take over some of the tasks previously assigned to the military aircraft fleet. Hence, the basic requirement for some classes of aircraft, bombardment type aircraft in particular, became less apparent than in previous years. Those people who had always been instinctively hostile to aircraft (and they have been with us since the days of Billy Mitchell and before) rather enjoyed this situation. "Now we can get rid of the bomber!"

246

But, as a nation, it seems to me that we have allowed the pendulum to swing too far. We should have remembered that a surface ship at sea, moving in two dimensions at thirty knots, is still a very useful and strategically vital instrument of war. Yet, by comparison, an aircraft flying at only half the speed of sound (less than the speed of commercial jet airliners) can go ten times as far and be in an area a hundred times greater, in the same period of time, as the thirty-knot surface vessel. The mobility and the flexibility provided by these air and sea platforms has lasting military significance for both.

As a nation we should also have remembered: first, that a land-based ballistic missile force is much like a Maginot line: it can be pre-targeted, and it is relatively inflexible in terms of response to a dynamic and fluid battle situation.

Second, that the sea-based component of our ballistic missile force (POLARIS), while a vitally necessary weapons system, is extremely expensive and can be produced only in limited numbers. It, therefore, offers a very limited number of aiming points to a hostile power.

The United States Joint Chiefs of Staff did recognize these relationships. However, their civilian superiors have taken the matter less seriously and have consistently overridden the judgment of the Joint Chiefs of Staff that a mixed strategic force of both ballistic missiles and long-range bombardment aircraft is mandatory for the national security. That this nation has a mixed strategic force as of today, is due only to the fact that it was inherited from previous administrations. The nation is fatefully moving toward a circumstance, because of lack of a sound strategic program, in which it will have to rely predominantly on ballistic missiles.

The second factor which I mentioned as having an adverse impact on U.S. aeronautical development was the basic research and development policies which came into being under the Kennedy Administration. As I view it, the over-centralization of power in the Offices of the Secretary

247

of Defense, the endless reviews and the detailed technical direction exercised by the Defense Secretary, and the "building-block" philosophy of safe, incremental progress in the development of new systems—all these practices—have tended to slow down military technology of all kinds, particularly progress in the aeronautical sciences.

A drastic cutback in production of fixed-wing aircraft of all types of course accompanied the new research and development policy. The net result is that in the autumn of 1965 we were trying to support the air war in Vietnam, and provide replacements for aircraft lost in combat, by the renovation of aircraft which were over ten years old and by cannibalization of our Air National Guard.

It is interesting to note what was actually accomplished in aeronautical development from the end of World War II up to the late 1950's, and to compare that performance with the performance of recent years. In this brief example, I will talk only about U.S. Air Force aircraft, but the Navy has had much of the same experience with respect to the development of its basic weapons systems.

Not counting the B-25's, B-26's, B-17's, B-24's, B-29's, et cetera of World War II (or the B-36), during the period 1945–1956 the Air Force developed and flight tested at least sixteen different bomber-type aircraft. Additionally, it also studied and carried part way to development, short of flight testing, another dozen designs. In counting these various types of bombardment aircraft, I, of course, do not include as separate numbers modifications which are designated by a letter preceding or following the basic system designation. For example, I have counted the B-47 as one aircraft. This one number includes the XB-47, the YB-47C, the XB-47D, the B-47A/H and RB-47E/H. What I wish to emphasize is that the Air Force brought to flight test sixteen substantially different conceptual designs of bombardment aircraft during the period 1945–1956. From this program of "prototyping" and testing was determined what was best for large-scale

248

procurement. The over-all program resulted in the bombardment force of Boeing-built B-52's, Boeing-built B-47's, Convair-built B-58's, Martin-built B-57's, North American-built B-45's, and Douglas-built B-66's, all of which the current Secretary of Defense inherited.

The initial development contract for the Boeing B-52 heavy bomber series was awarded in June, 1946, and the first aircraft flew in April, 1952—over thirteen years ago. The *last* U.S. Air Force bomber to go into operational inventory (the Convair-built supersonic B-58) had an initial contract date of December, 1951, and made its first flight in November, 1956. The supersonic North American-built B-70 had in initial contract date of January, 1958, and made its first flight on September 21, 1964; but this aircraft is not slated for production.

Hence, in terms of our fleet of bombers, design specifications for the backbone of the force (the B-52) were laid down in 1946, and the supersonic B-58 (only about 100 of which were built) was designed in 1951.

Now, if we were to assume that a follow-on bomber is needed to give flexibility to this nation's strategic posture (thus offsetting the Maginot line characteristics of our ballistic missile forces) and that the Air Force were authorized to go forward today with such a program, America might expect a new strategic bomber in the operating inventory no earlier than 1974. This would be about twenty-two years after the first B-52 flight and about eighteen years after the first B-58 flight.

Much the same pattern is found when examining our development program for new fighter-type aircraft. Following World War II, and through 1956, the U.S. Air Force and its partners in industry developed twenty-three separate and unique fighter-type aircraft. From among these competing prototype designs, produced in small numbers, the Air Force selected the F-84's, F-86's, and the 100 series of fighters which are now in the USAF combat inventory. Between

1956 and the end of 1964, a nine-year gap, there was no "first flight" of a new production series of high-performance USAF fighters.

Of course, the nation can point with pride to a few *special* things which were done in fighter aircraft development. Unfortunately, it cannot be reflected in a large *combat* inventory of fighting machines. For example, the U-2 high altitude reconnaissance aircraft was designed in the early 1950's and was operational from foreign soil by 1955. The existence of the A-11, an advanced supersonic follow-up to the U-2, was announced to the world by President Johnson in February, 1965. However, this aircraft was conceived in 1958 and its production approved in 1959. The A-11, incidentally, has been given several alias designations such as the YF-12 and the SR-71 in recent years. Whether or not these designations were for political purposes I cannot say. However, the press treatment was such as to generally credit the incumbent Administration with the results of a program conceived and implemented long before. Regardless of what it is now called, or the military uses to which it will be put, the A-11 family of aircraft was inherited by the Kennedy-Johnson Administrations.

In the construction of the A-11, extensive use was made of the lightweight, high-strength metal Titanium. This fact bears on the handling by civilian defense officials of another airplane which must be discussed—the highly controversial TFX fighter airplane.*

The Kennedy Administration can properly claim responsibility for the decision to go ahead with the TFX program, but serious questions have been raised with respect to the award of the contract and with respect to the decision by civilian defense officials that the aircraft should be used by both the Air Force and the Navy.

* The Air Force version of the TFX is now called the F-111A; the Navy version the F-111B.

It will be recalled that the contract for development and production of the TFX was awarded, in November 1962, to the General Dynamics Corporation while the uniformed officials of both the Air Force and Navy felt that the Boeing Company had the best design. Congress later investigated the award, and in that investigation one of the reasons given by civilian defense officials for awarding the contract to General Dynamics was that the Boeing design used too much of the "unproven metal" Titanium. This testimony was given at a time when the Secretary of Defense must have been aware of the substantial use of Titanium in the construction of the A-11. Military officials were aware, of course, but the A-11 was then a highly classified project and, as a consequence, the facts did not emerge until later. The professional military voice was effectively muzzled. The net result in my opinion was that the Congress of the United States apparently was given misleading information.

With respect to the use of the TFX by both the Air Force and the United States Navy, the record also needs some straightening out. The requirement for and the general characteristics of the TFX were developed during the later days of the Eisenhower Administration as an Air Force follow-on tactical fighter to replace the aging fleet of F-100's, F-84's and F-105's. Conceptually, the airplane was to be optimized for low-altitude nuclear attack, with all other roles secondary. Responsible Air Force planners wanted the airplane for this purpose and would still like to have it for this mission. It will be remembered that, at the time, our national military policy was founded on the use of nuclear weapons both tactically and strategically in any major military confrontation. A high-performance, high-cost aircraft was therefore both logical and necessary. The "go-ahead" on the program was considered by Secretary of Defense Thomas Gates, who preceded Secretary McNamara, but Gates decided, because of the short time he had to remain in office, to leave the final decision to his successor.

In the study of the program which followed, the basic concept behind the airplane became somewhat obscured, and decision was made by the new Secretary of Defense to make the airplane suitable to Navy requirements as well as Air Force requirements.

Under the new concept, the airplane was to be created to serve as a multiple-purpose aircraft, suitable for both carrier-based operations and land-based operations, and suitable for employment in a wide variety of missions by both the Navy and the Air Force. It was to be a cost/effectiveness miracle. It was to be a general air superiority airplane which could fight other aircraft at both high and low altitudes; a strike airplane which could deliver both nuclear and conventional weapons on surface targets; a direct-support airplane for joint operations with Army ground forces; a strike-reconnaissance aircraft; an airplane which could loiter for long periods of time while airborne; and an airplane with supersonic capabilities at both very low and high altitudes. This would indeed be an ideal aircraft—if you could get it, afford it, operate it, maintain it, and use it effectively in all these roles.

However, these various mission requirements involve different operational techniques and different methods of logistic support. When aircraft design compromises are attempted in order to meet competing requirements, past experience has indicated that the resulting hybrid machine cannot perform any one of its missions in an optimum manner.

As an example, a carrier-based aircraft can be designed with very hard tires and small wheels because it lands on the steel deck of an aircraft carrier or on a prepared hard-surface runway. A landing gear entirely suitable for such purposes might bog down in mud, or break up the runway in operations from relatively primitive, forward airstrips which base aircraft providing direct close support to Army ground forces.

In another design area, ordinarily the nature of the electronic gear carried in the aircraft is determined by the mission to be performed. It takes one kind of an integrated air-ground system to shoot at an air target, and a different kind of a system to attack targets on the ground. During my last review of the TFX program, it looked to me like the Navy had decided to equip its part of the TFX force with electronic gear focused on one basic mission—air defense of the Fleet. This was probably a sound decision under the circumstances. The Air Force, however, seemed to be going ahead in an attempt to make the airplane all-purpose, and was running into a nightmare of electronic and avionic problems.

When an engineer tries to jam all the electronics necessary to do everything into one airplane, three things normally happen: first, if the airplane is of reasonable size and weight, it becomes very dense, complicated, and difficult to maintain; second, it becomes very expensive; and third, the performance of the aircraft for any one specific mission is degraded because it is carrying around, as excess baggage, avionic systems not needed for the particular mission.

When the size and weight of the airplane get out of hand, serious consequences can result. In attempting to design an airplane suitable for both sea-based use and land-based use, the design becomes more of a problem for the Navy than for the Air Force. The reason is that carrier-based aircraft are more severely limited by the space aboard an aircraft carrier (in terms of gross dimensions and gross allowable weight) than are their land-based counterparts. Because of this fact, the TFX weight problem has been a major headache to the Navy since the inception of the paper study of the program.

The analysis of cost to the taxpayer of new weapons systems is also very complex and frequently misunderstood. And here again we run into some of the problems associated with the TFX. Under Secretary McNamara's concept, the aircraft was supposed to save money because of its

253

multi-service multiple-purpose application. But will it really save money when employed in combat? The TFX aircraft has become a very expensive machine, something on the order of three to seven million dollars per copy—the unit cost depending on specific configuration and the number of aircraft which will be built.

The cost factor assumes particular importance when the aircraft is limited to the use of conventional weapons. Many aircraft missions using conventional munitions are required to effect lasting damage to most targets of major military importance. This means that the aircraft and crews are exposed to enemy defensive fire many times. Even though it is generally cheaper in the long run—cheaper both in lives lost and in dollars—to use aircraft for certain operations, rather than ground forces, the competent military planner would like to have a flying machine which "does its job" favorably when all factors are considered during its lifetime of combat. The over-all problem constitutes the challenge to sound technical, logistical, and operational planning and, as such, receives detailed attention from the military services. And such attention is not confined purely to theoretical cost/effectiveness studies.

My own judgment on the TFX (F-111A, F-111B, B-111) is that the Air Force and the Navy need the technical, operational, and logistic experience with variable geometry aircraft which will accrue from the program.

However, the F-111 airplane is very expensive and I fear it is not adaptable, on an economical basis, to close support of ground forces when it employs conventional weapons. Who wishes to lose, as a matter of practice, a five- or six-million-dollar airplane to small-arms ground fire which costs the enemy next to nothing when compared to the price of the airplane and its highly trained crew? In terms of the air superiority role of the F-111, other aircraft already in the fighting inventory provide an acceptable substitute for its high-altitude performance capabilities as a fighter type air-

254

craft. With respect to the "strategic" version of the F-111 in a slightly modified form called the B-111, the range of the aircraft is limited and its over-all electronic capability is not really adequate for the strategic mission.

However, so much time has passed without initiation of other more suitable aircraft programs that the Air Force now faces a dilemma. In addition to acceptance of the TFX as an all-purpose fighter-bomber type airplane, it will necessarily have to accept the F-111 in the hashed-up B-111 version or have nothing at all to replace the strategic bombardment force which is being "phased-out."

The strategic nuclear B-47's (of which we once had about 1,400) have already been retired from the combat inventory and the B-52's and B-58's are on the way out. Under the current phase-out schedule, the B-52 force will be down to about 220 to 230 aircraft by about 1969 and the supersonic B-58 will be disappearing from the inventory. Even if decision were made in the fall of 1965 to go full speed ahead on the acquisition of a new strategic bomber, it would be about 1974 before it became a reliable weapon in the hands of the fighting forces.

The very rapid phase out of the B-52's and B-58's should raise some serious questions from the United States Congress. These aircraft have been bought and paid for, their logistic base and the trained crews are in-being. Some of the aircraft which are headed for the boneyard are still operable and maintainable. The questions which come to my mind are these: first, is this early retirement of the bombardment force related to the Wiesner concept of "parity" and "stability"? Or second, are we deliberately, on the basis of some secret understanding with the U.S.S.R., cutting our bombardment forces down to the size of the Soviet bombardment forces? Or third, having effectively blocked the development of a new bomber, are we now hastening the retirement of those already bought and paid for as a gesture of appeasement to the U.S.S.R.?

Whatever the reason for the policy decisions which are dominant, it is a fact of life that the strategic bombardment force of the Air Force will, in a few brief years, be about one-tenth of the force available in 1960. At the present time, this unhappy circumstance could be partially ameliorated by accepting a number of B-111's as an interim measure. Certainly, the B-111 would be better than nothing, particularly in helping to keep in existence the trained combat crews and the logistic base necessary for a strategic aircraft force. It takes a long time to build this kind of a base, and like the forces of World War II, the structure can be quickly destroyed by executive action.

The TFX series of aircraft will undoubtedly be fine flying machines. After all, they should be. They will cost millions of dollars per article, they represent the latest technology, and they are being built by reliable and competent industrial organizations. However, it seems to me that our Air Force would have possessed better all-around fighting capability across the spectrum of war if we had to put the six to nine billion dollars, which the planned production of this aircraft will cost, into two different aircraft:

1. A relatively simple and inexpensive direct support aircraft tailored specifically for support of our ground forces.
2. A modern bomber to follow the aging force of B-52's and B-58's.

Looking hopefully toward the future, the aerodynamic advances represented by the TFX series might yet be applied (belatedly) to a larger aircraft which would have the range and payload adequate for a strategic aircraft system, now designated as the Advanced Manned Strategic Aircraft. Such aircraft have already been through the preliminary design stage and can be built. In addition to meeting the military requirement, the acquisition of such aircraft would undoubtedly assist in the research and development effort which was necessary to meet the civilian requirement for a super-

256

sonic transport. However, in the light of current trends, this is all probably wishful thinking.

Paralleling the "gap" in strategic aircraft development, a startling picture of neglected security is discernible in examining the total number of aircraft in the operational inventory of the Air Force over the last several years. The active inventory of all types of aircraft in the Air Force in 1947 was about 25,000 aircraft. The inventory of 1965 is somewhat *less than half* this number. While some of this can be rationalized on the basis of greater cargo-handling capabilities of transport aircraft and a substitution of ballistic missiles for combat aircraft, I do not believe that an inflexible (and not fully tested) force of a thousand ballistic missiles can safely take the place of a flexible force of several thousand aircraft.

In retrospect, it may be argued that the Air Force built too many different types of airplanes during the period 1940–1960, and that by better preplanning, it would have saved some money. However, most of these aircraft were brought to prototype flying status only, and at reasonable expense. They were not put into production. The Air Force selected its flying hardware from flying models rather than theoretical designs. I am certain of one thing today—performance of the Air Force mission in the future stands in jeopardy because that service is not permitted to build enough experimental or prototype aircraft under today's politically oriented cost/effectiveness programs, nor is it permitted to add sufficient numbers of new aircraft to the combat force-in-being.

The United States actually faces two very real "gaps" in its combat inventory for the future. There is an "airplane gap" in both fighter and bombardment types, and there is a "very large-yield warhead" gap in this nation's follow-on ballistic missile program. If these two deficiencies are not corrected with the utmost speed, the announced policies of "flexibility" and "multiple-options" of the Johnson *nee* Kennedy Administration cannot be implemented by our future fighting forces.

257

There are those in the Department of Defense who wish to keep on "studying the problem" and "retaining options" for later decision. My question is—how much longer do we need to study an obvious obsolescence of our combat forces-in-being?

In the table on pages 260–61, I have summarized data on the more important aircraft systems of the Air Force which came into the USAF combat inventory for operational use during the last twenty years. In looking at this aircraft listing and the dates of the development program, it should be borne in mind that each of the dates indicated as an "initial contract date" was preceded by several years of study before the initial contract was awarded. Hence, in terms of total "leadtime" one must add two or three years for a true picture of the time required to develop a new aircraft weapon system.

Nuclear-powered Aircraft Carrier

Like all weapons of war, aircraft carriers (and air bases), are vulnerable to destruction. Carriers have been sunk in the past and they can be sunk in the future. However, this fact does not mean that we do not need them. Anything that man can create, man can destroy. This applies equally to the current myth of invulnerability of both the MINUTEMAN ballistic missile force and the sea-based POLARIS missile force. Even though it may be a convenient excuse for delaying new weapons-system development to claim invulnerability of forces already in the inventory, the theory is absolute nonsense. The theory is nonsense because neither the technology nor the tactics of the systems designed for attack of existing systems stand still. Whether we like it or not, technological progress is a fact of life and the Communist leaders fully understand it.

At the present time, the Navy says that it needs another nuclear-powered aircraft carrier. I would rather put my money on that judgment than on the more or less superficial brushoff given the project by the Secretary of Defense during 1963 and 1964. If this Nation survives, there *will* be another nuclear-powered aircraft carrier and there *will* be a follow-on to the B-52. How long these projects will be delayed by cost/effectiveness studies and other pressures, no one knows today and no one can predict the consequences of the delays. The delays could, of course, prove fatal to our survival as a free nation; but being a little ahead of schedule, and on the safe side, could do no major damage to our economy or to our way of life.

Nature of the Russian Military Apparatus

In our society there are alarmists who seem to believe that every Russian is ten feet tall, and there are others who have consistently deprecated the scientific and technological capability of this major Communist power. Neither group is right from the military viewpoint. Consequently, I would like to make a few personal observations which may have more substance than an impersonalized theory.

In mid-1956, Premier Khrushchev suggested to the President of the United States that a group of U.S. Air Force officers might enjoy a visit to the Soviet Union to witness a Soviet air review and to see Soviet developments in aviation. This suggestion was cordially accepted by President Eisenhower. As Chief of Staff, USAF, I headed the group and several Air Force officers were selected to make the journey with me. Our group included, of course, individuals who were well qualified in aircraft evaluation, intelligence, operations, research and development, and training techniques. The party left Washington on June 22, and arrived in Moscow on the afternoon of June 23. Marshall Georgi K. Zhukov, then the Defense Minister, and hero of the war, was to act as our host while we were in the Soviet Union. In addition to the United States contingent there were representatives from twenty-eight other countries, including England, France, East Germany, and Red China.

259

Aircraft Type	Contractor	Date of Initial Contract	Date of First Flight
BOMBERS			
B-45	North American	September 1944	March 1947
B-47	Boeing	February 1945	December 1947
B-52	Boeing	June 1946 (Development Contract)	April 1952
B-57	Martin	March 1951	July 1953
B-58	Convair	December 1951 (Gov. published)	November 1956
B-66	Douglas	February 1952	June 1954
B-70	North American	January 1958	September 1964
FIGHTERS			
F-84 (straight-wing)	Republic	November 1944	February 1946
F-86	North American	June 1946	October 1947
F-89	Northrup	June 1946	August 1948
F-94	Lockheed	October 1948 (Production Decision)	April 1949
F-84F (swept-wing)	Republic	December 1948	June 1950
F-100	North American	January 1952	May 1953
F-101	McDonnell	January 1952 (Production Decision)	September 1954

F-102	Convair	August 1950	December 1953
F-104	Lockheed	March 1953	February 1954
F-105	Republic	April 1954	October 1955
F-106	Convair	September 1951	December 1956
F-4C (F-110)	McDonnell	February 1962	May 1963
TFX (F-111A/B)	General Dynamics	November 1962	December 1964
		(Source Selection)	

261

The first thing on the program in Moscow was the air show, or Soviet Aviation Day. It was held at Tushino Airport on Sunday afternoon, the 23rd, in Moscow, of course. In this show, the defensive components of the Soviet Air Force were accentuated more than the offensive forces. In other words, fighters were stressed more than the bomber aircraft. Sixteen modern jet bombers were flown by in review as compared to 135 of their new fighters.

Khrushchev made the comment that for the edification of all, they were accentuating defensive systems rather than offensive systems, but that was readily apparent. The more spectacular of the bombers, of course, was the 4-engine jet-powered Bison bomber designed by Myasishchev (comparable to USAF B-52 airplanes), the 2-jet medium bomber, the Badger designed by Tupolev, and the long-range turbo-prop intercontinental bomber called the Bear.

Following the bombers were three Delta wing-types of the latest fighters, then large twin-rotor helicopters from which combat troops and supplies were landed for simulated battle. Single-rotor helicopters flew by in great numbers.

Prior to the military part of the air review, men and women of the ESOAF (the civilian defense component of the Soviet Air Force) flew by in precise formation. The sight of paratroopers jumping in the high wind was truly spectacular and greatly thrilled the crowd. The Russian women of this organization flew combat missions during World War II, and I asked one of the Russian officers how they performed in combat. He said that they were most courageous and did a very fine job. Their pilots appeared to be well trained and as good as they come. Incidentally, some of their combat glider demonstrations were among the finest I have seen anywhere.

The following morning we were the guests of the Air Force chief and his deputy, Pavel F. Zhigarev and Sergei I. Rudenko, at Kubinka Airport. During this inspection the aircraft we had seen in flight over Moscow the previous day were all on the ground. Some were their newest aircraft and they were operational, but had never been shown to any of the Western nations up to this time.

Following this inspection, I met with Defense Minister Marshall Zhukov, at his request. We conferred about two hours in connection with some military matters he wished me to relate to President Eisenhower. I took notes on it and gave the report to President Eisenhower on my return.

The following day our group visited the Zhukovsky Air Engineering Academy, located not far from Moscow. This Academy was responsible for the training of operational unit officers in advanced engineering and equipment maintenances. It was not a school for training scientists, as this was done at other institutions. There were about 500 students in attendance at the Engineering School at the time of our visit. The school had very fine facilities and equipment, including a twelve-inch Mach 3 wind tunnel. I don't think any of our training schools even today have any such kind of equipment. Although we did not witness any actual instruction in progress, our observation of facilities and people led us to believe their instruction was very good. It was obvious that the Russians were on the move and coming abreast and ahead of the latest technical developments. Undoubtedly the Russians have many schools. If this school which I saw was one of their "run-of-the-mill" examples, the Russians indeed have a fine system.

Our party also toured an aircraft-engine manufacturing plant in Moscow, plant No. 45. Our tour host was Marshall Vershimin. We followed the process of their construction of a Rolls Royce Nene engine. This was the engine that powered models of the MIG-15 and 17 which we fought in Korea. In touring the plant it was evident that the housekeeping was of very poor order compared to our own standards. They were using machine tools of World War II vintage, from Germany and England. However, with these relatively obsolete machine tools, we were told that this plant had built

10,000 Nene engines for the war in Korea. The Russians have no inspection system such as we do in our plants, where our supervisors watch over the work performance of a very few people. In Soviet Plant No. 45 the employee has no supervisor, but he stamps his code on each piece he works. If, when it comes to final assembly, this part that he has made doesn't work out, doesn't fit, strict action is taken and he probably goes to the salt mines somewhere. It's a pretty final inspection system! Everybody up and down the line knows that and does his best to make sure his work is satisfactory. Very good care is taken of the skilled mechanics in these plants. The higher grades especially receive awards and vacations for their good work. That's the incentive provided.

Our next visit was to the Central Aviation Assembly Plant in Moscow, Plant No. 3. They were building at that time the IL-14, a twin reciprocating-engine airplane, somewhere in performance between our DC-3 and our Convair. I had the pleasure of flying one of these planes later on a trip to Stalingrad. This factory is the oldest of its kind in the Soviet Union. The employers and the managers were very proud of the plant and the work that they were doing. We observed nothing new or unusual in the way of production procedures, tooling, or anything else. From what we saw, the United States is "out in front" in this stage of the operation. However, here again, we must be careful, and not prejudge, because the end product of these plants is excellent, top grade. Russian production efforts just reach the end result by a different method than that to which we are accustomed.

The next morning the group flew to the "Hero City," Stalingrad. I flew with the deputy chief of the Air Force, Marshall Rudenko. Accompanying us was the General of the Armies, M. S. Malinin. During World War II, Rudenko commanded three Air Force groups in the immediate defense of Stalingrad and Malinin was the Army Chief of Staff during the battle. These two Soviet officers were very close friends and took great delight in returning to Stalingrad. They were so excited

264

that I asked my interpreter what the problem was and he told me that this was the first time that either one of these two officers had returned to Stalingrad. The battle was fought in 1942. This seemed to me remarkable, because in our country we do things a little differently. Later on I asked Rudenko why he had not returned to Stalingrad before, instead of waiting for fourteen years. He said, "General, I have had no business in Stalingrad." That's the Russian way.

We were told by the Russians that 300 thousand German troops (22 divisions) were wiped out and 91 thousand captured in the battle for Stalingrad, and that none returned to Germany except a few from Siberia at a later date. History relates the tragic circumstances surrounding the terrible defeat and surrender of this unfortunate army.

The city of Stalingrad in 1956, with a population of about 500 thousand, was rebuilding from the terrible rubble of war and it promised to be a beautiful and modern city when completed. Everyone we contacted seemed to be very proud of what they were doing and delighted in showing us the master plan for the entire city reconstruction. The people in Stalingrad seemed even more friendly than they were in Moscow. They were fine in Moscow, but the people of Stalingrad manifested a genuine appreciation for the U.S. military representatives. I guess they remembered the great help Americans gave them during the battle of Stalingrad and, in fact, throughout the whole war. Some ten thousand people met our group when we came out of a restaurant and it was apparent that they were glad to see us. Apparently, the "word" hadn't got down to Stalingrad about America "today."

Flying back to Moscow late that afternoon, a flight of some three hours, we ran into some weather and immediately came down and flew on the deck through the low clouds and fog. I asked Rudenko why we didn't go up and fly through the clouds on instruments and get on in to Moscow. He replied, "the thunderstorms are too bad up there—too much turbulence." There were no thunderstorms that I could see. I am

265

sure, therefore, that they were a little behind our level in their blind flying equipment. The pilots were good, but apparently the electronics at the bases, the guidance ranges and so forth, had not been installed throughout Russia.

On our last morning we visited the site of the first Russian atomic reactor, about forty miles from Moscow. Here again, in walking through this reactor plant, I noticed that the housekeeping left much to be desired. It was not very clean, but the reactor was working *very* satisfactorily. It was actually furnishing electric power throughout this particular area.

When we had finished our tour, everybody in the group agreed that the Russians had come a very long way in the last few years in their research and development efforts, particularly as applied to weapons systems. They had made tremendous strides. During World War II, Russia really had no modern bombardment aircraft of any kind and concentrated her World War II aircraft efforts on ground attack types. She knew that the United States and Great Britain would furnish the strategic-type air forces. Russia started virtually from nothing in 1945, and by the time we arrived there in 1956, a little more than ten years later, that country had a fine array of locally produced jet engines and modern aircraft.

In looking broadly at industrial methods in Russia, an impression of mediocrity is obtained when measured by U. S. standards. However, such speculation is both idle and erroneous. Utility and purpose are the sole guides in the Russian scheme of achievement. It's the "packaging" by Russian standards that upsets the American sense of aesthetics. When Russian leaders feel that there must be a concentrated effort in a certain area to do something rapidly, or to do something expansively, its cost in manpower or in rubles is of little consequence. All of that nation's decisions are made unilaterally. It was only twelve years after the carnage of World War II when Russia put its first man-made earth-satellite into orbit. On a more homely scale, one aerodrome, when I visited, had barracks that were "policed-up" and looked fine. The flying field had long, smooth concrete runways, but the grass between the runways grew knee-deep. I asked why the grass wasn't cut, as it looked like a fire hazard to me. I was told that it wasn't necessary, and therefore a waste of manpower. Around the quarters on this same base, brand new and nice-looking quarters were available but there were no sidewalks. I was told that sidewalks weren't needed. There was a highway, a road to walk on, if they wanted to walk. The Russian just doesn't regard the comforts of life as we do, but I suppose some day they will get around to it. Russia definitely is a "first things first" nation—about that there can be no real question.

Probably the greatest tragedy of the world in which we now live is the control of the Russian people by a government which insists on world domination under a Marxist-Leninist concept of society. The Russian people are fundamentally warm, industrious, and capable. But they have accepted a government that does not appear to be either helpful or cooperative.

PART FIVE

WAY FOR THE
Future

Chapter XVI

ESSENTIAL
ELEMENTS OF POLICY

Terms of reference and adjustments of basic national security policy within the foreseeable future will be profoundly affected by the American government's judgment as to the intent and capabilities of the various Communist governments which exist throughout the world today.

It may be that in the process of governmental evolution, the Communist system can become sufficiently civilized to believe in a world that guarantees freedom and the dignity of man and subscribes to the rule of law and order. Certainly, the basic peaceful attitudes of the majority of the men and women behind the Iron Curtain indicate that such evolution would be inevitable. However, the leadership of a nation, as vividly demonstrated by Adolf Hitler, can coerce millions of people into circumstances, ideologies, and actions which they do not really desire. This can easily happen with respect to the militant, frustrated, narrow, and conspiratorial leadership characteristic of the Communist world. All civilized men on both sides of the Iron Curtain hope that this will not happen. However, it might happen.

271

The political-military problem of the United States and the Free World has become more complex because of what appears, at least on the surface, to be a gradual breakup of what we once referred to as the "monolithic Communist world" or sometimes as the "Sino-Soviet Bloc." We now seem to have three general types of Communist governments:

1. The governments of the Eastern European satellites— Poland, Hungary, Czechoslovakia, Bulgaria, Rumania, and East Germany.

2. The Red Chinese government, allied with such fanatic and inconsequential nations as Albania, North Korea, and North Vietnam.

3. The Russian government itself.

There are other Communist governments, quasi-Communist governments, and opportunistic governmental leaders scattered throughout the world, of course—Egypt, Algeria, Cuba, Indonesia, and some of the foundling states in Africa. However, these entities have no real power base with which to seriously threaten the security of the United States for many years to come.

The U.S. Joint Chiefs of Staff, in their constant study of the national defense problem, list and analyze all countries of the world, small or large, friend, foe, or neutral, as one of the many factors pertinent to their responsibilities for national security planning. However, I will confine myself to the three general types of major Communist powers which exist, as a matter of fact and as a matter of serious military concern in today's world.

The governments of the Eastern European Soviet satellites (Albania excluded), while generally communistic in nature, are not militant protagonists of the theory that the Marxist-Leninist concept should dominate the entire world. We could probably get along with them if they did not have an economic-political-military gun at their heads. Nevertheless, they usually vote against Free World objectives in the forum of

272

the United Nations, and their military forces constitute a potential threat to Western Europe as an augmentation of Soviet power in event of general war. However, if I were a Russian strategic planner, I would consider these countries as unreliable allies.

Red China under its present leadership seems to me at this writing to be practically a hopeless case. Naked force seems to be the only logic which the leadership of that unfortunate nation can comprehend. The ultimate objectives of China's leaders are certainly the subjugation and communization of all Southeast Asia, the Indonesian area, the Philippines, and Australia. However, their time schedule for conquest is probably not fixed—simply because they now lack the physical power to acomplish the objective. The aggressiveness and boldness of the Red Chinese government will undoubtedly increase as their nuclear stockpile and means of delivery continue to grow. At the moment, however, Red China is a paper tiger and constitutes no real military threat to the United States. In any war with mainland China in the near future we could knock them out practically overnight if we chose to use nuclear weapons. The Chinese Communists know this fact of life and will undoubtedly be careful during the near future. However, their ultimate objective is *Conquest*—and the future we face will become increasingly dangerous as their nuclear power develops. Consequently, in dealing with that government, I would have a very short fuse on the problem. If we are to prevent the present Red Chinese leadership from pursuing a pattern of violence and conquest, we should be prepared to identify the issues before that nation has developed an atomic arsenal.

With respect to Russia itself, the basic question is: Do we, or *do we not* now have a co-operative enemy?

If I were about to presume that the Russian government had gentled and modified its character to include earnest regard for human dignity and a world of law and order, I would

273

ask for some substantial proof before accepting the premise. The proof would be easy to come by. It would involve the four points I have mentioned on earlier pages.

1. The elimination of the Iron Curtain and the establishment of an open society such as that existing in the Free World.
2. The elimination of the ruthless controls which still enslave the Eastern European satellites, and concurrent permission for these enslaved ethnic groups to determine their own destiny.
3. The elimination of organized subversion throughout the world and the tampering of that subversive apparatus with the internal security affairs of other nations.
4. A governmental pronouncement, adopted as a matter of real policy, that the Communist movement no longer is dedicated to the destruction of all other forms of civilized society.

If the present leadership of the Communist conspiracy were sincere about "coexistence" and actually desired elimination of tensions between East and West, these four steps could be taken with no delay. In the absence of even one demonstrated move in this direction, I must doubt the sincerity of the apparent "coexistence" program and the peaceful intentions of the Sino-Soviet bloc.

I use the obsolete term "Sino-Soviet bloc" deliberately, even though much has been said recently about the ideological schism which exists between Russia and China. I cannot take this schism too seriously, or believe that it necessarily works in our own behalf, because two things are clear: if it does exist, the United States now has two enemies instead of one, both with the same announced objective—the destruction of the institutions and values of the Free World. And, when the chips are down, there can be no real doubt that the two would join forces to eliminate Western values, and then settle their own differences at a later time in history. So, in looking toward the future, the military establishment must assume that the objectives of the Communist credo remain *as stated by that conspiracy.* There has been no convincing evidence provided to the contrary.

If the United States were to assume the contrary viewpoint, it should disarm at once. If it does not make the assumption that the Russian Bear has gentled its fierce appetites during an evolutionary domestication, elementary prudence would indicate that America had better keep her guard up. Keeping the guard up, in this world of modern technology, means the elimination of constraints on our technological progress, gaining the lead, and remaining technologically ahead of the enemy at any point in time in actual fighting hardware. Actually, what is occurring is that this government has not made a clear decision with respect to either premise. It does not have sufficient trust in the enemy to disarm completely, nor will it allow the fullest preparation for the eventuality of deceit.

Because the Government fretfully clings to indecision, it has imposed constraints on vital areas of U.S. technological development which can be capitalized upon by the enemy, if he so chooses, at some future time. As specific examples, U.S. nuclear weapons programs, nuclear propulsion and power programs, aircraft programs, and national military space programs are moving along at a rate far below that which is attainable through the full application of the scientific genius and the industrial know-how of the Free World.

The Basic Premise

I can summarize my views on national security planning into two sentences. The leaders of an organized conspiracy have sworn to destroy America and the Free World by one means or another, and there is no real evidence available at this time to indicate that their objective has been changed.

275

Therefore, we had better be prepared to fight to maintain our liberty.

The Initiative

Having made the assumption that we do in fact live in a dangerous world and that we do confront an organized system dedicated to our destruction, the first element of national security policy would appear to be, in terms of elementary logic, the elimination or neutralization of that system.

Elimination, destruction, or neutralization requires initiative. In its definition of any of these nouns, the U.S. government should not constantly be in a position of defensive reaction to the subversion, probing, thrusts, and overt military actions initiated by its opponents. We should have a plan of our own which is focused on consciously and consistently probing and implementing actions to neutralize the enemy.

We may say that we have done some of the things necessary to take the initiative through such operations as economic and military aid and the Peace Corps, but these programs have had very limited objectives. As a nation, we have still said that we will "contain" rather than "neutralize." As a consequence, the United States seems to be fighting a battle in which it constantly retreats on the political, on the geographic, and on the technological fronts of war.

The power of the initiative might be related to the principle of surprise. Without initiative, the best one can do is to hold one's own. With the power of initiative, the opposition can be destroyed. It would therefore seem axiomatic that the first principle of our national security policy would be to seize and maintain the initiative in all dimensions of modern war; to include the economic, psychological, political, military, and the technological.

If the government were to implement a policy involving initiative for America, the first logical step would not be to start an indiscriminate nuclear war. But, the nation might be

276

able to revert to some of its earlier judgments with respect to the nature of communism. Over a period of years, in its attempts toward accommodation and creation of a peaceful world, our government has gone a long way toward accepting the basic immorality of the Communist system. Americans might now ask their government if it had the moral right to agree to a world in which millions of people were kept in a condition of slavery, and to accept such condition through continued recognition of the Soviet Union as a legitimate government. Many people have rationalized the recognition by the United States of the U.S.S.R. as a legitimate government with the argument that the United States obtains more from the relationship than does the U.S.S.R. The argument is that in the absence of recognition of the present Russian government, America would not have access to vitally needed intelligence information. I have never taken this argument seriously because, first, while a person is behind the Iron Curtain he sees mostly what has been determined for him to see, and second, because there are other intelligence techniques available which can provide us with much of the vital security information which we need. From this viewpoint it would appear thoroughly logical to *break diplomatic relations* with the U.S.S.R. and to insist on the payment of its overdue indebtedness to the United Nations of some sixty million dollars.

How can our government really rationalize the economic boycott against Cuba and our failure to recognize Communist China as a legitimate government when the United States maintains diplomatic relationships with the original villain, the U.S.S.R. The might of Cuba constitutes no threat, in a purely military sense, to the United States. Cuba cannot destroy this country and the United States could destroy that entire little island. Red China, likewise, constitutes no immediate military threat. At the present time, America could destroy the power base of Communist China in one overnight blow by utilizing only the power of the U.S. Navy's 7th Fleet which is already

277

deployed in Pacific waters. Red China *will* constitute a threat, in the near future, if allowed to continue with the development of nuclear weapons, and the development of means of delivery of these weapons. This can happen much quicker than most wishful thinkers are inclined to believe. However, at the moment, Red China constitutes no real military threat to the security of the power base of the United States, and could not defend itself effectively if we decided to attack with nuclear weapons.

The U.S.S.R. does constitute such a threat. And yet, by some curious quirk of logic, policy, and circumstance, the United States persists in exercising the diplomatic niceties usually reserved for co-operative and civilized nations.

Economic and Military Aid

A policy embodying initiative would affect our allies and the so-called "neutral" nations of the world, as well as our enemies. The ordinary citizen might say, with some evidence of substantiation in history, that you are either "for me" or "against me." This type of hard-boiled judgment could profoundly affect the world-wide application of U.S. military and economic aid.

I find it extremely difficult to rationalize the expenditure of United States taxpayers' dollars on aid to countries which align themselves with the enemy and which consistently vote against the principles of civilized behavior in the United Nations. If America believes that there is a conspiracy dedicated to her destruction, how can she really rationalize the vast expenditure of United States treasure in Poland and Yugoslavia, and how can America rationalize the subsidy of the U.S.S.R. through the provision of millions of tons of wheat to feed populations which are the victim of its own conspiracy? Such efforts seem to me to be a subsidy of communism and living proof to the peoples of those countries that the Communist system is working.

Even against this backdrop of self-contradiction and anomaly, the strictly military viewpoint would require a totally different treatment of so-called neutral nations than has been our practice during the last decade. The State Department argument for military and economic assistance to neutral nations is always premised with the conviction that if "you don't help them, you will drive them into the arms of the enemy."

I remember so vividly when, in the aftermath of World War II, the Chinese Communists were labeled by many people in the State Department as simple "agrarian" reformers. According to them, the Red Chinese leaders were really not Communists, they simply wanted a reform of the Chinese Nationalist government. I can also remember so vividly that at many National Security Council meetings, which I attended, the problem of the emergence of Castro in Cuba was discussed and his ultimate objectives were debated. The argument against firm United States action in Cuba, to prevent the establishment of a Communist beachhead in this hemisphere, was usually countered by the statement that "Castro is not a Communist, he is simply a patriot attempting to overthrow the dictator Battista; do not push him too far, because you will push him into the arms of communism." History shows what happened to both China and Cuba.

It is therefore difficult to understand the favored treatment of neutrals, as opposed to the positive help which might be given to real friends who actually oppose communism. In the face of the stark realities of the world in which we live, my judgment would be against squandering the wealth of the United States in support of neutralist governments. Let them alone until they make up their minds. If they want to "go Communist," let the U.S.S.R. support them, rather than the United States taxpayer, because, after all, most of them can contribute very little to defense of the Free World.

The question of colonialism and support of our Western Allies, of course, presents somewhat the same problem. Colon-

279

ialism is an ugly word these days in most of the press of the world, but unfortunately, it has never been subjected to the type of critical analysis that our government is attempting to employ through the cost/effectiveness procedure with respect to its own weapons of war. I have never seen a State Department "white paper" on the subject of colonialism.

This problem might be reduced to a single question as follows: do human beings want to live in a primitive society, or do we prefer the values of civilization? After all, colonialism developed because some people of the earth, living in a land of splendid natural resources, did not develop the genius nor the inspiration to capitalize upon the fruits of a bountiful nature. It was only through the genius and the work of the colonialists that the latent capabilities of these areas of the world were brought into a reality. Now that his genius has been successful, in some cases for many generations, the colonialist is suddenly "an unwanted oppressor" holding down the people who inhabited the area before he arrived. The point is that justice would indicate that the colonialist should have some rights.

As a nation we have not done very well in supporting some of our allies with military aid in respect to the colonial issue. We have gone along with the concept that the vote of one man or the vote of one nation in world affairs (that one man or that one nation having no real responsibility) is as good as that of the vote of a responsible, creative, people. We have thereby abdicated the world of reality and the world in which power factors are still important.

Apologists for our aid policy insist that the United States should give economic and military aid "without strings attached." I do not understand this philosophy. Why shouldn't we have "strings attached," as a *quid pro quo*, for the resources and the wealth which our government takes away from our people, and our own industrial development, and gives to others? "Strings attached" seems to have some kind of an obnoxious political connotation. However, I see absolutely no point in giving either economic or military aid to neutral countries who do not care to support our fundamental beliefs before the United Nations. I see even less reason for providing economic and military aid to Communist countries that conspire toward our ultimate destruction. We are digging America's grave when we permit our government to rescue Communist countries from the pitfalls and failures of their own economic system, feeding them and giving them other material aid paid for out of the pockets of the American taxpayers.

A reversal of American policy toward neutral countries would, of course, generate a violent emotional reaction around the world. However, no one seems to love us anyhow. We cannot buy love, but at least we might re-establish respect.

A Superior Military Technology

Today, a third major element of basic national security policy should be the absolute determination to maintain a superior military technology in the fighting forces of the United States. This is no easy task. The first problem, if our nation had such determination, arises from the imbalance in technical intelligence opportunities which exist between the Communist world and the Free World.

Ours is an open society and most of our scientific and technical intelligence information is widely published in trade journals, in newspapers, in various periodicals, scientific works, and often is exhibited on television. The Communists, on the other hand, have a second Iron Curtain within their political Iron Curtain. This second barrier is the "technological" curtain which deliberately conceals from the rest of the world any Soviet technological progress which might have military significance.

Our military establishment and our defense industry consciously and constantly feed back the results of research and development programs into the consumer industry. Most of the material, metallurgical, and electronic advances of that past twenty years have had their roots in military research and development. The civilian aircraft in which we ride across the United States in four hours owes its existence to military propulsion and aerodynamic innovations. The now universally available new cooking utensils to which food will not stick while cooking, and which need no scouring, owe their development to the work which the military establishment did on ballistic missile re-entry systems. Computer technology, electronic and communications systems, all of which support the functioning of industry, grew out of military research and development. The radar systems which control air traffic and prevent collision of civilian aircraft in flight, and which guide such civilian aircraft into safe landings in fog and bad weather, were perfected by the military. There are many other such innovations too numerous to mention.

The application of our Free World military technology to civilian life is proper and is a natural consequence of an open society. There is no such similar application behind the Iron Curtain.

This circumstance is what the military professional calls the imbalance of opportunity for acquiring and exchanging scientific and technological information. What it amounts to is that the Soviets have access to, and know, just about everything that this nation does while our government has only fragmentary information on Russian programs.

If this nation were to assume that the geographic, demographic, and logistical power factors provided certain military advantages to the Soviet system, and if it were to assume that, because of this relationship, the United States should maintain superior Free World fighting forces, our government would have identified a major problem. It would worry more about the "imbalance" in opportunity for acquiring technical intelligence. We might even call a part of the Cold War a "technological war," the winner of which could easily become dominant in world affairs. If the United States is indeed involved in a technological war, it must seek the answer to a simple question: How does the United States keep ahead, or stay even, when the enemy has access to practically all of this nation's scientific and technical information, and, in addition, has the benefits of his own innovations, and the United States has only what it produces by itself?

America therefore has "two strikes" against her in fighting the technological war of the future. If our government further compounds this difficulty by the self-imposition of constraints on the progress of our own military technology, logic would indicate that we are creating an insoluble problem. And this the nation seems to be doing that, particularly as it affects U.S. space technology, U.S. nuclear technology, and the modernization of air and naval combat forces-in-being.

Free World Collaboration in Research and Development

In addition to the pessimistic observation given above, there are two reasons which convince me that the United States should do far more in fostering collaboration of the Free World powers in all disciplines of scientific research and development.

The first consideration is that of the phenomenal growth of scientific institutions within the U.S.S.R. and the equally phenomenal growth of their annual output of trained scientists and engineers from higher institutions of learning. Informed projections of the rate of training of Soviet scientists and engineers, when compared to the rate of training of people in these hard disciplines in our own country, shows quite clearly that, under present trends, the Soviets will be doubling our own output by 1970.

It can, of course, be argued that the quality of the Soviet university output is not equal to our own. I consider such an argument to be highly debatable and, furthermore, begging the issue. In any event, no one in position of authority in the

283

Government disagrees with the judgment that a massive effort has been undertaken by the U.S.S.R. to improve the number and the quality of its scientific institutions as well as trained scientists and engineers. The Russian technological explosion suggests to me that the scientific and engineering brain power of the entire Free World should be working in unison to stay ahead of the inevitable progress of the Communist countries. After all, this battle for men's freedom is not limited singly to the United States. It involves all free nations. Therefore, it seems to me to be elementary that the brain power of all free nations should join harmoniously in a common effort in their own defense.

A second important circumstance which influences my judgment on this matter is the fact that America certainly cannot proclaim herself the sole birthplace of genius and inventions of significance to the future. I remember so vividly that during World War II, the British pioneered radar and were well ahead of us in the development of jet engines. Most of the scientists associated with our nuclear energy program were foreign born or of immediate foreign extraction. The Germans were ahead of both England and the United States in jet engine technology and certainly far ahead in applied ballistic missile technology. These lessons of the past indicate to me that an essential element of America's national security policy must be to cultivate to the maximum practicable extent Free World collaboration in scientific research and development. Careful selection of participants would, of course, be necessary; and, on our side of the fence, we would have to do two things: first, the United States government would have to eliminate some of the artificial security barriers which now prevent a free relationship with respect to military technology; and second, the United States government would have to have the moral courage to select some allies for collaboration, and reject other allies, for valid reasons which are not too difficult to define.

284

U.S. Attitude Toward Disarmament

There are a large number of people in the Free World who claim credit for participation in war, when as a matter of fact they have never smelled gunpowder and were never subjected to enemy fire. This observation bears directly on the pros and cons of the current world emphasis on the problem of disarmament. Some people seem to believe that the possession of arms and armament creates a circumstance which can lead to war. They seem to think that if our Government could eliminate military forces and armaments it would have eliminated war itself. This logic is totally at variance with the history of man. Under the terms of this logic the nation could eliminate its police force and thereby eliminate crime. This viewpoint also contradicts military history from well before the time of Caesar.

In this currently popular and superficial analysis of war and peace (the "cause and effect" which relates the possession of arms to the instigation of war), the cause and effect relationships have been totally reversed. We actually have arms and armaments and military forces-in-being because of political tensions. The armament is a result of political tensions, not the cause of political tensions. If the political objectives and the economic objectives of competing nations did not collide in the mainstream of life, there would be no arms. Consequently, any thinking on the problem of disarmament which starts with the reduction of armed forces, the elimination of arms-in-being, or the elimination of new armament that might be developed, is wishful thinking. The cart has been placed before the horse. The solution to disarmament, on both sides of the Iron Curtain, is therefore a political problem, not a military problem.

If the politicians could really agree, and if their agreements were supported by solid evidence of good faith on both sides, there would be no requirement for military forces, and any military man who has actually fought a battle, a campaign, or a war would be the first to subscribe to the arrangement. In the absence of such validated political agreements, a fundamental element of our basic national security policy should therefore be: *no disarmament without prior proof.*

It can be claimed that America is not disarming at the present moment. The truth is that we are involved in a creeping disarmament, for this nation has accepted international constraints and is adding additional self-imposed constraints on the progress of its nuclear, aerodynamic, and space technologies.

Internal Management Practices

I have already described the overcentralized management of the detailed activities of the Department of Defense, but the subject must be mentioned again when we think about essential elements of policy. We should not forget that:

1. In war, we get by on our "margins"—that is, the over-all depth and availability of the material of war.
2. That what one service forgets or neglects, another remembers, and that this is a form of insurance.
3. That when all control over procurement and supply is fixed at the top, service responsibility and accountability tend to wither, with attendant reduction in a logistic base of adequate depth. The deficiencies in a logistic system under single control at a very high level may not be apparent to the responsible combat commander until, in a battle situation, it becomes too late to do anything about them.

Accordingly, an essential element of defense policy would appear to be a reversal of the trend toward complete and detailed control at the top which came in with Secretary of

286

Defense McNamara. The Secretary of Defense should certainly sit on top of the defense establishment with respect to the general policies of business administration, management procedures, and in the adjudication of differences of military viewpoints. However, he should not be in position to ride rough-shod over professional military judgment and at the same time to be able to invoke pressures which tend to muzzle the professional establishment in its traditional dealings with both the public press and the Congress of the United States.

Chapter XVII

THE JOHNSON ADMINISTRATION

In this summary of contemporary military affairs, as I have reported them, it has been necessary to move from the area of purely military affairs into the area of political-military affairs. This has been necessary because the two areas are inseparable and mutually interacting and I have been in a position to see, very vividly, the impact of political action on the capability of our military forces to ensure and maintain the physical security of this free land. After all, America maintains a military establishment for a single purpose—to defend and maintain our freedom.

People see the events of the times from their own limited perspective. Mine is a military perspective—it was my life and my career for forty-four years. I am aware that there is no special virtue necessarily associated with long service in any kind of an organization. Quite to the contrary, an organization may frequently become ineffective if the "Old Guard" stays too long and the young, the fresh are held in check, are not allowed to emerge when changing times and circumstances demand change. However, when dealing with the most vital problem of humanity—freedom itself—some reasonable continuity of responsibility, in terms of logic, would seem to have merit. I do not know whether a man in uniform should stay on for one war or three wars, or for twenty years, thirty years, or forty years—but I do know that men and women both in uniform and as career civil servants in government generally have a greater sense of continuity of responsibility than do transients on the scene. Nevertheless I am compelled to view the current trends of national security organization and planning with some apprehension.

Heritage

The next four years can be very critical years of our brief life as a nation. President Johnson has inherited, among other problems, the following circumstances:

1. The results of this nation's post-World War II compromises, including the loss of China to communism, the German problem, De Gaulle and the enslavement of the Eastern European satellites.
2. The growth to significant power of the world-wide Communist movement.
3. The policy of containment; the progressive loss of freedom in Southeast Asia; the Congo, Cuba, and still unresolved stalemate in Korea, South Vietnam, Laos, Cambodia, and hostile Indonesia.
4. The emerging dominance of the new, small, and sometimes irresponsible members of the United Nations.
5. The U.S.S.R. as a massive nuclear and technological power.
6. The emergence of Red China as a nuclear power.
7. The deterioration of solidarity in NATO, SEATO, and CENTO.
8. The results of the 1958 uninspected moratorium on

289

nuclear weapons testing and the Test Ban Treaty of the Kennedy Administration.

9. The precedent of governmental fear of escalation and proliferation.

10. A highly centralized defense establishment under a single civilian Chief of Staff and a civilian General Staff.

11. International economic problems of great difficulty and great importance, sometimes referred to as the "Gold Flow Problem."

12. The basic orientation of our national space program to "space for peaceful purposes."

This last heritage deserves special attention. Earlier in these pages we have discussed the possible military utilization of the medium of space as a national security problem of the United States. The problems of the past few years in getting a military space program going have been just about as difficult as were the problems of the years during which Billy Mitchell was a symbol for the fight for the progress of military aviation. A close look at the record will show that the Johnson Administration inherited five circumstances affecting military space technology when he took office as Chief Executive.

1. That the nation started late in the space race.

2. That the basic national vector of "space is for peaceful purposes" had its seeds under the Eisenhower Administration.

3. That the Kennedy Administration, aided and abetted on the Department of Defense side by the Secretary of Defense himself, further compromised and slowed down military exploration and evaluation of the potentiality of this new medium.

4. That it was the existence of military developed rockets which allowed the United States to start even a belated move toward space exploration. (The Air Force de-

290

veloped ATLAS missile, built by the General Dynamics Corporation, put the MERCURY astronauts into orbit and the Air Force developed TITAN missile, with the Martin Company as contractor, put the GEMINI spacecraft into orbit. In addition, the THOR missile developed by Douglas Aircraft became a reliable workhorse for many unmanned satellite ventures into space.)

5. That our national preoccupation with "space for peaceful purposes" has even denied the astronaut regular officers the privilege of wearing their uniforms. The civilian space agency had to choose, in the majority, uniformed test pilots to do the work—Marine, Navy, and Air Force pilots. Yet these regular career men have had to go around in semi-masquerade as civilians. In this regard I feel that as a nation we went overboard in our efforts to show our peaceful intent.

On the positive side of the equation, the thirty-sixth President has inherited a powerful military force-in-being, laid down under the administrations of Presidents Truman and Eisenhower; a healthy industrial base and resources for meaningful and timely military research and development programs; an international system of alliances and bilateral treaties which, though now in some difficulty, provide the basis for Free World collaboration; and a generally sound economy.

Current Trends

It is much too early, as this book goes to press, to judge the performance of the Johnson Administration from a national security viewpoint or, for that matter, from any other viewpoint. It can easily be observed, however, that the policies of this Administration will not be a blueprint of those of the Kennedy years; changes are in process. I will not comment on the fabric of legislative and executive actions which relate to the current emphasis on the Great Society, but the more significant trends in political-military affairs should be mentioned.

Policy With Respect to Vietnam

It is probably fair to observe that the increased pressure on North Vietnam, through air strikes against targets on North Vietnamese territory and through build-up of American ground forces in the area, is a form of escalation which the policy-makers of the Kennedy Administration would have been extremely reluctant to undertake. The Johnson Administration apparently is not going to give up easily in Vietnam.

It was only a few short years ago that American military personnel (ordered by their government into Vietnam as "Military Advisors") were not allowed to wear the United States uniform, and even the commanding general was officially known as "Mister." Our government has discarded this practice and the Johnson Administration has gone part way in carrying the war to the enemy.

On the negative side, sanctuaries are still granted to the seat of government of North Vietnam and to logistic support lines leading into Red China. And, of course, detailed control of tactical military operations by the White House still persists. Additionally, our government has advised the enemy that Hanoi is safe and that the United States will not use even small nuclear weapons tactically.

Therefore, at this writing, while it seems that the Johnson Administration has been bolder in Vietnam than the Kennedy Administration, still the Johnson Administration has not gone full out in the change of policy. The United States continues to operate under self-imposed restrictions and seems to be getting mired down in a man-to-man war of attrition on the Asian land mass. (A war in which for many years we have said we would never become involved.)

292

The Chinese Communist Camp

Behind the North Vietnamese invasion of the territory and the sovereign rights of the South Vietnamese lies Red Communist China. The Viet Cong could not possibly undertake the types of operations which have been employed without both political and matériel support from Red China. During the latter days of the Korean War, under the Administration of President Eisenhower, this nation shied away from direct involvement with Red China. U.S. military forces could neutralize sufficient military targets in Red China overnight and set that nation back to an industrial and technical base more consistent with its medieval concept of government, law, and order. If ever there was a "paper tiger" in fact, it was not the United States of America. It was Red China—and still is.

However, Red China is moving with more than the bluff and the bluster which is only the current tactic of its irrational and suspicious leadership. If we give the Hitler-type mentality which now dominates Red China a little more time, we will have a real problem. Up to this writing, the current Administration has done nothing about this clearly developing threat.

In short, the Johnson Administration has thus far given no assurance that it will face up to the Red Chinese leadership at places and times which are most favorable to the destiny of free men.

The Dominican Republic

In April, 1965, the United States moved military forces into the Dominican Republic during a situation of civil revolt. The prompt action by the Johnson Administration in quelling another Communist takeover in the Caribbean deserves mention and credit. As usual, the Communist nations issued bitter denunciations of the action, but they did nothing more in an overt military sense. Our own domestic grouping of left-wing

293

pacifists, compromisers, appeasers, and ill-informed adolescent students also objected to the act. If these American groups could only think in terms of the power factors which exist in the world today, they would realize that they were supporting Communist policy in their criticism of the actions of our own government.

The facts of the case appear to indicate quite clearly that the President's actions were fully justified and were necessary to the long-term preservation of freedom in this hemisphere. It is one thing to have true wars of national liberation, such as our own War for Independence; a totally different circumstance exists when a foreign power uses a smaller nation to engineer a revolution which will be controlled from the outside. Such revolutions lead only to slavery, to communism, and to the loss of free institutions. No proof of this allegation need be made other than the simple question: "Where are the plebiscites which would give self-determination to the Eastern European satellites?"

The Goldberg Speech to the United Nations

On September 23, 1965, Arthur Goldberg, the United States Ambassador to the United Nations, succeeding the late Adlai Stevenson, made a major address. While no one can disagree with the philosophic objectives of the speech (peace, disarmament, productive human enterprise), I was disturbed by his offer to retire from the United States arsenal a vast amount of nuclear weapons material on the condition that the U.S.S.R. reciprocally would retire about two-thirds of the same amount. All of this, of course, was to be done with proper safeguards and inspections.

My concern with respect to this speech is based on the fact it must have represented Administration policy, and this policy includes a glaring blind spot carried over from policies of the past. I have seen this nation's negotiating teams go into nuclear matters on an international basis, time and again, with an initial mandate of mutual inspection and guarantees and come out eventually with the substantive terms of the agreement in force and *no* mutual inspection and verification system. This nation always honors the uninspected agreement; the Communist enemy does not.

The speech also indicated that what each country did with the nuclear matériel which it had left (after the elimination of sixty thousand kilograms of enriched uranium on the part of the United States and forty thousand kilograms on the part of the U.S.S.R.) was its own business. A military question with respect to such an arrangement naturally comes to mind. Assuming, which I do not, but even assuming that the U.S.S.R. would keep faith, what would be the world balance of power if that nation put its remaining weapons material into one-hundred-plus megaton systems and we put our remaining material into weapons of far less strategic power?

Finally what does this formula for a massive retirement of United States nuclear material do about the Red Chinese equation? Is the United States going to allow the Red Chinese to make a nuclear power out of themselves while we destroy our own nuclear arsenal?

Earlier in this book I outlined eight steps which could be taken to effect a unilateral nuclear disarmament of the United States. If you will remember, the fifth step in the process was the transfer of nuclear weapons material back to "peaceful" purposes. The speech of our Ambassador to the United Nations concerned me because we now seem to be at step number five.

Civilianization of the Department of Defense

There have been some serious suggestions of late for recruiting several scores of thousands of civilians to do "military" jobs. This would be convenient for the Secretary of

Defense, who has attempted to show "savings" while the actual cost of the military establishment (under the limited war philosophy) has constantly increased.

This latest effort reminds me, in a tactical sense, of one of the circumstances of the World War II Air Transport Command. As a result of the Topsy-like growth of World War II forces, we had civilian contract pilots on some of the Air Transport Command lines who were making about 1,500 dollars per month, and who could and did fly transport aircraft up to the edge of the combat zone. But there they had to stop; they were civilians. The same aircraft would then be taken over by a Second Lieutenant in uniform—making 250 dollars per month—and the uniformed Lieutenant took the aircraft on into where it had to go under combat conditions. This is "civilianization" of the military establishment in a tactical sense.

On the strategic side, or policy-planning side, what confidence can one really have in a procurement and production system run by people who will never have to stand the test of fire as a result of their own decisions? The Johnson Administration would probably do well to look at this question, not for the sake of protecting Defense Secretary McNamara's reputation, but for the sake of the fighting men of the United States.

Military Man in Space

Against the background of inherited circumstances, the Johnson Administration has taken a step to break the block against investigation of the military defense of space. This Administration has approved the development of a military Manned Orbiting Laboratory (MOL) to be built and operated by Douglas Aircraft for the Air Force. However, as the MOL now stands, it is so heavily circumscribed by restrictions and narrow technical goals that its ultimate usefulness can be seriously questioned. Again, the Johnson Administration has taken a first step, but the shadows of a sterile past still haunt the program.

Basic National Security Policy

As of the date of this writing in 1966, I do not believe there is a written Basic National Security Policy.

Decisions Facing the Administration

The thirty-sixth President of the United States is confronted with a monumental task in leading this nation through the labyrinth. Some leading and possibly prophetic questions might be asked as follows:

1. How will he reverse the ever-growing "status quo" philosophy, the "no-win" philosophy and again make the United States the master of its own destiny?
2. Will he retain the appeasers in Government, and in some of the advisory committees to the White House, or will he discard them?
3. What will be his continuing attitude toward escalation, proliferation, and safe sanctuaries to enemy forces which are engaged in or are supporting aggression?
4. What will be his attitude toward giving aid to those nations who oppose America's principles and/or constantly vote against America in the United Nations?
5. What will be his attitude toward this nation's alliances and how will he strengthen and unify the forces of freedom throughout the world?
6. What will be his attitude toward civil defense measures, super-megaton nuclear warheads (now possessed by the U.S.S.R. but not by the United States), military activities in space, a follow-on bomber to replace the B-52, and modernization of the Navy?
7. Will he keep the United States task force for nuclear-

297

weapons testing ready to go in event of a Soviet abrogation of the nuclear test ban treaty?

8. What will he do to re-establish the legitimate freedom of speech of the uniformed members of the armed forces?

9. What will he do about the "building block" philosophy of technological development of military weapons systems?

10. What can he, or will he, do about restoring the prestige of the professional military establishment and placing military decisions on weaponry and tactics back into professional military hands?

Probably no man, in four years, can take actions which can compensate adequately for the mistakes of a generation. But he may be able to reverse the trend of the past five years.

Appendix A

NOTES ON THE
BALLISTIC MISSILE PROGRAM

It has been said that Air Force military executives were strongly opposed to the ICBM and that the scientific fraternity *forced* the program into effect. This is simply not so. As a matter of fact, the Air Force strongly supported an ICBM program even during the mid-forties, but could not get scientific support to proceed. However when the Von Neumann Committee Report was issued in February of 1954, as Chief of Staff I personally supported the ICBM program to the utmost, as did all the senior Air Force commanders who had responsibility for the development of the ICBM. Even the Strategic Air Command, though I must admit there were some doubters, certainly supported the program all the way through.

The U.S. ballistic missile program got haltingly under way shortly after World War II. However, studies of that time militated against a development program because formidable guidance, weight, and propulsion problems associated with first-generation nuclear weapons indicated that a long-range ballistic missile was then an impractical weapon. It wasn't until the thermonuclear breakthrough in 1952 that a practical

ICBM could be considered in the realm of possibility. The "new" thermonuclear technique made it possible to achieve high megaton yield weapons at much lower weights than were previously possible with fission-type weapons. Also contributing to the slow early development of the ballistic missile was the reluctance of the Atomic Energy Commission to divulge any planning data which the Air Force could use in ballistic-missile weapons analyses and design. The Air Force had, on several occasions, asked the Atomic Energy Commission to forecast weapon-technology capability to five- and ten-year projection schedules. The reason for these requests, of course, is that the lead time for research, development, and production tooling of a delivery system (airplane or missile) is on the order of seven or eight years. Unfortunately, the Atomic Energy Commission consistently refused any scientific summary beyond a two-year projection.

In February, 1953, following several meetings between Dr. John Von Neumann and Dr. Edward Teller in discussions of nuclear-weapons technology, the Air Force Scientific Advisory Board finally established a committee headed by Dr. Von Neumann and including this nation's top scientists—Bradberry, Teller, Herb York, Gene Root, and Dave Griggs, among others equally qualified. In June, 1953, the Von Neumann Committee issued its report. Projecting weapon technology into 1959–1960, the report, among other significant disclosures, predicted that, employing thermonuclear technology, it would be possible to devise a warhead which would be light enough and powerful enough to make the intercontinental ballistic missile a practical weapon.

Although the Von Neumann Committee had no official status within the AEC, its report, because of the irrefutable stature of its authors, nevertheless was considered completely acceptable to the Department of Defense. Because it was difficult to argue with scientific genius such as that of Teller, Von Neumann, Bradberry, and York when predicting the future of nuclear-weapons technology, the AEC also accepted their forecast. From that time forward, all Defense Department planning with respect to nuclear-delivery systems has found basis in the thermonuclear-weapon technology heralded in that unprecedented and historical report.

About the time the Von Neumann Report was issued in June, 1953, the late Trevor Gardner was named Assistant Secretary of the Air Force for Research and Development. A tireless and aggressive man, he exerted a considerable influence with respect to the future of the Air Force and the translation of nuclear technology into weapons equipment for the operational Air Forces.

In the fall of 1953, Secretary of Defense Charles E. Wilson established a committee to examine guided-missile service activities throughout the Department of Defense. Mr. Gardner, fortunately for the Air Force, and the nation, was given the job as Director of the Task Group to examine the strategic and intercontinental ballistic missile category which, at that time, included the SNARK and NAVAJO missile programs. Heretofore, as I have said, ICBM development had been given only scant official attention. Actually, this was logical in view of the fact that early studies had indicated that a tremendously large missile would have been necessary as a booster for the large and heavier "old-fashioned" warhead demanded for intercontinental use. As a matter of fact, these studies indicated that such a missile would "weigh-in" at more than a million pounds; would be very difficult to operate and to maintain; and finally, would be extremely expensive to manufacture.

Considering the state-of-the-art in the late forties and early fifties, the decision not to proceed with the program at that time can be rationalized as correct. However, even in Fiscal Year 1954, two years after the thermonuclear technique was discovered, the budget for the ICBM development was only four million dollars. But, in several of the previous fiscal years, I might point out, the *ICBM had not been supported at all.* The General Dynamics Corporation deserves a great deal of

301

credit for whatever continuity this nation's ICBM development enjoyed historically in the late forties and early fifties. It was largely the General Dynamics research and development team and the company's own money which kept the ICBM effort alive. There had been a little government support for the ICBM for study and experimental work during the period from about 1946 to 1951, but that sum was almost negligible. In 1951, even that funding was dropped and not resumed until 1954.

The Von Neumann Committee made its recommendation to the Secretary of the Air Force, Harold Talbott, February 8, 1954. Its key recommendations, in summary, were as follows:

1. The ICBM was technically feasible. The re-entry, guidance, and warhead problem could be resolved.
2. The Air Force should proceed as fast as technology permitted to achieve an operational ICBM; the program should be accorded the highest priority.
3. The Air Force should establish a special management approach to ICBM development. Under normal management procedures, the report found, it would be impossible to achieve an operational ICBM capability for years. The 1954 report stated that a special management approach augmented by *highest* priority *might make it possible* to achieve an operational ICBM by the early 1960's (a six-year leadtime).

The Air Force Secretary in forwarding the report to me (then Air Force Chief of Staff) stated that he agreed with the Von Neumann Report and that I should immediately initiate action to get the ICBM program under way. Brig. General Bernard A. Shriever was given the job as project officer for ICBM development. I also charged him simultaneously with full field responsibility for the program once the necessary administrative and organizational matters had been established.

302

During March, April, and part of May, 1954, Mr. Gardner aggressively pursued the project from the civilian executive level, and General Shriever worked on the necessary directives for approval at the Air Staff level. By mid-May, the Air Force arrived at a workable approach for carrying out the program. Basically, the plan established within the Air Research and Development Command (ARDC) an autonomous organization to manage the ballistic missile program. The commander of this organization was given, through ARDC, authority for direct channels to the Office of Chief of Staff and Office of the Air Force Secretary and the operating and logistic commanders of the Air Force. This approach departed from normal procedures, but, as time was to show, did get the job done.

I think it well to point out at this time that oddly enough although the Air Force had given the ICBM program the highest priority among all its projects, similar action was not taken by the Department of Defense. As a matter of fact, it was not until late fall, 1955, *after* the President had been briefed, and by his action had accorded ICBM development the highest national priority, that civilian Department of Defense approval was obtained.

In August of 1954, the management approach taken was designed to exploit the best talent and competence in American industry, but retained the responsibility for over-all systems engineering and technical direction of the ICBM program *under* direct management of the military establishment through creation of a technical organization to provide systems integration and technical direction on a fee basis—but being excluded from the actual manufacture of systems, components, and hardware. This unorthodox procedure assured that the USAF retained direct control over the rocket, the guidance system, the warhead, and the re-entry vehicle. This was a significant reversal of normal procedures, but the expedient did permit the Air Force to go directly to all contractors on an associate basis.

The main objective, of course, was to go to where competence existed for the nose cone, guidance, propulsion, and the integration of the entire system. The procedure, needless to say, found little favor among major elements of industry. However, no manufacturer then possessed the over-all systems engineering capability or technical competence to manage the entire program. Nevertheless, the prime contractor approach was the one strongly pressed by the aircraft industry. They saw in the prime contractor approach, the capability of expanding their manufacturing effort not only in the airframe, but in propulsion and guidance development as well. While this method would have given considerable strength to a single prime manufacturer, such an approach would have doubtlessly cost the government more money and, more importantly, time.

In addition to the pressures on the management approach, there were also a number of skeptics among the scientific fraternity who constantly derided the soundness of the ICBM program. I need only to mention Vannevar Bush's book which emphasized *logically* that this nation could not develop an ICBM for many, many years to come. In this connection, many adherents to the Bush philosophy were generally in favor of the incremental approach. They would move ahead, first with an intermediate-range ballistic missile (IRBM) and then go to the ICBM. Their beliefs were tritely backed with such comments as "let's walk before we run." Fortunately, the position of these scientists did not prevail. It could easily have been so if it had not been for the knowledge, strength, and stature of the Von Neumann group within the Defense establishment.

From the beginning, military planners realized that "hardened" underground (permanent concrete and steel) operational facilities would be the most practicable in a nuclear war environment. However, in the interests of expediting the program, the first ICBM installation was a "soft" facility; this meant above ground and vulnerable to enemy attack. Al-

304

though this was not operationally the best, the political and psychological aspects of reaching an operational capability at the earliest date made it mandatory. Because of the state-of-the-art, there were many aspects of the program which would have made it far too great a gamble to fire the pioneer ICBM, ATLAS D, out of a hardened environment. The ATLAS follow-on weapon system, the TITAN program, was designed for hardened facility operations. But it wasn't easy. The TITAN program, developed by the Martin Company, proceeded on schedule. However, there were a number of critical phases in the TITAN development cycle when the program was almost canceled by Washington political planners for reasons that were "the wrong reasons." Fortunately, these political considerations were side-tracked. Cancellation of the TITAN program would have reduced this nation's strategic deterrence far below the safe minimum during the very critical time period of late 1960–1962.

In addition, the TITAN program had several military advantages, not achievable in the first generation ATLAS missile. TITAN II was not only hardened, and fired from an underground silo, but it also used storable liquid propellants which permitted a short count down and very quick military reaction time in event of war. The TITAN family of missiles also had growth potential, because of large payload and because of the adaptability of its structure to accommodate "strap-on" solid-fuel auxiliary propulsion motors.

As a result, the TITAN missile system carries the largest warhead of any of our current ballistic-missile weapons, and a man-rated version of the TITAN II serves as the booster for the Gemini Astronaut program. It was a modified TITAN II which placed Astronauts Grissom and Young into orbit on March 23, 1965, McDivitt and White on June 3, 1965, and Cooper and Conrad on August 21, 1965, as well as making possible the highly successful Gemini 6 and Gemini 7 space rendevous of December, 1965.

The latest of the Titan series, the TITAN IIIC, is in acceler-

305

ated tests at this writing and will become this nation's standard workhorse for boosting payloads on the order of 25,000 pounds into earth orbit, for some time to come.

Concurrently with the TITAN program, we were pushing ahead as rapidly as possible with the solid-fueled MINUTEMAN. It is a matter of history, of course, that the first flight of the MINUTEMAN in early February, 1961, was a complete success and it achieved a Circular Error Probable (CEP) of less than a mile. The military gamble to deliver security paid off. The Air Force, of course, did experience some flight failures subsequent to the first flight, but it was well worth its cost. I am absolutely convinced that the MINUTEMAN is one of the most successful military programs that has ever been undertaken in this country. Its solid-fuel motor development has given this nation a large measure of strategic security. But it was a hard-won victory.

Solid propellants have always intrigued missile engineers because of their inherent safety, reliability, and ease in handling. However, their use was eliminated during the early days of the ballistic missile program for several reasons. First, there were no large-grained solid propellants in 1954. The Army Short Range SERGEANT missile, which was about twenty-four inches in diameter, was the largest solid-fuel rocket in the U.S. arsenal. The weight-to-power factor of solid fuels was not good. Also, the state-of-the-art offered no sure way of directional thrust control. There were no movable nozzles, none had ever been developed for solid propellants, and this is absolutely essential for a long-range missile. There was no precise method of stopping or starting a solid propellant motor. In stopping a solid-fuel motor, for example, a residual flame always remained to cause some additional thrust. Analysis indicated that best accuracy at target *might* be an unacceptable "within fifty miles." As a result, solid propellant engines were shelved temporarily for the more positive results and controls possible with exotic liquid fuels. Nevertheless, the solid propellant had great potential. Based on this, the

Air Force undertook a ten-million-dollar feasibility study in 1955. Under today's Defense Department cost/effectiveness methods, incidentally, such a project would be impossible. Today the Air Force would have to get time-consuming approval of innumerable echelons in the Defense Department before it could undertake anything of this magnitude.

At any rate, the Air Force requested all of the solid propellant companies in the country to become involved. Following some eighteen months of study, analysis, and experiments, the Air Force was finally convinced that the feasibility of overcoming the shortcomings of solid-fuel motors mentioned previously was proven. Another six months completed the project definition phase and out of this work came the detailed specification of the MINUTEMAN program. The missile configuration with its three stages, its weight and size, was determined in late 1956. It is identical with the configuration of the MINUTEMAN missile now operational.

The proven MINUTEMAN design was presented to the USAF for approval. Then it was presented to the Ballistic Missile Committee. From there the presentation went to the Secretary of Defense (who was also Chairman of the Ballistic Missile Committee at the DOD level). All of this took approximately three days. Today such an accomplishment would be utterly impossible. A program of this magnitude simply could not get under way without years of justification in today's sterile defense environment.

In 1958, Air Force Chief of Staff, General Thomas D. White, directed that the Air Force make every effort to reduce the timetable on the MINUTEMAN by at least one year. With that directive, an objective and detailed analysis of development capability was undertaken. There was a great deal of development time risk involved. It was decided that the first flight test of the MINUTEMAN *would be* a complete missile. In other words, all three stages of the missile must function; they must separate; the re-entry vehicle must separate; the guidance system must function; and the re-entry vehicle must re-enter the atmosphere and target to its CEP in one single test. No other missile test program has ever been as comprehensive or demanding either previously, or since. In ballistic missile programming, the procedure normally is to test-flight the guidance system open-loop; then fly it closed; then separate the re-entry vehicle. It is usually well after the tenth firing before flight experience permits a complete missile firing.

There is one other historical aspect of the MINUTEMAN program as it relates to the Navy POLARIS program that needs clarification. The POLARIS fleet submarine missile became operational slightly ahead of the MINUTEMAN. Because of this a general misconception exists that the MINUTEMAN program was based on POLARIS technology. Actually, the reverse is true. The original POLARIS program undertaken by the Navy was designed around a bundle of SARGEANT rockets. The Von Neumann Committee in its examination of the POLARIS program recommended that it be re-oriented to the Air Force technology and solid propellant feasibility program. This was subsequently directed. As a result, all USAF technology and know-how in solid propellants, guidance, and re-entry was made available and utilized in the POLARIS program.

There are lessons to be learned from the MINUTEMAN program:

1. The degree of flexibility which permitted the Air Force to take wide research latitudes, such as the advanced technology required for the solid propellant, was essential and does not exist today.
2. Streamlined management procedures allowed rapid decision-making. The Air Force could not have accomplished what it did in today's environment. A new weapons breakthrough simply cannot develop now. The Department of Defense cost/effectiveness theories and building block approach to new systems preclude it.
3. Delegation of authority to the operating management level was essential. The ballistic missile program pro-

ceeded rapidly because there was little technical interference from the Defense Department paper passers.
The Minuteman program, I am sure, would have been
delayed at least a year if technical decisions could not
have been made in the field. However, delegation of
major systems authority to field management levels has,
of course, been completely abandoned in recent years.

Appendix B

GLOSSARY OF TERMS

(Approved JCS Definitions)

General War—Armed conflict between the major powers of the Communist and Free worlds in which the total resources of the belligerents are employed, and the national survival of a major belligerent is in jeopardy.

Limited War—Armed conflict short of general war, exclusive of incidents, involving the overt engagement of the military forces of two or more nations.

Cold War—A state of international tension, wherein political, economic, technological, sociological, psychological, paramilitary, and military measures short of overt armed conflict involving regular military forces are employed to achieve national objectives.

Civic Action—The use of preponderantly indigenous military forces on projects useful to the local population at all levels in such fields as education, training, public works, agriculture, transportation, communications, health, sanitation, and others contributing to economic and social development, which would also serve to improve the standing of the military forces with the population. (U.S. forces may at times advise or engage in military civic actions in overseas areas.)

Counterguerrilla Warfare—Operations and activities conducted by armed forces, paramilitary forces, or nonmilitary agencies of a government against guerrillas.

Counterinsurgency—Those military, paramilitary, political, economic, psychological, and civic actions taken by a government to defeat subversive insurgency.

Covert Operations — Operations which are so planned and executed as to conceal the identity of or permit plausible denial by the sponsor. They differ from clandestine operations in that emphasis is placed on concealment of identity of sponsor rather than on concealment of the operation.

Insurgency—A condition resulting from a revolt or insurrection against a constituted government which falls short of civil war. In the current context, subversive insurgency is primarily Communist inspired, supported, or exploited.

Paramilitary Forces — Forces or groups which are distinct from the regular armed forces of any country, but resembling them in organization, equipment, training, or mission.

Paramilitary Operation—An operation undertaken by a paramilitary force.

Psychological Operations—These operations include psychological warfare and, in addition, en-compass those political, military, economic, and ideological actions planned and conducted to create in neutral or friendly foreign groups the emotions, attitudes, or behavior to support the achievement of national objectives.

Psychological Warfare—The planned use of propaganda and other psychological actions having the primary purpose of influencing the opinions, emotions, attitudes, and behavior of hostile foreign groups in such a way as to support the achievement of national objectives.

Unconventional Warfare—Includes the three interrelated fields of guerrilla warfare, evasion and escape, and subversion. Unconventional warfare operations are conducted within enemy or enemy-controlled territory by predominantly indigenous personnel, usually supported and directed in varying degrees by an external source.

Evasion and Escape (E&E)—The procedures and operations whereby military personnel and other selected individuals are enabled to emerge from an enemy-held or hostile area to areas under friendly control.

Guerrilla Warfare (GW)—Military and paramilitary operations conducted in enemy-held or hostile territory by irregular, predominantly indigenous forces.

311

INDEX

A-bomb
  cost of, 39
  estimates on Soviet possession of, 38, 196
  not used in Korean War, 52, 53–54, 56
  Truman's decision to use, 146–147
  trusting France with, 83
Acheson, Dean, defensive perimeter of U.S. defined by, 35–36
aid programs, American military and economic, 75–81
Airborne Early Warning (AEW), 125
aircraft
  acquisition of new combat, 245–258
  Advanced Manned Strategic, 256
  bomber-type, 248–249
  carrier-based, 252, 253
  fighter-type, 249–250
  multiple-purpose, 252, 253
  strategic, 17, 255–257
aircraft carriers, 31
  nuclear powered, 258–259
aircraft development program (table), 260–261

air defense, North American, 123, 125–126
Air Defense System for Europe, 85
Air Force, U.S.
  autonomy of, from Army, 15, 26, 27, 31
Air Force Scientific Advisory Board, 300
airlift of troops, 193
Air Research and Development Command (ARDC), 299, 303
Air Transport Command, W W II, 296
alliances, 72–73
Allies, Free World, W W II, 7
American States, Organization of, 73
analysts, operations, 191–192, 199
Anderson, Adm. George, 182
Anderson, Maj. Gen. Orville A., 18, 19, 22
antinuclear scientists, 101, 118, 135
armament race, 40, 203–204
armed services, U.S., competition between branches of, 13
Arnold, Gen. H. H., 191
astronauts, 291, 305
ATLAS missile, 143, 291, 305

312

313

314

315

National Military policy founded
on, 251
retirement of, 294–295
Soviet development of, 42
testing of, 137, 297–298
nuclear weapons capability, 159
French, 82, 84
nuclear weapons delivery, U.S.
foreign policy based on, 33–34
nuclear weapons technology, progress of, 25

Objective, principle of, 200–202
operations analysts, 191–192, 199
Oppenheimer, J.R., 39
organization, military, 129–133
overseas deployments of U.S.
Forces, 126

pacifists, 110, 113, 203
Pakistan, 67, 76, 201
paper tiger,
America as a, 56
Red China as a, 293
parity, 175, 176
Patton, Gen. George S., attitude of,
toward taking Berlin, 5–6
peaceful coexistence. See coexistence
peace in space, 153, 177–178, 290
peacetime strategy, U.S., 40
Pearl Harbor, xiii, xiv, 206, 212
point system, for demobilization,
8-9
Poland, 12, 77, 201, 213, 278
blitzkrieg in, xiv, 208
enslavement of, 5
POLARIS submarine, 39, 94, 143,
173, 179, 247, 258, 308
policy, military, in support of containment, 121–143
political leaders, responsibility of,
6
political scientists, pacifistic, 110–
111
population, a basic power factor,
229–230
Potts, Ramsay D., Jr., 37
Power, Gen. Tom, 299
power, balance of, 33
power factors, basic, 226–236
pre-emptive action, 48, 49
Presidents' Advisory Commission
on Universal Training, 41

prestige, U.S. National, 63–68,
127
preventive war, 19, 49
principles of war, 198–225
Air War College students' opinions on, 217–220
Joint Chiefs of Staff approval of,
221–225
priorities, service, 125
proliferation, 84, 159–161, 297
Pursuit, principle of, 212, 216

Quemoy-Matsu islands, 74

radar, 282, 284
radiation fallout, 95
reciprocity, 79–81
Red China, 272–273, 293
as a military threat, 277, 278,
293
See also China, loss of to
Communism;   Commu-
nists, Chinese
Reorganization Act of 1958, 130–
133
research and development
a basic power factor, 234–235
Free World collaboration in,
283–284
military, 133–143
requirements for, 122
Research and Development Board,
28
research and development policy,
176–182, 247, 248
Richardson, Brig. Gen., R.C., 96–
101
Ridgeway, General, 56
rivalry, interservice, 31–33
See also interservice conflicts
rocket technology
German lead in, 177
Soviet exploitation of, 42
Root, Gene, 300
Royal Air Force Fighter Command, 208–209
Rudenko, Marshal, 264, 265
Russian military apparatus, 259,
262–267

SACEUR, 68, 79, 81, 161
satellite,
first man-made earth, 205, 206,
266

satellite countries,
Eastern European, 294
European, 19
Scientists with a bad conscience,
106–108
security, collective, 46, 69, 86
Semi-Automatic Ground Environment (SAGE), 125
SERGEANT missile, 306
Shriever, Brig., Gen. Bernard A.,
302, 303
Sino-Soviet Bloc, conflict with, 59
SKYBOLT program, cancellation of,
174
SNARK missile, 301
Sokolovskey, Marshal, quoted on
Soviet use of space, 178–179
source selection, 183
South East Asia Treaty Organization (SEATO), 71, 72, 73,
76, 147, 289
membership of, 67
Soviet Aviation Day, 262
Soviet land force, 20–21
Soviets
B-29 bomber copied by, 42
Eisenhower's dealings with, 5, 6
hostility of, toward Western
World, 17, 18, 19
participation of, in U.S. war
against Japan, 7
See also Russian military apparatus; U.S.S.R.
Soviet Union, U.S. Air Force officers visit to, 259, 262–267
U.S. recognition of, 277–278
space
military use of, 37, 42, 136, 176,
178–181, 195, 290, 296, 297
peace in, 177–178
space agency, civilian, 291
space technology
military, 37
U.S. position in, 177
space vehicles, military use of, 94,
178
Spitfire, 209
status quo, 19, 35, 61, 108, 297
Strategic Air Command, U.S.
(SAC), 87–89, 94, 115, 299
strategic bombing theory, 33, 34,
195, 196
strategic force, U.S., 93
submarine potential, Soviet, 21

submarines, U.S. See POLARIS
Suez crisis, 201, 206
Surprise, principle of, 206–207,
216, 223
surrender, unconditional, policy of,
6, 200, 215
survivability, 175–176
"Survival in the Air Age," 40
Symington, Stuart, 33, 37

Talbott, Harold, 302
Teller, Dr. Edward, expert on
nuclear problems, 39, 135,
136, 300
Test Ban Treaty, 290
testing, nuclear weapons, 137–139
THOR missiles, 81, 86, 291
TITAN missile, 291, 305–306
Training, Universal, President's
Advisory Commission on, 41
Tripoli, 104
troop requirements, U.S., 64
Truman, Harry, 50, 153
Soviet detonation of atomic device announced by, 37, 38, 44
Finletter Commission established by, 40
NSC-68 approved by, 47, 144
Truman Administration, 18, 93
specific actions of, 145–147

unconditional surrender, policy of,
6, 200, 215
unilateral disarmers, 112–114, 118
United Nations
aggression checked by, 36
establishment of, 26
Goldberg speech to, 294–295
and the Korean War, 53
Russian indebtedness to, 277
votes against U.S. in, 77, 201,
278, 297
United States
military-political development in,
xv–xvi
World War II activities of, 3–13
Universal Training, President's Advisory Commission on, 41
U.S.S.R.
first propaganda victory of, 8
nuclear power of, 22–23
See also Russian military apparatus; Soviets; Soviet
Union